"*Eschatological Discipleship* is a brilliant book. In it, Trevin Wax argues that Christian discipleship cannot be reduced to the transmission of timeless truths that float above history and culture. Instead, Christian discipleship always and necessarily involves confronting the ideologies and rival eschatologies of our own contemporary context. In our own era, he argues, we must confront the Enlightenment, the Sexual Revolution, and modern consumerism as rival eschatologies, exposing them as frauds and offering the gospel as our one-and-only hope."

—**Bruce Ashford,** provost and dean of faculty, Southeastern Baptist Theological Seminary

"Trevin Wax's *Eschatological Discipleship* is a much-needed book that teaches that followers of Jesus are shaped in their thinking and actions by Jesus's kingship, and by the coming kingdom. God's future—including our future in it—constructs a worldview and supplies us with wisdom for living in the current age. Ultimately, every worldview, whether secularist or Islamic, has a view of the 'end.' By knowing God's plan for the end, we will be better equipped to work for the kingdom here on earth."

—**Michael F. Bird,** lecturer in theology, Ridley College, Melbourne, Australia

"With the publication of *Eschatological Discipleship*, Trevin Wax has solidified his role as an important Christian voice for the next generation. The call to biblical faithfulness, serious cultural engagement, careful worldview thinking, and long-term eschatological discipleship is masterfully and winsomely presented. Wax has provided us with a clearly written, insightful, well-researched, and illuminating work that will be essential reading for thoughtful Christian leaders in the church and in the academy. It is a genuine joy to recommend this outstanding work."

—**David S. Dockery,** president, Trinity Evangelical Divinity School

"Discipleship and eschatology are not often thought of in tandem. Discipleship is about following Jesus here and now, while eschatology is about what happens then and there. But in this important book, Trevin Wax shows the coinherence of these two biblical themes. An impressive theological study written with an eye for Great Commission reflection and praxis."

—**Timothy George,** founding dean, Beeson Divinity School of Samford University

"It is not a matter of whether eschatology will shape the church's life but only a matter of which one. Discipleship, a burning need in the syncretistic American church, surely needs to be reenvisioned in terms of equipping God's people to more and more live out of a biblical eschatology of the kingdom. In this book Trevin Wax takes up this challenge and encounters the two most powerful rival eschatologies of our day—the Enlightenment notion of progress, and consumerism. I pray that God will use this book to enable the American church to reimagine discipleship in its missionary setting."

—**Michael W. Goheen,** director of theological education, Missional Training Center, and adjunct professor of missional theology, Covenant Theological Seminary

"The philosopher Martin Heidegger famously defined human existence as 'being-toward-death,' a posture that generates anxiety in view of our limited time. Trevin Wax does him one better: the Christian life is a matter of being-towards-discipleship, and discipleship is a matter of being-towards-*end*-time. Disciples take their bearings from the story of Jesus, especially its end: the hope of resurrection. Wax convincingly sets out the biblical basis for 'eschatological discipleship,' which means the importance of waking up (and staying awake) to the reality that our citizenship in heaven begins now."

—**Kevin J. Vanhoozer,** research professor of systematic theology, Trinity Evangelical Divinity School

ESCHATOLOGICAL

DISCIPLESHIP

TREVIN K. WAX

ESCHATOLOGICAL

DISCIPLESHIP

Leading Christians to Understand Their Historical and Cultural Context

NASHVILLE, TENNESSEE

Eschatological Discipleship

Published by B&H Academic
Nashville, Tennessee

ISBN: 978-1-4627-7638-2

Dewey Decimal Classification: 248.84
Subject Heading: DISCIPLESHIP \ ESCHATOLOGY \ EVANGELISTIC WORK

Printed in the United States of America

1 2 3 4 5 6 7 8 9 10 • 23 22 21 20 19 18

VP

To

Corina,

whose love and sacrifice enabled this pursuit.

Contents

Acknowledgments

I must first express gratitude to my wife, Corina, for her constant encouragement and sacrificial support during my studies and the writing of this work.

I also thank my children, Timothy, Julia, and David, for their patience with me and for their prayers during the writing process, a lengthy time that demanded so much of my time and attention.

I am grateful to have a heritage of faith that extends to my parents, grandparents, and great-grandparents on both sides of my family, a heritage that prized love for Jesus and using our minds to the glory of God.

I am thankful for Eric Geiger, Bill Craig, and other friends at LifeWay for the freedom to pursue doctoral studies as part of my responsibilities.

Further, I am thankful for my colleagues in ministry and in the classroom. Their comments and pushback sharpened my thoughts on this and other topics.

J. D. Greear and Keith and Amy Whitfield opened their homes to me while I was involved in the study that made this book possible. Their hospitality made the time away from family and friends something to enjoy, not merely endure.

Most of all, I am thankful for Bruce Ashford for challenging me, sharpening me, and supporting me throughout the process.

INTRODUCTION

Eschatological Discipleship and Contemporary Christianity

> It is sometimes said of people who constantly think about or speak of eternal matters, "They are so heavenly minded they are of no earthly good." The popular saying gives the impression of a believer whose head is "in the clouds," isolated from the hustle and bustle of everyday life and the practical needs that impinge upon us here below. The saying intends to downplay the importance of eschatology in the life of a Christian by suggesting that looking too much to the future will undermine obedience or, at the least, rob the effectiveness and relevance of such obedience in the present.

The problem with this statement is that it fails to do justice not only to Scripture but also to church history, most notably the evidence of Christian influence on society. C. S. Lewis once countered this notion and made an opposing claim, "If you read history you will find that the Christians who did most for the present world were just those who thought most of the next. . . . It is since Christians have largely ceased to think of the other world that they have become so ineffective in this one."[1] Was Lewis right? Or does the popular saying remain true?

A cursory glance through some contemporary discipleship books may, at first, lend credence to the idea that one should take care not to be "too heavenly minded." We find a disconnect between books on discipleship, many of which focus on spiritual disciplines or our motivation for obedience, and "end times" titles, which seem to surface in every generation and offer new applications of the apocalyptic imagery of Revelation. Is it possible that evangelical Christians have simultaneously amplified *and* reduced

1. C. S. Lewis, *Mere Christianity*, C. S. Lewis Signature Classics (San Francisco, CA: HarperSanFrancisco, 2009), 134.

the importance of eschatology? (Amplified in the sense that so much attention is given to a narrow sliver of debates about the end times. Reduced in the sense that the broader vision of eschatology no longer has much to do with our day-to-day lives or discipleship as a process.)

If, as Lewis writes, believers have become "ineffective" in this world because they fail to think of the next, then perhaps the separation of discipleship from eschatology is partially to blame. Divorced from eschatology, discipleship may lead us to adopt personal interior-focused practices but fail to give sufficient attention to the kind of spiritual formation that helps us recognize the present context and our role in it. Likewise, eschatology, divorced from a larger vision of discipleship (or eschatology reduced to debates about the timing of Christ's return), may lead us to an inordinate focus on historical and interpretative curiosities rather than sound exegesis that helps us discern the Bible's overarching vision of the world and our future.

Here is the problem: our understanding of discipleship is deficient if it includes only a nod toward our eschatological hope or if it reduces our eschatological hope to its personal dimension (living in light of our coming death and afterlife). Likewise, our understanding of eschatology is deficient if it fails to encompass the broader sense of the Bible's grand story, which motivates and informs many New Testament ethical exhortations. A shrunken view of discipleship misses eschatology, and a shrunken view of eschatology fails to impact discipleship. The result is that Christians may be left without the necessary tools to read the signs of our own times or navigate the darkness of the contemporary age. We may fail to see how discipleship equips us to see current challenges in the light of God's coming kingdom.

Bringing together eschatology and discipleship is the primary purpose of this book. However, as soon as we begin this task, we are faced with a number of pressing questions. *What do we mean by eschatology? Are we speaking of eschatology as the future of the world, the church, and the individual believer? Or are we speaking of eschatology in its broader reference to the great story of our world? Is there biblical precedent in the Old or New Testaments for linking our obedience as Christ's followers to eschatological realities? If so, where and how do these links occur?*

The questions concerning discipleship also multiply. *What is discipleship, and how does it relate to the mission of the church? How is our obedience motivated by eschatological reality? How do we contextualize our mission for the times in which we live? What role does worldview formation play in the making of disciples, and what role does eschatology play in the formation of a worldview? How does our mission of proclaiming the gospel as the true story of the world interact with and confront rival eschatologies? How can we strengthen various conceptions of discipleship by giving more attention to their eschatological dimension?*

These are the questions we will examine at length in the course of this work.

What Is Eschatological Discipleship?

Because discipleship in a New Testament sense is holistic (encompassing all of life) and contextualized (the way believers put Jesus's teachings into practice will look different in various cultural contexts), discipleship is also "eschatological"; that is, it is a type of spiritual formation and obedience that takes into account the contemporary setting in which one finds oneself, particularly in relation to rival conceptions of time and progress.

In this book I make a case for an eschatological understanding of discipleship on the basis of the New Testament authors' consistent appeals to eschatology when exhorting Christians to live according to biblical ethics. My goal is to demonstrate the need for churches to reenvision disciple making as spiritual formation that goes beyond the adoption of personal spiritual disciplines or engagement in church-related activities to a missionary encounter and confrontation with the world. Additionally, I hope to show the importance of asking the question "What time is it?" in order to understand a worldview properly and then illustrate the importance of this question for missiology by countering the prevailing rival eschatologies of our current cultural moment in order to display our unique identity as kingdom citizens.

An Outline of This Book

In chapter 1, we define four key words that help explain what is meant by the term *eschatological discipleship*. These words are *discipleship*, *worldview*, *eschatology*, and *wisdom*.

In part 2 (chaps. 2–4), we focus on the biblical foundation for seeing an eschatological component to the forming of disciples. We begin with Old Testament examples of spiritual formation in historical and wisdom literature, particularly the connections to the New Testament's further fulfillment of spiritual development. We continue (chap. 3) with an examination of some of Jesus's teachings in both propositional and parabolic form, showing how discipleship is often viewed as "living in light of what time it is," according to the eschatological timetable. We examine the eschatological dimension of the commissioning texts of Jesus in Matthew and Luke (Matt 28:16–20; Luke 24:44–49; Acts 1:6–9) in light of Jesus's ethical teachings. Chapter 4 includes an exposition of Paul's ethical exhortations rooted in his distinctive eschatological vision, showing how eschatology both shapes and motivates Christian ethics.

In part 3 (chaps. 5–8), we build on the definition of and biblical examples of eschatological discipleship by showing how a Christian answer to the worldview question, "What time is it?," necessarily counters rival eschatologies in North America in the twenty-first century. These chapters examine three rival worldviews with their own eschatological visions: (chap. 6) the Enlightenment (a view of history that sees society as shedding the supernatural superstitions of the past on the march of progress toward a future of technological and scientific advancement); (chap. 7) the sexual revolution (a view of history wherein the staid morality of previous generations is rejected in favor of a wide-ranging embrace of any and all consensual sexual pleasure as a mark of progress and tolerance); and (chap. 8) consumerism (a view of life and history that sees a progressive line toward happiness found in what is created and consumed). Eschatological discipleship includes the equipping of contemporary disciples in the church to understand and counteract these rival eschatologies in light of their identity as God's kingdom people.

In part 4, we survey common evangelical conceptions of discipleship that fall into three distinct categories: (1) discipleship conceived of as primarily evangelistic reproduction, (2) discipleship in terms of personal piety (expressed through the adoption of spiritual disciplines), and (3) discipleship that is gospel centered in its motivation. The purpose of this brief survey is not to argue for one approach to discipleship over another, or even to make the case that these three conceptions are the most common ones found in evangelicalism, but rather to show how each approach would benefit from training people to think eschatologically—to ask and answer the worldview question "What time is it?" in the culture in which they are called to submit to Jesus as Lord.

PART 1

Defining Eschatological Discipleship

CHAPTER 1

Toward a Definition of *Eschatological Discipleship*

Defining the term *eschatological discipleship* requires a clear explanation of what is meant by *eschatology* and *discipleship*. Furthermore, *worldview* and *wisdom* relate to the definition toward which we are working. Because these terms will be used throughout this book, we will analyze them one-by-one before combining them into a definition.

Discipleship

Discipleship involves a holistic vision of life as a believer seeks to follow Jesus. Discipleship entails more than the transfer of biblical information or the affirmation of correct doctrines because it includes certain actions and sentiments that bear witness to the gospel.

Defining *discipleship* in a holistic manner such as this is in line with a number of contemporary theologians. For example, Kevin Vanhoozer defines a disciple as "one who seeks to speak, act, and live in ways that *bear witness to the truth, goodness, and beauty of Jesus Christ.*"[1] Vanhoozer's definition emphasizes discipleship as something people *do*, not something they *are* or *say* they believe. The focus is on "bearing witness."

Similarly, Anthony Thiselton points out that one's faith is "*action-oriented, situation-related,* and embedded in the *particularities and contingencies* of everyday living."[2] Discipleship, then, is not only understanding the truth about Jesus in a cognitive manner but also presenting the truth through words and deeds in a particular time and place. Discipleship

---

1. Kevin Vanhoozer, *Faith Speaking Understanding: Performing the Drama of Doctrine* (Louisville, KY: Westminster/John Knox, 2014), 20 (emphasis in original).

2. Anthony C. Thiselton, *The Hermeneutics of Doctrine* (Grand Rapids: Eerdmans, 2007), 21 (emphasis in original).

necessarily bends toward practice, as is made clear by Jesus Christ's command to "Follow me!"[3] There is a sense, then, in which true understanding of Christian doctrine has not occurred until the one who has faith has put that faith into action.

1. Discipleship Is Balanced

If a disciple is one who follows and bears witness to Christ, then the goal of discipleship must be Christlikeness, and Christlikeness is a holistic notion including not only right belief but also right practice and right sentiment. Baptist ecclesiologist Gregg Allison rightly notes that the disciple-making process should consist of a balance between these three elements. First, followers of Christ should be characterized by orthodoxy (sound doctrine). Second, followers of Christ must be known for orthopraxis (right practice). Third, the follower of Christ must exude *orthopatheia* (proper sentiment).[4] When any one of these three elements is excluded from a disciple's development, the other two elements are adversely affected, and the mission of the church is hindered because Christlikeness suffers.[5]

Discipleship, then, includes the educational ministry of the church, but this education transcends the classroom because it includes more than merely the transfer of information. Indeed, Allison recommends a discipleship model that consists of indoctrination,[6] character building, and worldview development, the latter of which he defines as "the formation of gospel-oriented disciples in terms of their feelings, assessment of moral and social issues, and purpose for living." This development is necessary in equipping people to be effective in their abilities "to evangelize, disciple,

---

3. Matthew 4:19; 8:22; 9:9; 10:38; 16:24; 19:21; 19:28; Mark 1:17; 2:14; 8:34; 10:21; Luke 5:27; 9:23; 9:59; 18:22; and John 1:43; 8:12; 10:27; 12:26; 21:19; and 21:22.

4. Gregg Allison, *Sojourners and Strangers: The Doctrine of the Church* (Wheaton, IL: Crossway, 2012), 441.

5. Francis A. Schaeffer, *Letters of Francis A. Schaeffer: Spiritual Reality in the Personal Christian Life* (ed. Lane T. Dennis; Wheaton, IL: Crossway Books, 1985). Additionally, these three elements of balanced discipleship may refer to the church corporately. Responding to a letter in which someone asked him for advice on finding a church, Francis Schaeffer used the terms "orthodoxy of doctrine" and "orthokardia of community."

6. Vanhoozer, *Faith Speaking Understanding*, 53. The term *indoctrination* often has a negative connotation, as if it means people are being brainwashed or forced to accept something against their will. These negative associations should not deter us from using the term, properly understood, which refers to the fact that, in the words of Kevin Vanhoozer, "Doctrine is inevitable. We've all been *indoctrinated:* everyone has absorbed some system of beliefs and values. . . . Indoctrination is always happening: in homes, schools, the workplace, sometimes even in church. The only question is whether it is truly Christian."

show mercy, and engage in other church ministries."[7] The question of worldview development will be treated in more detail below.

2. Discipleship Is Modeled

Disciple making is accomplished by modelers, not just messengers. We develop not merely through cognitive transfer but also through witnessing the lives and choices of other disciples we encounter on our way. Perhaps this is the reason the Old Testament emphasizes the meditation and memorization of Scripture *alongside* conversations about the law that take place in the daily rhythms of life.[8] As Oliver O'Donovan points out, "The disciple is, literally, 'a learner,' but at the same time, given the patterns of rabbinic learning current in Jesus' day, a 'follower.' The cognitive and affective are bound together in the life of the disciple who learns by following and follows by learning."[9] This emphasis corresponds with the New Testament picture of Jesus with his disciples. Jesus was always teaching, not just through his public discourses but also through his actions.

The idea of "modeling," and specifically "imitation," seems to have fallen out of favor among some contemporary evangelicals, perhaps because of an overemphasis on practicing virtues that has sometimes led to a tiresome moralizing of biblical texts,[10] or perhaps the reason is that imitation is no longer thought of as part of the discipleship process. People are more likely to see spiritual direction as the individual's responsibility to fulfill certain requirements common to Christians. However, a neglect of "imitation" and "modeling" language in the discipleship process leads to other problems, including an overemphasis on technique or a classroom

---

7. Allison, *Sojourners*, 443.

8. Psalm 119, for example, is heavy on the need for learning and internalizing the law of God, while Deuteronomy 6 focuses on the frequent discussions of the law's significance and application in everyday life. Widder says, "YHWH's instructions are taught *so* they can be done. Implicit in much of this kind of teaching is the need for repetition—both by the teacher and in the practice of the student." Wendy L. Widder, *"To Teach" in Ancient Israel: A Cognitive Linguistic Study of a Biblical Hebrew Lexical Set* (Boston: Walter de Gruyter, 2014), 118.

9. Oliver O'Donovan, *Finding and Seeking: Ethics as Theology* (Grand Rapids: Eerdmans, 2014), 2:117.

10. Sidney Greidanus, *The Modern Preacher and the Ancient Text: Interpreting and Preaching Biblical Literature* (Grand Rapids: Eerdmans, 1988); Bryan Chapell, *Christ-Centered Preaching: Redeeming the Expository Sermon* (2nd ed.; Grand Rapids: Baker Academic, 2005); Dennis Johnson, *Him We Proclaim: Proclaiming Christ from All the Scriptures* (Phillipsburg, NJ: P&R, 2007); and Jonathan Pennington, *Reading the Gospels Widely: A Narrative and Theological Introduction* (Grand Rapids: Baker Academic, 2012), 163. Many preaching manuals and hermeneutics texts counter an overdependence on biblical characters as examples of morality. The caution against moralistic preaching warns about the potential loss of the redemptive thread of the Bible's story line. Still, as Jonathan Pennington reminds us, "A crucial part of understanding the identification role of the Gospels is recognizing that other characters in the stories provide important models either for emulation or avoidance" (163).

experience. A biblical understanding of discipleship involves "modeling" at two levels, imitation of behavior (what one does) and imitation of reasoning (how one thinks).

Modeling takes place through the imitation of behavior. Modeling is a central component of being a disciple and of making disciples. Surveying the landscape of various approaches to spiritual direction (often under terms such as "spiritual director," "spiritual guide," "spiritual friend," "mentor," or in evangelical parlance, "discipler"), Victor Copan provides a working definition of the concept: "Spiritual direction is the (variegated) means by which one person intentionally influences another person or persons in the development of his life as a Christian with the goal of developing his relationship to God and His purposes for that person in the world."[11]

Using this definition as a baseline, Copan turns to the example of the apostle Paul. Interestingly, the Gospels do not include any specific commands from Jesus concerning imitation, even though numerous calls were present to follow him. In Paul's letters, the reverse is true. Paul urged people to imitate him as he followed Christ (1 Cor 4:16; 11:1). Copan shows that the emulation of human beings was widespread in ancient literature, with particular focus on the classical virtues, specific actions of respected individuals, or the overall mimicking of another person's lifestyle and character. Paul utilized the relational spheres common to ancient literature (parent-child, teacher-student, and leader-people), often choosing to rely more heavily on one sphere or another, depending on his particular intentions. As Copan notes, imitation in the ancient world was directed toward the improvement of character, and it was viewed positively (although thoughtless mimicry was viewed negatively).[12]

In Paul's Corinthian correspondence Copan notices a specific and a general referent in Paul's desire for the church to imitate him. Specifically, he points to Paul's life of humble, sacrificial service to others and his rejection of the world's view of wisdom, strength, and honor. Generally everything in Paul's life ("actions, virtues, emotions, and lifestyle") that flows

---

11. Victor A. Copan, *Saint Paul as Spiritual Director: An Analysis of the Concept of the Imitation of Paul with Implications and Applications to the Practice of Spiritual Direction* (Eugene, OR: Wipf and Stock, 2007), 39.

12. Ibid., 70–71; and Vanhoozer, *Faith Speaking Understanding*, 117. Vanhoozer also distinguishes between mimicry and imitation, as he states, "It is one thing to *mimic* faith, quite another to achieve a true mimesis (from Gk. *mimesis*, imitation) of the great cloud of witnesses that make up the biblical roll call of faith (Heb. 11:1–38)."

from his service to Christ is in view when he called the Corinthians to imitate him.[13]

Other theologians support the contention that modeling is essential for being a disciple and making disciples.[14] Missionary theologian Lesslie Newbigin, for example, writes that "a true Christian pastor will be one who can dare to say to his people: 'Follow me, as I am following Jesus.'" He goes on to say, "A true pastor must have such a relation with Jesus and with his people that he follows Jesus and they follow him."[15] Notice the double relationship here, the relationship with Jesus and the relationship with people. In relationship with Jesus, the pastor is a disciple; in relationship with people, the pastor is a discipler. Both of these aspects are included in discipleship, and both of these aspects point toward a definition of discipleship that includes modeling. Though Newbigin was speaking of pastors, the same truth is relevant for all those who follow Christ and make disciples.

Similarly, Jason Hood writes, "A maturing believer in Jesus can present herself as a model for others to imitate. In fact, if she is faithful to her identity in Christ, she must become a model."[16] A key component of the discipleship process, then, is imitating the behavior of people who are following Christ.

Modeling takes place through the imitation of reasoning. In emphasizing discipleship as something that is modeled, we might be tempted to think of "imitation" as merely a matter of activity. In other words we might be inclined to think of discipleship in two stages: (1) the inculcation of Christian doctrine (information), and (2) the imitation of Christian behavior (modeling). However, the New Testament does not distinguish between these stages. Instead, it brings together the informational and imitational aspects of discipleship and, in the process, transcends them.

---

13. Copan, *Saint Paul*, 124.

14. Vanhoozer, *Faith Speaking Understanding*, 123–24, reclaims imitation language and specifically applies it to disciples. He insists, "Imitation (*mimesis*) is an important biblical principle. Saints are to imitate both good (3 John 11) and God (Eph 5:1). If this direction was all disciples had to go on, they would have difficulty determining what to do; it is hard to imitate abstractions. Fortunately, most biblical references to imitation are more specific. . . . Disciples imitate their masters. Masters are role models because their actions provide a template that guides the actions of their followers."

15. Lesslie Newbigin, *The Good Shepherd: Meditations on Christian Ministry in Today's World*, accessed August 28, 2015, http://newbigin.net/assets/pdf/77gs.pdf.

16. Jason B. Hood, *Imitating God in Christ: Recapturing a Biblical Pattern* (Downers Grove, IL: IVP Academic, 2013), 156; and Stanley Hauerwas and William H. Willimon, *Resident Aliens: Life in the Christian Colony* (Nashville: Abingdon Press, 1989), 102. Similarly, Hauerwas and Willimon describe Christian ethics as "aristocratic," that is: "It is not something that comes naturally. It can only be learned. We are claiming, then, that a primary way of learning to be disciples is by being in contact with others who are disciples."

One of the most important ways the New Testament vision of discipleship transcends the boundary between "information" and "imitation" is its emphasis on the believer's union with Christ. What keeps imitation from slipping into hypocrisy is the reality that disciples are acting in accordance with the Christ who indwells them. "What disciples act *out* is their being *in* Christ."[17] It is not surprising, then, to see that biblical imitation is not described as thoughtless mimicry but as having the mind of Christ (Phil 2:5) in order to respond to new circumstances with the humility and wisdom of the Savior who indwells believers by his Spirit.

Another way the New Testament vision of discipleship transcends the line between information and imitation is in revealing the connection between imitation and reasoning in Paul's interactions with the Corinthians. There Paul's focus on imitation is more comprehensive than a mere correspondence between his own activities and what he desires the church to do. Paul wanted the people to follow the same "reasoning process" that led him to such actions; he wanted the Corinthians to display the same "ethos."[18] To put it another way, modeling the Christian life includes the cultivation of wisdom from within a biblical framework, wisdom that leads to the right decisions when the circumstances are difficult. Passing on the capability of wise reflection is an important aspect of discipleship, leading to the next element of the discipleship process, a worldview.

3. Discipleship Is Worldview Oriented

Disciple making presupposes a worldview, viewing the world through a Christian lens. If disciple making begins with conversion, believers must ask themselves the question, What is conversion? Missiologist Paul Hiebert argues true conversion is comprehensive, encompassing three levels: behavior, beliefs, and the worldview that underlies those behaviors and beliefs.[19] The neglect of this latter element (worldview transformation) is largely responsible for syncretism, where people convert to Christianity by adopting certain beliefs, or by changing certain behaviors, without

---

17. Vanhoozer, *Faith Speaking Understanding*, 125.

18. Copan, *Saint Paul*, 137. Similarly, when Paul wrote to Timothy about what the younger disciple had learned from him, he mentioned "teaching," and then added elements that were only available through imitation of behavior and reasoning: "conduct, purpose, faith, patience, love, and endurance, along with the persecutions and sufferings that came to me" (2 Tim 3:10–11).

19. Paul G. Hiebert, *Transforming Worldviews: An Anthropological Understanding of How People Change* (Grand Rapids: Baker Academic, 2008), 11.

ever having the structural issues, the scaffolding of their old worldviews, challenged.[20]

Why do these dimensions of a worldview matter? Because people matter, and if one is to get to know people in their efforts to present the gospel, they must take their belief systems seriously.[21] Worldviews matter for both the calling of disciples (believers should know and love other people in order to be effective in sharing the gospel) and in the formation of disciples (believers should be transformed by the renewing of their minds as they seek to follow Christ).

Biblical faith presupposes a worldview because faith is directed toward the God who directs this world. As Albert Wolters suggests, believers "look to the Scriptures for a 'biblical worldview'—now taking that term in an expanded sense to refer to an overall perspective on the world and human life in general."[22] He elaborates:

> Biblical faith in fact involves a worldview, at least implicitly and in principle. The central notion of creation (a *given* order of reality), fall (human mutiny at the root of all perversion of the given order) and redemption (unearned restoration of the order in Christ) are cosmic and transformational in their implications. Together with other elements . . . these central ideas . . . give believers the fundamental outline of a completely anti-pagan *Weltanschauung*, a worldview which provides the interpretive framework for history, society, culture, politics, and everything else that enters human experience.[23]

Building upon all that has been seen about discipleship up to this point, our focus now turns to the formative worldview aspect of disciple making and the definition of *worldview* as a term.

---

20. Paul Hiebert, R. Daniel Shaw, and Tite Tienou, *Understanding Folk Religion: A Christian Response to Popular Beliefs and Practices* (Grand Rapids: Baker Academic, 2000).

21. Tim Keller, *Center Church: Doing Balanced, Gospel-Centered Ministry in Your City* (Grand Rapids: Zondervan, 2012), 120. Keller sees the first step in contextualization as seeking to understand and "as much as possible, identify with your listeners. It involves learning to express people's hopes, objections, fears, and beliefs so well that they feel as though they could not express them better themselves."

22. Al Wolters, "No Longer Queen: The Theological Disciplines and Their Sisters," in *The Bible and the University*, Scripture and Hermeneutics Series (ed. David Jeffrey Lyle and C. Stephan Evans; Nashville: Zondervan, 2007), 8:73.

23. Albert M. Wolters, "Gustavo Gutierrez," in *Bringing into Captivity Every Thought: Capita Selecta in the History of Christian Evaluations of Non-Christian Philosophy* (ed. J. Kapwijk, S. Griffioen, and G. Groenewoud; Lanham, MD: University Press of America, 1991), 237.

Worldview

If disciple making includes the inculcation of a Christian worldview, then we must ask what we mean when we use this term. In this section we engage in a brief historical overview of the term *worldview*, consider what it is, how it functions, the questions it answers, and respond to a few contemporary criticisms of the concept.

History of Worldview as a Concept

The German word *Weltanschauung* was first used by Immanuel Kant in 1790.[24] By the 1840s, it was commonly accepted in the vocabulary of the educated German. Describing the idea behind this word, Albert Wolters writes, "Basic to the idea of *Weltanschauung* is that it is a point of view on the world, a perspective on things, a way of looking at the cosmos from a particular vantage point. It therefore tends to carry the connotation of being personal, dated, and private, limited in validity by its historical conditions."[25]

Whereas Kant introduced the term in reference to one's understanding of the world and where one fits in it, other philosophers, such as Friedrich Schelling (1775-1854) and William Dilthey (1833-1911), emphasized the comprehensive nature of worldview thinking and the inherent plurality and relativity of worldviews.[26] Historians and anthropologists adopted the term to refer to "the deep, enduring cultural patterns of a people,"[27] and in this way they were able to distinguish one period of history from another in terms of a people's underlying structures of belief that give shape to all subsequent thinking.[28]

James Orr (1844-1913) and Abraham Kuyper (1837-1920) are most responsible for bringing the term into Christian academic circles.[29] Both Orr and Kuyper emphasized Christianity as a comprehensive vision for every sphere of life, the ability to see the world with new eyes, "guided by

---

24. Immanuel Kant, *Critique of Judgment* (N.p.: N.p., 1790).

25. Albert M. Wolters, *Creation Regained: Biblical Basics for a Reformational Worldview* (2nd ed.; Grand Rapids: Eerdmans, 2005), 9.

26. Bartholomew and Goheen, *Living at the Crossroads*, 11-14; and David K. Naugle Jr., *Worldview: The History of a Concept* by (Grand Rapids: Eerdmans, 2002), 55-67.

27. Hiebert, *Transforming Worldviews*, 14.

28. Ibid., 16. Hiebert mentions the anthropological study of culture and the notion that "culture is not a random assortment of traits but an integrated coherent way of mentally organizing the world."

29. Naugle, *Worldview*, 6-13, 16-25.

love, by an abiding desire to care about what God cares about—to rejoice in what makes God's heart glad and to grieve about what saddens him."[30]

More recently the concept of worldview has been popularized by Christian thinkers and communicators, such as James Sire ("a set of presuppositions which we hold—consciously or unconsciously—about the world in which we live"),[31] Charles Colson, and Nancy Pearcey.[32] From the examples above, it seems clear that Christians who use the term *worldview* generally consider it as something that precedes philosophy. Their vision is of "a worldview yielding or being developed into a Christian philosophy;"[33] that is, a worldview provides the underlying and usually unconscious framework for further belief and action.

What a Worldview Is

In order to define "worldview" for our present purposes, it is best to start with the most basic, fundamental premise and then dig under the surface until we unearth additional elements that aid us in understanding the breadth and depth of the concept. At its most basic level, a worldview is the lens through which one sees the world. N. T. Wright defines a worldview as "the basic stuff of human existence, the lens through which the world is seen, the blueprint for how one should live in it, and above all the sense of identity and place which enables human beings to be what they are."[34] Comparing a worldview to a lens reminds that most of us do not spend our time looking *at* the lens of our glasses, but rather looking *through* them. In a similar manner, we do not spend most of our time looking *at* our worldview, but rather *through* it, a fact that makes worldview analysis a

30. Richard Mouw, *Abraham Kuyper, A Short and Personal Introduction* (Grand Rapids: Eerdmans, 2011), 92–93. Mouw gives his explanation of Kuyper's idea of worldview, although he cautions that worldview is not something people "possess," as in "having a worldview," but rather is something people practice, as in "engaging in worldviewing."

31. James W. Sire, *The Universe Next Door: A Basic Worldview Catalog* (5th ed.; Downers Grove, IL: IVP Academic, 2009), 16; and Sire's *Naming the Elephant: Worldview as a Concept* (2nd ed.; IVP Academic, 2015).

32. Charles Colson and Nancy Pearcey, *How Now Shall We Live?* (Wheaton, IL: Tyndale House, 1998); Nancy Pearcey, *Total Truth: Liberating Christianity from Its Cultural Captivity* (Wheaton, IL: Crossway, 2004); and idem, *Finding Truth: 5 Principles for Unmasking Atheism, Secularism, and Other God Substitutes* (Colorado Springs, Colo.: David C. Cook, 2015).

33. Craig Bartholomew and Michael Goheen, *Christian Philosophy: A Systematic and Narrative Introduction* (Grand Rapids: Baker Academic), 23; and Albert M. Wolters, "On the Idea of Worldview and Its Relation to Philosophy," in *Stained Glass: Worldviews and Social Science*, ed. Paul Marshall et al. (Lanham, MD: University Press of America, 1983), 14–25. This view is in contrast to other models of conceiving the relationship between worldview and philosophy, in which a worldview might be the crowning achievement of building philosophy, or that worldview and philosophy repel each other.

34. Wright, *New Testament and the People of God*, 124.

difficult endeavor and the discernment of our own perspective a perennial challenge.[35]

The illustration of a worldview as a lens is helpful, as long as we take care to not reduce a worldview to *seeing* alone. We can see above how Wright mentions a worldview's "blueprint for how one should live"; likewise, Brian Walsh and J. Richard Middleton caution against reducing a worldview to "a vision of life" that does not "lead a person or a people into a particular way of life."[36] Conduct is essential both in the outcome and in the understanding of worldview.

Describing a worldview is a way of giving voice to what we see or what others see—the perspective that we have adopted or the framework from which we interpret reality. Michael Goheen and Craig Bartholomew define the term as "an articulation of the basic beliefs embedded in a shared grand story that are rooted in a faith commitment and that give shape and direction to the whole of our individual and corporate lives."[37]

This definition contains three significant points in relation to the present discussion. First, it locates these basic beliefs within a shared story, a narrative in which these beliefs make sense, and as we will see below, the storied structure of a worldview is important when considering how human beings interpret their existence in light of their surroundings. Second, this definition shows that a worldview story is rooted in a faith commitment. This reminds us that not only people of religious faith have a worldview but every person acts out of faith—including the secularist, the agnostic, or the atheist. We take the shared story by which we interpret our world, at least at some measure, by faith, even if we are not religious at all.[38] Third, this definition helps broaden a worldview beyond an individualistic interpretation by allowing "worldviews" to describe the corporate life of a society. As inherently social beings, we never develop a worldview in total isolation from others. The differences of our beliefs and practices bump up against one another to the point that we cannot help but be shaped by others' distinctive beliefs and to influence the beliefs of others.

---

35. Sire, *Naming the Elephant*, 143, states, "We think *with* our worldview and *because of* our worldview, not *about* our worldview." On a related note, it is usually when our perspective on the world has let us down in some way (either through cognitive dissonance or affective incoherence) that we question our foundational beliefs.

36. Brian J. Walsh and J. Richard Middleton, *Transforming Vision* (Downers Grove, IL: InterVarsity Press, 1984), 54.

37. Bartholomew and Goheen, *Living at the Crossroads*, 23.

38. This understanding of a "faith commitment" severs the tie between "secularity" and "objectivity," as if religious adherence disqualifies itself by having a faith commitment.

Paul Hiebert approaches the concept of worldview from the standpoint of an anthropologist. He provides a social scientific definition of worldview, one which is confluent with that of Bartholomew and Goheen's but at the same time expands it as "the foundational cognitive, affective, and evaluative assumptions and frameworks a group of people makes about the nature of reality which they use to order their lives. It encompasses people's images or maps of the reality of all things that they use for living their lives. It is the cosmos thought to be true, desirable and moral by a community of people."[39] The three dimensions here are cognitive, affective, and evaluative.

Because the term *worldview* comes through philosophy, it could easily lend itself to an overemphasis on the cognitive aspects of worldview analysis (hence, the term *worldview thinking*). Hiebert points to the comprehensiveness of a worldview by his use of the terms "images" and "maps" that refer to our affections and moral decision making. Hiebert's definition focuses on "assumptions" and "frameworks"—the unconscious categories used to interpret our experiences.

The cognitive dimension refers to the way humans perceive the world around them. For example, do we view time in a linear fashion (from past to future) or in cyclical events? How do we view space? What are the mental maps we have of the world? Likewise, this dimension raises the issue of perception: does a person see oneself primarily in terms of individual autonomy or as connected to a group? Zoom out from the view of the individual, and we have another level of cognition related to how one views his or her "group" versus "other groups." Zoom out further, and we see issues regarding how one views this world and the forces in it. Do we see nature as mechanistic and natural? Or do we believe in the existence of supernatural forces that affect our lives? These are all examples of cognitive themes in a worldview.[40]

The affective dimension refers to the kinds of personal emotions stirred up as we encounter the world around us. What produces joy or sorrow? What produces fear or revulsion? What elements inspire worship and create a sense of awe and wonder? How do we determine what is beautiful? Why do we create certain styles and find them attractive? Although not often treated in worldview studies, these themes are important for understanding the perspective of an individual or society.[41]

39. Hiebert, *Transforming Worldviews*, 25-26.
40. Hiebert, *Transforming Worldviews*, 50-59.
41. Ibid.

The "evaluative" or "moral" dimension relates to the judgments human beings make. What do we consider to be virtues worthy of emulation, standards worth keeping, morals worth modeling, or manners worth employing? These themes concern the moral order of the world. They help us understand why certain types or figures are consistently seen as heroes in literature and why other types are considered villains. These themes unconsciously form the way we view and value human achievements.[42]

In studying worldviews, Hiebert recommends both a synchronic model (that helps one understand how people view the structure of the world) and a diachronic dimension (that helps one see how people interpret the human story).[43] This narratival aspect is crucial to understanding a worldview because it indicates how people view their history and their future, thus infusing the present with eschatological meaning. We will return to this aspect of a worldview when defining the term *eschatology*.

What a Worldview Does

We turn now to the question of a worldview's *function*, not simply what it is but rather what it does. N. T. Wright's understanding of worldview is consonant with Bartholomew, Goheen, and Hiebert and includes a helpful enumeration of four things a worldview accomplishes. First, worldviews provide the stories through which human beings view reality. Wright states, "Narrative is the most characteristic expression of worldview going deeper than the isolated observation or fragmented remark."[44]

Second, building upon this narrative, a worldview helps us answer "the basic questions that determine human existence."[45] Walsh sees these questions as forming plausibility structures that reveal the assumptions behind the beliefs and actions that make sense.[46] Third, Wright points out that a worldview is expressed in cultural symbols[47] that reinforce the interpretive frameworks for a society and open the door to a worldview's fourth

---

42. Ibid., 60–65.

43. Ibid., 25–28. Hiebert limits worldview to cultural analysis; hence, his emphasis on a "group of people," not individuals. I am using worldview language in a more expansive way, referring to both culture and individual persons.

44. Wright, *New Testament and the People of God*, 123.

45. Ibid.

46. Brian J. Walsh, "From Housing to Homemaking: Worldviews and the Shaping of Home," *Christian Scholar's Review* 35, no. 1 (2006): 237–57; and Sire, *Naming the Elephant*, 132–36.

47. Wright, *New Testament and the People of God*, 123.

function—the inclusion of "praxis, a way-of-being-in-the-world."[48] Wright's explanation of a worldview's function centers primarily on giving answers to the basic questions of life, which, in turn, lead to a particular kind of involvement in the world. We will examine these worldview questions below, but first, we should consider an additional function of a worldview, as indicated by Paul Hiebert.

Not surprisingly, given Hiebert's emphasis on affective and moral dimensions of a worldview, Hiebert sees "emotional security" as one of the primary gifts of a worldview. In a world of sorrow and loss, he writes, "People turn to their deepest cultural beliefs for comfort and security." He then points to life's most significant rituals (births, marriages, funerals, harvest celebrations, etc.) as evidence. He adds, "Our worldview buttresses our fundamental beliefs with emotional reinforcements so that they are not easily destroyed."[49] This emotional security gives "psychological reassurance" as we view the world as it really is and protects us from a "worldview crisis" that erupts when our experience of reality differs starkly from our worldview.[50] The emotional underpinning of comfort and security in interpreting life through our worldview explains why a "worldview crisis" is rarely the result of a cognitive clash of logic alone.

Because our tendency is to turn to our worldview for psychological reassurance, we should be ever cautious about the way worldviews can be marshaled in support of idolatrous ideology. Oliver O'Donovan warns against mistaking the conception itself with false imaginations of the world. As an example, he mentions Christian appropriators of worldview terminology who so emphasized a "plurality of spheres of knowledge" that the result was a "civil conformity in the form of a political pluralism with which the sovereignty of Christ had little to do."[51] The danger here is seeing the function of a worldview in largely neutral terms, without recognizing that even its best-intentioned observers can succumb to its inherent, idolatrous bent.

48. Ibid., 124; and Hiebert, *Transforming Worldviews*, 29. Hiebert concurs, "Our worldview validates our deepest cultural norms, which we use to evaluate our experiences and choose courses of action."

49. Hiebert, *Transforming Worldviews*, 29.

50. Paul G. Hiebert, *The Gospel in Human Contexts: Anthropological Explorations for Contemporary Missions* (Grand Rapids: Baker Academic, 2009), 158, writes, "To question a worldview is to challenge the very foundation of life, and we resist such challenges with strong emotional reactions. Few human fears are greater than the fear of a loss of a sense of order and meaning."

51. O'Donovan, *Finding and Seeking*, 112–13.

What a Worldview Asks

If one of the functions of a worldview is to provide answers to the basic questions of life, as seen above, we must now consider these questions and what they signify. N. T. Wright lays out four basic questions at the heart of a worldview: "Who are we?"[52] "Where are we?" "What is wrong?"[53] and, "What is the solution?" That final question is what leads to praxis, as Wright insists, "The implied eschatology of the fourth question ('what is the solution?') necessarily entails *action.*"[54] Goheen and Bartholomew add "What is life all about?" and "In what kind of world do we live?" as additional, foundational questions prompted by the worldview story.[55] Asking this question another way, Mark Sanford and Steve Wilkens sum up the "problem" and "solution" questions by claiming that every worldview attempts to answer the question, "What must we do to be saved?"[56]

In the decades since he listed four foundational worldview questions, Wright has come to see the value of a fifth question. He has decided to make the "implied eschatology" of the fourth question ("What is the solution?") explicit. He writes, "Since writing *The New Testament and the People of God*, I have realized that 'what time is it?' needs adding to the four questions I started with (though at what point in the order could be discussed further). Without it, the structure collapses into the timelessness which characterizes some non-Judeo-Christian worldviews."[57] For Wright, asking the question, "What time is it?" clarifies the shape of worldview thinking and keeps one from losing the important "this-world" dimension of

52. Some might add, "Where have we come from?" as a subset of the question "Who are we?" The reason debates over human origins continue to provoke such heated controversy in our day is because the existence or nonexistence of a personal Creator is a foundational plank in a person's worldview. If humans have arrived here as the result of a purely naturalistic process, then the answers to "Who are we?" and "Where are we?" are radically altered.

53. The question regarding what is wrong with the world is closely linked to, What is the solution? For example, if the biggest problem in the world is ignorance, then the solution will be education. The reason some find "education" as a superficial answer to the world's problems is because they believe "what has gone wrong" cannot be answered by appealing to ignorance.

54. Wright, *New Testament and the People of God*, 123.

55. Bartholomew and Goheen, *Living at the Crossroads*, 24. Sire, *Naming the Elephant*, 154–55. Sire's worldview questions are arranged philosophically rather than narratively: (1) What is the prime reality, the really real? (2) What is the nature of external reality, that is, the world around us? (3) What is a human being? (4) What happens to a person at death? (5) Why is it possible to know anything at all? (6) How do we know what is right and wrong? (7) What is the meaning of human history? Sire sees his questions as comprehending the more story-based questions of Wright and others. I prefer to see Sire's philosophical angle as a subset of the "worldview as master story" approach.

56. Wilkens and Sanford, *Hidden Worldviews*, 14.

57. N. T. Wright, *Jesus and the Victory of God*, Christian Origins and the Question of God (Minneapolis: Fortress, 1996), 2:443.

discipleship. This question situates people not only in the world—a place in space ("Where are we?")—but also in a cultural moment—a place in time ("*When* are we?"). Just as humans cannot conceive of themselves apart from their geography and physicality, they cannot conceive of themselves as timeless beings.

If a worldview leads to praxis, a way of being in the world, then practice must inevitably be linked to moral deliberation that goes beyond mere rule keeping to include "discerning the time." O'Donovan writes,

> What is it, then, that the moral law cannot tell us? It cannot tell us what is to be done *next.* It gives generic forms by which we can understand the moment in which we find ourselves placed, but it does not tell us what time it is. It casts no light on the immediate horizon. And so it cannot formulate an agenda in which things that demand to be done can be ordered by their timeliness.[58]

Therefore, the question "What must I do?" is closely connected to the preceding question, "What time is it?"

Much of this book will focus on Wright's fifth worldview question, "What time is it?" Without this eschatological dimension we are unable to comprehend fully the contextual nature of our discipleship task. If the church is a sign and an instrument of the coming kingdom of God, then we cannot see our obedience as a timeless expression of God's will. We are, instead, witnesses to a God who has done something in history, in this space-time universe, and who is moving all of humanity and the world to the ultimate fulfillment of his purposes. Understanding the times is vital if Christians believe we are witnessing to a God who has a plan for the future.

Criticisms and Cautions of Worldview

In recent days, certain scholars have questioned the helpfulness of the concept of "worldview." Goheen and Bartholomew note several objections often made by such scholars and then offer a response to the objections. The first is that the worldview approach intellectualizes the gospel. While recognizing the dangers of modernism's overemphasis on reason, Goheen and Bartholomew reaffirm the importance of "thinking Christianly," and they believe they overcome this objection by showing how the Christian worldview is connected to one's personal experience of Jesus Christ.

58. O'Donovan, *Finding and Seeking*, 216.

The affective elements of relationship are at the heart of a worldview, and because the starting point is God's revelation, not human reason, we cannot accept this criticism that a worldview is too dependent on human thought to be valid.[59]

This charge of over-intellectualism is leveled against worldview thinking in another way. It is at the heart of James K. A. Smith's concern that worldview terminology focuses primarily on education as something one knows rather than something one loves.[60] Smith sees much Protestant discipleship as being overly fixated on doctrines and ideas, leading to "an overly intellectualist account of what it means to be or become a Christian," which in turn leads to "a stunted pedagogy that is fixated on the mind."[61] Appealing to Augustine, Smith believes, "The way we inhabit the world is not primarily as thinkers, or even believers, but as more affective, embodied creatures who make our way in the world more by feeling our way around it."[62]

How does this criticism influence an understanding of a Christian worldview? For Smith a worldview is no longer about distinctly Christian "knowledge" but rather about a Christian "social imaginary." It is "a distinctly Christian understanding of the world that is implicit in the practices of Christian worship."[63] The difference between a "social imaginary" and a "theory" is that the former emphasizes the way people's stories, narratives, myths, and icons capture their hearts and imaginations and thus form their view of the world. Instead of a trickle-down approach that begins with beliefs and then moves toward desires and actions, Smith sees the reverse taking place; human practices contribute to their imaginations, which then lead to the formation of knowledge of doctrines.[64] He adds, "What we do (practices) is intimately linked to what we desire (love), so what we do determines whether, how, and what we can know."[65]

---

59. Bartholomew and Goheen, *Living at the Crossroads*, 19–21.

60. James K. A. Smith, *Desiring the Kingdom: Worship, Worldview and Cultural Formation (Cultural Liturgies)* (Grand Rapids: Baker Academic, 2009), 18.

61. Ibid., 12–13.

62. Ibid., 47.

63. Ibid., 68; and Charles Taylor, *A Secular Age* (Boston: Harvard University Press, 2007), 171–72. The term "social imaginary" comes from Taylor, who defines it as "the way ordinary people 'imagine' their social surroundings, and this is often not expressed in theoretical terms, it is carried in images, stories, legends, etc." Smith uses "social imaginary" instead of "worldview" in order to capture the imaginative aspect more clearly.

64. Smith, *Desiring the Kingdom*, 69.

65. Ibid., 70.

Smith's criticism of an approach to spiritual formation that is overly intellectualized is a helpful caution against focusing only on the cognitive aspect of worldview formation. However, as long as we remain fully aware of the "affective" and "moral" dimensions of a worldview, as noted by Hiebert and as affirmed by Wright in his consideration of cultural symbols as expressions of practice, then we should be able to avoid many of the dangers Smith mentions.[66] The best way to incorporate Smith's critique of the worldview approach is not to dismiss or downplay the cognitive element but to see how beliefs and practices work in a dialectic manner, with our social imaginary influencing what we can know and how we know it and our beliefs simultaneously impinging on our social imaginary and how we interpret the world around them. The reality is neither a trickle-down approach, like a river that rushes from knowledge to beliefs to practices; neither is it a trickle-up approach leading from practices to imagination to knowledge. Instead, we should view the relationship between the imagination and knowledge more like ocean waves, where the ocean thrusts water onto the shore (our practices) and the water that returns is taken up into the sea (our beliefs) and becomes part of the next wave (knowledge that now encompasses beliefs and practices).

Goheen and Bartholomew mention a second objection made by critics of the worldview approach: it might lead to relativizing the gospel. Confronted with a perplexing diversity of worldviews, we might begin to see truth as relative, since it seems impossible to adjudicate between competing worldview claims. On a similar note, does not the diversity of worldviews (and the specific nature of individual belief and practice) lead to incoherence when speaking of worldviews in general terms? If everyone has a worldview and every worldview is different, then how can one avoid reductionism when speaking of worldviews in general terms?

Goheen and Bartholomew answer the first aspect of this objection in two ways. First, they see the gospel as the true story of the world despite the plurality of perspectives that exist. Second, they believe one's articulation of worldview should not be confused with the gospel itself, but it is always

66. N. T. Wright, *Paul and the Faithfulness of God*, Christian Origins and the Question of God (Minneapolis: Fortress Press, 2013), 4:28, n. 80. Contra Smith, I side with N. T. Wright who prefers to "expand the notion of worldview to incorporate these and other elements rather than abandon it and launch out with a different term."

open to critique from Scripture.[67] These responses help answer the objection of relativism.

James Sire responds to the second aspect of this objection, the idea that pluralism makes any general discussion of worldviews incoherent. Sire sees discussion of worldviews as "ideal types" that may not be held in the same way by every individual and yet still hold value in describing the general characteristics of that society. For example, within a Christian worldview, distinctions may be present between denominations—more or less consistent or coherent versions of seeing the world through a biblical lens, despite the differences that still exist. However, recognizing these differences do exist does not negate the helpfulness of generalizing worldview discussion as "ideal types," just as one would not find it problematic to speak generally of a Hindu worldview, a naturalist worldview, and so forth.[68]

A third objection is that "the worldview approach may become disconnected from Scripture and thus vulnerable to the spirits of the age."[69] This objection is not a criticism per se but a warning against an ever-present danger. Perhaps in an attempt to ward off this danger, Oliver O'Donovan recommends the language of testimony and witness rather than a "worldview." What is to be had here is "a message about the order of God's works which we may both receive and give, a testimony to receive and amplify as it is passed through the thought and experience that is given to us to live with." Furthermore, O'Donovan sees the language of "faithful repetition" as less vulnerable to the perils of idolatry, the idea of "extending or amplifying the testimony we have received." The goal is for Christians to "in our time" take up the confession of those who have gone before them and then learn "to think and say for ourselves what has been thought and said before us on our behalf."[70]

Although O'Donovan's cautions are helpful in reminding of the necessity of faithful witness to the apostolic testimony, as revealed in Scripture, they need not lead us to dispense with worldview terminology altogether. The answer to this warning is to heed it. If we are to embrace a worldview formed by the drama of Scripture, we must return again and again to the

67. Bartholomew and Goheen, *Living at the Crossroads*, 22.
68. Sire, *Naming the Elephant*, 131-32.
69. Bartholomew and Goheen, *Living at the Crossroads*, 22.
70. O'Donovan, *Finding and Seeking*, 137.

true story of our world in order to have our own blind spots exposed and mistaken ways corrected.[71]

Some criticisms of the use of worldview terminology are well founded, and we benefit from incorporating these warnings and concerns into our overall project. As long as we are clear on the affective and imaginative elements of worldview formation (as opposed to what is primarily a cognitive approach), the biblical drama as the true story of the world (as opposed to the relativizing tendencies of a pluralistic diversity of worldviews), and the need to be constantly immersed in Scripture (as opposed to extrabiblical or antibiblical visions of the world), then we can continue to use the idea of worldview as a way of helping to understand the interpretive framework from which people know, believe, and act in the world.

Eschatology

A third term that requires further reflection is *eschatology*. At the beginning of this chapter, we examined the term *discipleship* and showed that one important element of discipleship is that it includes a worldview. Then we examined the term *worldview* and showed that one of the questions a worldview seeks to answer is, "What time is it?" This worldview question leads to a consideration of eschatology, for no one can properly answer the question of what time it is without considering where he or she is in the narrative of world history and what the future is or should be.[72]

If discipleship includes the mission of making more disciples, then the fulfillment of the Great Commission depends on faithful obedience to Christ in a particular place and time. Regarding *place*, most missionaries instinctively recognize that the shape of Christian obedience will change depending on the context in which that obedience is fulfilled. For example, a family in sub-Saharan Africa existing in impoverished conditions will have a Christian life of obedience that looks different from an underground

71. Bartholomew and Goheen, *Living at the Crossroads*, 22.

72. Sire, *Naming the Elephant*, 155. "What time is it?" is not the only eschatological question a worldview asks. Sire asks the worldview question, "What is the meaning of human history?" He makes clear that this question includes Wright's "What time is it?" Orr poses a similar question, "What is the true end of existence?" Walsh and Middleton offer yet another, asking, "What master story ties my life to the lives of others living and dead?" I prefer "What time is it?" because it not only presupposes a meaning given to human history, but it directs our attention to what we do in the present in light of history's ultimate significance.

church in China or a wealthy suburban businessman in south Florida.[73] We recognize that discipleship—following Jesus—will vary from place to place as different churches seek to follow Jesus in their context. Likewise, the methods of leading people to faith in Christ may vary depending on where they are and what is effective in a certain cultural milieu.[74] Geography matters, and even though there is an underlying unity in the gospel and what it demands of believers, the day-to-day vision of discipleship may appear different when the situation requires wisdom and discernment of how best to follow Jesus in areas not specifically spelled out in the Scriptures or in cultures where scriptural interpretation diverges.[75]

If we recognize that geography shapes the form of one's Christian discipleship, why should we not also recognize that time does so as well? It is not just geography that shapes us but also our situatedness in a particular time. When we speak about "living on mission" in a particular place and time, it is not enough for us to consider *place* apart from *time*. As God's emissaries to a lost world, we are to understand our cultural "moment"—the time in which we have been put on earth.[76] To say that *time* matters for

---

73. Samuel Escobar, "Mission Studies—Past, Present, and Future," in *Landmark Essays in Mission and World Christianity* (ed. Robert L. Gallagher and Paul Hertig; Maryknoll, NY: Orbis Books, 2009), 243. Escobar explains how Christianity embraces the paradoxical dynamic of the gospel and pluralism. Christians believe in plurality in the sense that every culture is equal in terms of access to God, and at the same time, Christians believe no culture is adequate in presenting the transcendent truth. He writes, "The gospel does not find expression outside of a cultural form; however, the gospel cannot be restricted to any given cultural form—it transcends all of them."

74. David Clark, *To Know and Love God: Method for Theology* (Wheaton, IL: Crossway, 2003), 78. Regarding our task of recognizing the differences in culture, Clark believes evangelicals should: (1) "recognize the reality of cultural influence on all theological interpretation," (2) "purposefully adopt a self-critical stance toward any and all cultures," while (3) asserting "the need for theology to achieve cultural relevance," and (4) yielding "to the priority of Scripture over any and all cultural assumptions."

75. Timothy Tennent, *Theology in the Context of World Christianity: How the Global Church Is Influencing the Way We Think about and Discuss Theology* (Grand Rapids: Zondervan, 2009), 12. When it comes to exercising this discernment, Tennent contrasts the universal truth of Christianity (the "pilgrim principle") with the particular force of the gospel in a culture (the "indigenizing" principle) and recommends a healthy balance between the two. Tennent writes, "An undue emphasis on the pilgrim principle assumes that all the issues we face in our culture are the same faced by every culture. In other words, our own theological reflection is universalized for the entire world. Because our issues must surely be the same as theirs, and we are confident in our own theological and exegetical abilities, there is no point in humbly listening to the insights of Christians outside of our cultural sphere. By contrast, an undue emphasis on the indigenizing principle assumes that every issue the church faces is, in the final analysis, so contextualized and conditioned by the particularities of the local setting and the time in which we live that we become skeptical of the ability of any theologian to speak with authority or confidence about the claims of the gospel on someone outside his or her own cultural arena."

76. Michael Goheen, *Introducing Christian Mission Today: Scripture, History, and Issues* (Downers Grove, IL: IVP Academic, 2014), 27). Goheen claims, "The church's mission is always contextual. The church must always ascertain what the issues *of the day* are and address those. Missiology must remain rooted in the gospel and the Word of God. But it also must address *the times* and places in which it lives. Thus missiology will vary from place to place and *time to time*" (emphasis in original).

our mission is one way of saying that our conception of discipleship itself, which is both the result and the process of mission, is thoroughly eschatological. To make this case, I must explain what I mean by "eschatology."

A General Definition of *Eschatology*

Generally speaking, eschatology is not a distinctively Christian concept; that is, people who adhere to other religious faiths or no religious faith at all still maintain a vision for humanity's future, and this vision is part of the narrative that gives them meaning and significance. German theologian Hans Schwarz defines the term broadly enough to encompass multiple religious perspectives when he writes,

> In its broadest sense the term "eschatology" includes all concepts of life beyond death and everything connected with it such as heaven and hell, paradise and immortality, resurrection and transmigration of the soul, rebirth and reincarnation, and last judgment and doomsday. Eschatology also is determined by and determines our understanding of humanity, of body and soul, and of value systems and worldviews.[77]

Note how there is nothing particularly Christian about this definition since multiple religious perspectives are included here. Similar to the way the term *worldview* can apply to Christianity or to other religions (for example, "the Hindu worldview"), eschatology can also apply to other belief systems and visions of the future. Even those without religious faith have an eschatological viewpoint. For example, the committed naturalist may believe that the physical universe is in a state of entropy and will eventually lead to the dissolution of the planet and all humanity. This perspective is eschatological (albeit a pessimistic one!), but it plays an important role in one's thought. Schwarz continues,

> Eschatology always influences and determines the conduct of life and vice versa. In an individual eschatology the conduct of this life will determine the destiny of the individual after death, whereas in a collective eschatology the destiny of all humanity is taken into consideration. A cosmic eschatology even goes beyond

77. Hans Schwarz, *Eschatology* (Grand Rapids: Eerdmans, 2000), 26.

> the scope of humanity and includes the destiny of this earth or of the whole cosmos.[78]

The three elements of eschatology here are personal, collective, and cosmic. In most worldviews, these three are held together like different plot points in the overarching story people believe about humankind.[79] Not only are these elements operative in the work of Christian and non-Christian religious scholars, but they also are operative in scholars who are not religious at all. Take, for example, Julian Barnes, the British novelist who has written a popular memoir on death. Barnes is an atheist whose *cosmic* eschatology is that the world is doomed to eventual destruction, and thus, his *collective* eschatology is that all humanity will perish with it, so his *personal* eschatology is that no hope exists for life after death.[80]

It would be inconceivable for Barnes to believe in a personal afterlife with God while simultaneously arguing that the story of humanity ends with the universe and all the people in it ceasing to exist. These three elements of his vision of the future naturally hold together and help us see that, although Barnes is not religious at all, he adopts an eschatological position as part of his overarching story of humankind. Within the framework of this overarching story, we make decisions based on the kind of world we believe we inhabit. For this reason O'Donovan reminds us, "Narrative is an important condition for moral thought."[81] The understanding of a narrative is what distinguishes merely "doing something" from "how one thinks what one is to do."

The reason we must first consider eschatology in its broadest sense, even without its distinctively Christian contours, is so we can later contrast Christian eschatology with rival eschatological perspectives. However, since we are also affixing "eschatological" as a modifier for "discipleship,"

---

78. Ibid.

79. Lesslie Newbigin, *The Gospel in a Pluralist Society* (Grand Rapids: Eerdmans, 1989), 178. Newbigin warns against reducing eschatology to only one of these elements—in this case, the personal. He writes, "The question we have to ask is not, 'What will happen to this person's soul after death?' But 'What is the end, which gives meaning to this person's story as part of God's whole story?'"

80. Julian Barnes, *Nothing to Be Frightened Of* (New York: Alfred A. Knopf, 2008), 242; and James K. A. Smith, *How (Not) to Be Secular: Reading Charles Taylor* (Grand Rapids: Eerdmans, 2014), 5–6. Barnes writes hauntingly about a person's inevitable death and eventual irrelevance ("just as every writer will have a last reader, so every corpse will have a last visitor") as part of the collective demise of humanity on a planet doomed to eventual destruction. James K. A. Smith notes how Barnes's meditations on death and extinction lead him to questions about God and divinity.

81. Oliver O'Donovan, *Self, World, and Time: Ethics as Theology* (Grand Rapids: Eerdmans, 2013), 1:3.

it is important that we define the distinctively Christian understanding of humanity's future.

The Christian Understanding of Eschatology

Many Christians assume that discussion of eschatology refers to the "last things" doctrines in the back of systematic theology textbooks. These doctrines generally refer to the second coming of Christ, the timing and interpretation of the millennium, and the future, final state of humanity. In this book we will be using *eschatology* in a broader sense, as encompassing the Christian vision of time and the destiny of the world. Therefore, to say discipleship is eschatological is not to say that discipleship is caught up in debates about the time line of events surrounding Christ's second coming but to say that discipleship is grounded in the larger story of the world and where the world is going, as articulated in Scripture.[82]

In fact, viewing eschatology as only the "end times" is derivative, according to Dermot Lane, because it comes from "the broader and more biblical understanding of eschatology which is founded on the Christ-event: the announcement of the coming reign of God, the public ministry of Jesus, and the outpouring of the Spirit. This primary meaning of eschatology should be the basis of any particular understanding of death, judgment, heaven, hell and the second coming."[83] In other words, we derive our understanding of the end times from the larger story of salvation, not as an isolated appendix of doctrines clustered around "the future." We now turn our attention to this larger story of salvation, the story of God's work in world history, the coming of Christ, and the promise of his return.

Christian Eschatology as the Story of World History. Perhaps no one has emphasized the eschatological nature of Christian theology in recent centuries more than Jürgen Moltmann. In his monumental *Theology of*

---

82. In broadening my definition of eschatology, I hope to include various perspectives on the end times within an overarching framework of God's ultimate promise. In the past century the prominence of dispensational thought within evangelical circles sought to make particular prophecies relevant for Christian behavior, with urgency around evangelism in light of Christ's imminent return. But it would be a mistake to label all dispensationalists as pessimistic in cultural outlook. B. M. Pietsch's important work, *Dispensational Modernism* (Oxford: Oxford University Press, 2015), shows an "afflictive model of progress" at work, in which the present is getting better and worse at the same time, with ultimate hope in the rule of Christ on earth (158). Although I recognize that different millennial views will impact a Christian's perspective of future hope, I believe a detailed treatment of specific eschatological beliefs would lead beyond the main thesis for this book. For this reason I will focus on eschatology as a general understanding of the Christian vision of time and the ultimate destiny of the world.

83. Dermot A. Lane, "Eschatology," in *New Dictionary of Theology* (ed. Joseph A. Komonchak, Mary Collins, and Dermot A. Lane; Wilmington, Del.: Michael Glazier, 1987), 329–42.

Hope, Moltmann argues that only in the presence of a certain worldview, a "confidence and a hope for the world," will Christian mission be truly transformative.[84] Moltmann sees eschatology not as the end itself but as the entire course of history in its movement toward the end. He writes, "The eschatological is not one element *of* Christianity, but it is the medium of Christian faith. . . . Hence eschatology cannot really be only a part of Christian doctrine. Rather, the eschatological outlook is characteristic of all Christian proclamation, of every Christian experience and of the whole earth."[85]

Moltmann is not alone in his broader conception of eschatology and its centrality within the Christian story. For example, Trevor Hart shows how the eschatological time line of humanity's future reaches back into the present and the past when he states,

> Eschatology concerns the fact that, just as God spoke the primordial word which called the world into being, so too he will have the final say about its future, a word that he has already uttered under the form of promise. While, therefore, eschatological doctrine certainly has to do with final destinies—of individual people, human history, and the cosmos as a whole—beyond the threshold of finitude and death, in a vital sense it is not just about the "end" (the final few pages) of the world's story, but about the story as a whole (past, present, and future) and as

84. Moltmann, *Theology of Hope*, 288–89.

85. Ibid., 16; and Scaer, "Jürgen Moltmann and His Theology of Hope," 69–79. No doubt exists that Moltmann has strong justification in Scripture for his emphasis on eschatology, and even his critics commend him for resurfacing this often-neglected element of missiology and ecclesiology (ibid., 69). The problem with this theology of hope is that Moltmann, at times, overstates his case to the point that God appears to be subject to the process of time and not outside of it. The result is a biblical-sounding version of process theology. For a healthy critique of Moltmann's proposal, see ibid. Additionally, Oliver O'Donovan credits Moltmann for bringing the distinctiveness of hope into view but claims "his exposition of hope has been bipolar" because of the way it insists on intrinsic possibilities, while also promoting an ethico-political program. He writes, "Hope does not and cannot ground the program Moltmann elicits from it." O'Donovan, *Finding and Seeking*, 163–65. Pentecostal theologian Simon Chan appreciates Moltmann's emphasis on eschatology, but he argues against Moltmann's tendency to "free" the Spirit from his ecclesial location and release him into the world. Chan makes the case for a unique working of the Spirit in the church, writing, "Not only is the church Spirit-filled, but the church is also the place where the Spirit is present on earth." Simon Chan, *Pentecostal Theology and the Christian Spiritual Tradition* (Sheffield, UK: Sheffield Academic Press, 2000), 110–11. Missionary and theologian Lesslie Newbigin manages to make many of the same points as Moltmann yet without the problems of process theology. In this dissertation, wherever I quote from Moltmann, it is to affirm his theological and biblical reflection where he is helpful and should not be interpreted as advocacy for his overall theological project.

> individual parts of it read now consistently in the light of that promised end.[86]

Similarly, Karl Barth grounded eschatological hope in Christology, arguing that "Christianity that is not entirely and altogether eschatological has entirely nothing to do with Christ."[87] Likewise, Stanley Hauerwas claims that "every loci of the Christian faith has an eschatological dimension, making impossible any isolated account of eschatology."[88] Seen in this light, eschatology functions as something of an umbrella that encompasses all of Christianity and its doctrines. To put it another way, eschatology refers to the story line as it moves to its climax and culmination; it is the element that drives the plot forward to the promised resolution.

Christian Eschatology and the Coming of Christ. Why is it not only possible but also necessary to see eschatology in this broader sense? Perhaps it is because the gospel infuses time with redemptive significance. The reason eschatology matters for understanding Christianity is the same reason geography and physicality matter for understanding Christianity; Jesus entered this world in a particular place *and* time.

Theologians write about the miracle of the incarnation—the reality of God the Son taking on human flesh and dwelling among humanity. The terminology of incarnation refers to God's *enfleshment*. Though it may not receive the same amount of attention, *temporality*—just as much as *embodiment*—is at the heart of this spectacular miracle. Timothy George reflects, "At the heart of the Christian faith is this stupendous claim, that the eternal God of creation, the God who *is* eternity . . . has so opened himself to our creaturely existence, to our history, to our time, that he has come among us as one of us." George recommends we recognize this truth not only is the incarnation but also "the Intemporation." He continues, "In Jesus Christ, God in his own being—and not as a surrogate—has come into our own world *and also into our own time*, and in doing so he has taken unto himself our hurt, our pain, and indeed our sin."[89]

---

86. Trevor Hart, "Eschatology," in *The Oxford Handbook of Evangelical Theology* (ed. Gerald R. McDermott; New York: Oxford University Press, 2010), 262–75.

87. Karl Barth, *The Epistle to the Romans* (London, UK: Oxford University Press, 1933), 314.

88. Stanley Hauerwas, *Approaching the End: Eschatological Reflections on Church, Politics, and Life* (Grand Rapids: Eerdmans, 2013), xii.

89. Timothy George, "St. Augustine and the Mystery of Time," in *What God Knows: Time and the Question of Divine Knowledge* (ed. Harry Lee Poe and J. Stanley Mattson; Waco: Baylor, 2005), 40.

Because the incarnation is just as much about the Son of God entering time as it is his entering humanity's space, we should not be surprised to see the theme of "fulfilling the times" running throughout the scriptural story line, primarily in reference to Christ's coming.[90] According to O'Donovan, this theme "summons us to bring our different historical moments into relation with a focal community of obedience evoked by that moment."[91] In other words, we read our own history and interpret our present moment in light of the times being fulfilled in Christ.

The events that make up the heart of the Christian understanding of eschatology are not, in the first place, the return of Christ and his judgment of all things but the cross and resurrection. The crucifixion is not a metaphor; neither is it an appeal to a timeless ethos of forgiveness and love. Instead, the crucifixion is a moment of time that tears history in two and gives it "meaning, a direction that it never had before."[92] Likewise, to speak of the resurrection as the "center of history" (as does O'Donovan) is to elevate this event from being "a mere extent of time" and to see it, instead, as "the narrative logic that underpins whatever has been undertaken or will be undertaken in time,"[93] or as Newbigin put it memorably, "The resurrection cannot be accommodated in any way of understanding the world except one of which it is the starting point."[94] The cross and resurrection are the climactic point in the story of the world, not simply because of their place in the biblical time line but also in how they impact our reading of history before and after. The apostolic testimony to the truth of the cross and resurrection, therefore, "renarrates the whole of human life" so that one sees the world in light of God's action in the person and work of Jesus Christ.[95]

Christian Eschatology and the Return of Christ. Broadening the Christian understanding of eschatology beyond "end times" doctrines must not exclude these future events. The return of Christ and final judgment are key moments in the future that infuse our present choices with significance and purpose. As O'Donovan writes, "At the heart of eschatology is the promise that we all must appear before God to be judged according to our works.

---

90. Mark 1:15; Luke 1:1; 1:20; 21:24; and 24:44; Acts 1:6; 3:18, 20; and 13:33; Gal 4:4; Eph 1:10; and 1 Pet 1:20.

91. O'Donovan, *Finding and Seeking*, 116.

92. George, "St. Augustine and the Mystery of Time," 43.

93. O'Donovan, *Self, World, and Time*, 92.

94. Lesslie Newbigin, *Truth to Tell: The Gospel as Public Truth*, Osterhaven Lecture (Grand Rapids: Eerdmans, 1991), 11.

95. Hauerwas, *Approaching the End*, 53.

Our deeds are to be events in history, subject to ultimate appraisal."[96] The three elements of eschatology (personal, collective, and cosmic) find their Christian particularity in this place. *Personal* eschatology refers to our hope of eternal life with God that will outlast physical death. *Collective* eschatology refers to our hope in a bodily resurrection and our unending fellowship with God and one another. *Cosmic* eschatology refers to the regeneration of the universe and the establishment of the new heavens and new earth.

Once we consider Christian eschatology in its personal, collective, and cosmic conceptions, we see how it shapes our decisions in the here and now. N. T. Wright sees our present behavior as shaped by the ultimate goal for humanity. If the goal is the new heaven and new earth ("with human beings raised from the dead to be the renewed world's rulers and priests"),[97] and if the goal is achieved through God's work through Jesus and the Spirit, then "Christian living in the present consists of anticipating this ultimate reality through the Spirit-led, habit-forming, truly human practice of faith, hope, and love, sustaining Christians in their calling to worship and reflect his glory into the world."[98] Christians live today in light of the future, as people who trust in the promises of God and anticipate the return of Christ. Christian obedience, therefore, is grounded not merely in what God has done but also in what God will do.

Eschatology and the Worldview Question, "What Time Is It?"

As we consider a definition of *eschatology*, we must give more attention to the worldview question mentioned in the earlier section, "What time is it?" This question leads us not merely to reflect on the nature of time and its significance but also what we are to *do* in light of the time we have and the time in which we live.

How does our obedience work out in time? For that matter, what is time, and how do we see ourselves situated in it? For Augustine the Christian perspective on time is "a way of coming before God and offering our lives to him as a form of faith seeking understanding, leading toward vision."[99] Time is "ecotonic"—always fluid, insecure, and "midway between the vanished past and the unknown future."[100] The term he uses—*distentio*

96. O'Donovan, *Self, World, and Time*, 130.

97. N. T. Wright, *After You Believe: Why Christian Character Matters* (New York: HarperOne, 2010), 67.

98. Ibid.

99. George, "St. Augustine and the Mystery of Time," 31.

100. Ibid.

animi—refers to time as "a distension of the mind or the soul," where three realities are in the mind: (1) the past (in memory), (2) the present (in attention), and (3) the future (in expectation).[101]

O'Donovan recognizes the innate difficulty of comprehending the meaning of "the present time." He writes, "What the present cannot be is a *period of* time, with dimensions and extension. As soon as we sandwich it in between past and future, it disappears into nothingness. . . . We find ourselves like salmon leaping in the stream, the present being our point of purchase on our upstream journey, *disposing of* the past and *appropriating* the future."[102]

This difficulty of the conceiving of time, particularly in the relationship of the past and future to the present, does not mean that we reduce time to mind games. One could interpret Augustine's claim, "It is in you, O mind of mine, that I measure the periods of time. Do not shout me down that it exists [objectively]; do not overwhelm yourself with the turbulent flood of your impressions"[103] as if he were making time *merely* a matter of the mind, but this would be to confuse his emphasis on *measuring* time with *time* as it truly is. The measurement of time is indeed a mental activity, but time itself is something that exists outside the mind, something created by God (the "eternal Creator of all times"). Augustine's point in emphasizing the tension and strain is, rather, "to show us that time is never at our disposal. It is never ours to claim and control and command."[104] It is another way of showing how humanity's restless hearts will not find healing in the passing of time but in the God who is beyond the time he has created.

Living in the Present as People of the Future. As Christians who see time as a gift from God, we must see ourselves as people who inhabit a particular place and occupy a specific time *for a purpose*. Therefore, the question "What time is it?" cannot linger in philosophical and theological reflection but must move toward action as we seek to walk in obedience. "What time is it?" draws a line from eschatology to ethics. It moves from the question of timing to the question, "What do we do in light of what time it is?" The action question presupposes the temporal reality.

Christian ethics are grounded in eschatology and ecclesiology. The grand narrative of the Bible not only shows us what the future is but marks

101. Augustine of Hippo, *Confessions* (Nashville: Thomas Nelson, 1999), 269.

102. O'Donovan, *Self, World, and Time*, 15.

103. Augustine, *Confessions*, 277–80.

104. George, "St. Augustine and the Mystery of Time," 36.

us out as a people belonging to that future. We not only *know* the ultimate future of the world, but we also *embody* that future.[105] Eschatological discipleship intends to help "disciples learn how to interpret everyday experience eschatologically."[106] We see the world through the eyes of faith, through the testimony of Scripture, and then we fulfill our particular roles within that overarching story. Stanley Hauerwas and William Willimon are right when they claim, "We can only act within that world which we see," which means the ethical question Christians should ask is not simply, "What ought I now to do?" but first, "How does the world really look?"[107]

On a similar note Alasdair MacIntyre asserts, "I can only answer the question, 'What am I to do?' if I can answer the prior question, 'Of what story or stories do I find myself a part?'"[108] Christian obedience takes place within a narrative of history. Asking, "What time is it?" leads to an eschatological interpretation of everyday decisions based on the future promise of God and our belonging to the people of that promise.

Embracing an eschatological understanding of redemption leads us to ask, "What time is it?" in order to ground our efforts at disciple making within the cosmic story of God's plan for the universe. Goheen and Bartholomew define our task, insisting, "Following Jesus, we are called to make known God's rule over all of human life, embodying it in our lives, demonstrating it in our actions, and announcing it with our words."[109] Making known God's rule and obeying Christ in our daily lives is inevitably contextual. This work will appear different from culture to culture, even from person to person.[110] For this reason Goheen and Bartholomew rely on John Stott's concept of "double listening," whereby believers keep one ear

---

105. Richard B. Hays, *The Moral Vision of the New Testament: A Contemporary Introduction to New Testament Ethics* (New York: HarperOne, 1996), 198. Hays notes, "The church embodies the power of the resurrection in the midst of a not-yet-redeemed world." Additionally, he uses this memorable image when he writes, "The church community is God's eschatological beachhead, the place where the power of God has invaded the world." Ibid., 27.

106. Vanhoozer, *Faith Speaking Understanding*, 45.

107. Hauerwas and Willimon, *Resident Aliens*, 88.

108. Alasdair MacIntyre, *After Virtue: A Study in Moral Theory* (3rd ed.; Notre Dame, Ind.: University of Notre Dame Press, 2007), 216; and James K. A. Smith, *Imagining the Kingdom: How Worship Works (Cultural Liturgies)* (Grand Rapids: Baker Academic, 2013), 108. On a similar note, James K. A. Smith claims "narrative is the scaffolding of our experience."

109. Bartholomew and Goheen, *Living at the Crossroads*, 60.

110. Simon Chan, *Spiritual Theology: A Systematic Study of the Christian Life* (Downers Grove, IL: IVP, 1998), 96. Chan sees a dialectical relationship between Christian virtue and cultural values. Chan says, "While cultural values shape the way Christian virtues are expressed, Christian virtues, as a coherent pattern of living out the Christian story, must challenge values that contradict the Christian story. Only in maintaining this dialectic can the Christian be theologically and culturally authentic."

listening carefully to Scripture and Christian tradition and the other ear listening to the surrounding culture.[111] Though Stott does not ask the specific question of "What time is it?" his concept of double listening implies it.

Goheen and Bartholomew explain why the worldview question of eschatology matters for our mission when they observe, "Failure to know what time it is in our culture will render us unable to discern the crossroads at which we are called to live for Christ. Such failure may well betray us into accepting, however unintentionally, the idols of contemporary culture."[112] Knowing what time it is in our culture is a crucial aspect of being a disciple of Jesus Christ, for only in this manner will we be able to show forth a way of life and holiness that confronts the prevailing idolatries of our age.

Where does this eschatological worldview question leave us? It leaves us with a clear sense of who we are, where we are, and *when* we are. O'Donovan states, "In outline we may suggest that the opportune time is a time *in the world*, when the act will correspond truthfully to the conditions that obtain; it is a time *for the agent*, who may realize him—or herself according to God's calling; it is a time *of the future*, which opens a way to the realization of God's purposes."[113]

Biblical eschatology—the time line of Scripture climaxing with the death and resurrection of Jesus Christ and moving inexorably toward his return—is what grounds and informs ethical choices, but those choices are not made clear by eschatology alone. Asking, "What time is it?" is the precursor to wisdom and deliberation, a way of discerning the current moment in light of one's past, present, and future. Cognitive knowledge of the world's future is not all that is necessary for eschatological discipleship. What we also need is wisdom, and that leads us to the fourth and final term we must define.

Wisdom

Discerning the answer to the worldview question, "What time is it?," requires wisdom and deliberation. The missionary task of the follower of Christ is to receive the apostolic testimony and then faithfully transmit it into a new time and place, to a generation that will once again pass it along to the next. This transmission requires great wisdom.

---

111. John Stott, *The Contemporary Christian: Applying God's Word to Today's World* (Downers Grove, IL: InterVarsity Press, 1995), 24-29.

112. Bartholomew and Goheen, *Living at the Crossroads*, 108.

113. O'Donovan, *Finding and Seeking*, 147.

Recent years have brought a renewal of wisdom studies in contemporary theology. In the field of systematic theology, for example, David Ford has written an entire monograph on wisdom.[114] In the field of biblical studies, Bartholomew has taken up the subject.[115] Meanwhile, as seen below, scholars such as N. T. Wright, Oliver O'Donovan, and Kevin Vanhoozer frequently speak of wisdom as integral to Christian living. Benefiting from these recent studies on wisdom, we will seek to define the term biblically, show its importance for the Christian life, and how the Spirit's guidance relates to Christian discernment.

Living according to God's Good World

What is wisdom? According to Craig Bartholomew, wisdom is about "the paths that lead to life, shalom (peace) and flourishing";[116] it refers to "a very wide range of desires, behaviors, skills and beliefs—all of which, like the spokes of a wheel, find their hub in the order God has created into our world."[117] In this sense "wisdom teaching" refers to instruction that puts believers in a position to live in harmony with nature and events.[118] Wisdom is not something we create but something we discover. It is coming to terms with reality and then adjusting our lives accordingly. Goheen and Bartholomew draw on this historic definition in their discussion of wisdom when they write, "Wisdom is the discovery of the order of creation found in both nature and society, and it implies a willingness to live in conformity with that order as it is discovered. God's wisdom is manifested in the order that he has established in the creation; true human wisdom is manifested in recognizing and conforming to that order."[119]

On a similar note, O'Donovan draws on the portrait of wisdom as a "master workman" (Prov 8:22, 30 ESV) to explain wisdom's purpose. He states, "What wisdom demands is a response to the goodness of God's world, which is to say, to know it and to love it, to realize ourselves in engagement with it." O'Donovan's definition of wisdom pushes beyond Goheen and Bartholomew's idea of living in light of the created order.

114. David F. Ford, *Christian Wisdom: Desiring God and Learning in Love* (Cambridge, MA: Cambridge University Press, 2007).

115. Craig Bartholomew and Ryan O'Dowd, *Old Testament Wisdom Literature: An Introduction* (Downers Grove, IL: IVP Academic, 2011).

116. Ibid., 19.

117. Ibid., 24.

118. O'Donovan, *Self, World, and Time*, 60.

119. Bartholomew and Goheen, *Living at the Crossroads*, 39.

O'Donovan sees wisdom as not something we employ when needed but something that employs us. It makes a demand on people; it requires a "reflective and critical relation to knowledge, exercised in judging what this or that item of knowledge is worth, how it is contextualized among other items, and what it licenses us to conclude and what it does not."[120] Putting O'Donovan's insight together with Goheen and Bartholomew's definition, we conclude that, because wisdom concerns living in harmony with the truth of God's good world, wisdom is something to which we submit as we seek to live faithfully with discernment.

Wisdom Lived Out in Time

Wisdom not only considers *what* we are in this world but *when* we are as people who inhabit this world. Living in harmony with God's created order means we must put our faith into practice in particular times and places. Kevin Vanhoozer focuses attention on practice when he distinguishes between wisdom and knowledge by claiming, "Disciples need more than knowing *that* (knowledge); they need to know *how* to live out their knowledge of Jesus Christ (wisdom). Wisdom is lived knowledge, the ability to transpose what we know here to that problem over there." According to Vanhoozer's metaphor of a drama, to have doctrinal wisdom is to see oneself on the stage and instinctively "know what to say and do in order to advance the main action of the play, and to do so in a contextually fitting way that effectively communicates to others."[121] Wisdom, therefore, means understanding the story we are part of and what temporal place we occupy in the unfolding of that story and then living accordingly.

Vanhoozer's distinction between "knowledge" and "lived knowledge" is helpful in that it includes the element of moral discernment and judgment. For Christians who view the Bible as a rulebook, offering timeless wisdom for life and a series of commands to obey, holiness turns into a timeless moral code that brings reward from God and earns his favor, or a moral code followed out of gratitude for being saved by God's grace. Either way we conceive of holiness as following a moral code that is universal for all Christians.

The problem with this view is that many moments in our lives do not require obedience at the basic level of discerning God's commandments

120. O'Donovan, *Finding and Seeking*, 48.
121. Vanhoozer, *Faith Speaking Understanding*, 204–5.

(for example, the Decalogue) but rather a deeper, more fundamental obedience that requires wisdom and discernment in understanding the times and acting accordingly. Simon Chan defines *discernment* this way:

> Discernment is knowing God's will in particular situations. And knowing God's will, as we learned earlier, is not just a matter of grasping a piece of information. It has to do with our whole attitude toward God and ourselves, with an ongoing relationship with God and loving him. Discernment, therefore, is more than just the scientific application of principles to particular situations. It requires practical wisdom that no amount of formal study can impart, that is, a kind of spiritual sensitivity that comes with long experience.[122]

Discernment is on display when, before we can answer the question, "What am I to do?," we ask the question, "What am I to do *in this state of affairs?*,"[123] which is another way of asking the question, "What time is it?"

Eschatological discipleship, then, is not a timeless moral code but rather a timely application of moral wisdom that is cultivated through growth in Christian character, immersion in the grand narrative unfolded in the Scriptures, and reliance on the Spirit's guidance. Included in this search for moral wisdom is a sense of urgency. For this reason David Ford is correct to link the pursuit of wisdom to the discernment of cries—both cries of blessing as well as warning when he writes, "Discernment of cries and crying out with discernment are near to the heart of the meaning of a prophetic wisdom that is involved in history and oriented to God and God's future."[124] This pursuit of wisdom is grounded in a desire to see God's ultimate purposes come to fruition.[125]

Although wisdom transcends time (because it is what we need in whatever epoch we finds ourselves), it is cultivated and applied *in* time. Wisdom draws on the resources of the past, looks to the promise of the future, and

---

122. Chan, *Spiritual Theology*, 201.

123. O'Donovan, *Self, World, and Time*, 32.

124. Ford, *Christian Wisdom*, 19.

125. Ibid., 50. Ford states, "Desire is in many ways the embracing mood of a life immersed in history and oriented towards the fulfillment of God's purposes."

relies on the Spirit's guidance in the present.[126] O'Donovan says, "The disciple is a figure who identifies with more than one time and place: a time and place to inhabit, another time and place to be centered upon." The disciple

> has recognized a time and place in history, there and not elsewhere, then and not before or after, where the possibility of wisdom was decisively given. In understanding *this* moment in relation to *that* moment, in finding in *that* moment the key to *this* moment's meaning and purpose, the disciple has overcome what was most threatening and destructive about historical relations, their contingency and moral arbitrariness.[127]

O'Donovan's insight is key to eschatological discipleship; our actions in the current moment find their significance because of God's salvific events in the past and eschatological promises of the future.

Wisdom and the Spirit

Before moving on from this definition, we must reiterate the importance of the Spirit's guidance when it comes to moral decision making in light of "what time it is."[128] Life in the Spirit should not be contrasted with a contextually aware, morally discerning knowledge, as if the Spirit's guidance must always be spontaneous and surprising, rather than the result of reflection and depth. O'Donovan is correct to view life in the Spirit as "a condition of moral *maturity*," and he defines maturity as understanding the order and destiny of the world and then distinguishing certain elements of moral experience (norms, goods, demands of other people) until a discernment of God's will occurs. He observes, "The maturity of the believer is set against the background of a world-historical narrative of new creation through the Son of God, a story of a once-for-all recovery of humankind that reaches its crisis in Christ's death and resurrection."[129]

Once again we see the connection between the wise course of action today and the salvific moment in the past. To follow Christ under the

---

126. N. T. Wright, *Simply Christian: Why Christianity Makes Sense* (New York: HarperOne, 2006), 124. Wright notes that the first thing to know about the Spirit is that he "is given to begin the work of making God's future real in the present," so that we can learn "to live with the life, and by the rules, of God's future world, even as we are continuing to live within the present one."

127. O'Donovan, *Finding and Seeking*, 118.

128. Ford, *Christian Wisdom*, 192. David Ford writes, "Learning to live in the Spirit is the encompassing activity of Christian discipleship after Pentecost."

129. O Donovan, *Finding and Seeking*, 9.

guidance of the Spirit, relying on wisdom in reading the times, and acting accordingly is to speak, to offer "a meaningful and contoured account of what it is to live, here in this place and time, under the guidance of the Spirit which the ascended Christ poured out upon His followers."[130] As disciples, we do not simply ask the question, "What would Jesus do?" as Charles Sheldon famously recommended.[131] We must ask the deeper and richer questions, "What would Jesus have me to do in this state of affairs? What time is it? What is God calling us to do in this time?"[132]

An element of improvisation is necessary in our walk with Christ, something Vanhoozer dubs "improvisatory wisdom"—a way of continuing obedience "in the *same* way, but *differently.*" Returning to his metaphor of a play, he writes, "The company of faith plays the same drama, but in ten thousand different places, each with its own particular social setting and cultural scenery."[133] Likewise, Brian Walsh and Sylvia Keesmaat speak of "imaginative improvisation" that is, nevertheless, "so deeply immersed in the text, and so completely absorbed in the story, that our imaginations are transformed and liberated by the vision the story sets before us."[134] However, the Spirit empowers our improvisatory performance—the Spirit who is "a gift of the end time" that brings the future into the present, giving the "life of the new creation" to God's people.[135]

An additional reason for relying on the Spirit's guidance in the application of wisdom is that the moment of decision is not always up for

---

130. Ibid., 139.

131. Charles Sheldon, *In His Steps* (Greensboro, NC: Empire Books, 2012).

132. Chan, *Spiritual Theology*, 208. My use of the plural "us" is intentional here. It is not the individual believer who, on his or her own, must discern the way forward but is, instead, a communal process. Simon Chan is correct when he writes, "Discernment . . . is ultimately a communal undertaking, based not on some private revelation that gives us access to privileged information about ourselves, others and the world but on the corporate reality that shapes our identity. In short, the church is the locus of all discernment because God's will is truly revealed there."

133. Vanhoozer, *Faith Speaking Understanding*, 201; and Ford, *Christian Wisdom*, 202. This focus on improvisation should not be used as an excuse to take a sharply different direction than what the wisdom of the past or the historic tradition of the church has countenanced. David Ford recommends believers "be open to surprises on the scale of resurrection from the dead or Peter's baptism of Cornelius" as one of the ways we learn to live in the Spirit and exercise wisdom. I worry, however, that appeals to the Spirit's "surprising" moves can be used to downplay or deny the authority of Scripture on controversial matters, thus pitting the Spirit against Scripture or tradition.

134. Brian J. Walsh and Sylvia C. Keesmaat, *Colossians Remixed: Subverting the Empire* (Downers Grove, IL: InterVarsity Press, 2004), 134.

135. Goheen, *Introducing Christian Mission Today*, 77; and Justo L. González, *Mañana: Christian Theology from a Hispanic Perspective* (Nashville, TN: Abingdon Press, 1990), 163. Similarly, González defines genuine spirituality as based in the presence of the Holy Spirit who directs believers to the future when he states, "To have the Spirit is to have a foot up on the stirrup of the eschatological future and to live now as those who expect a new reality, the coming of the Reign of God."

deliberation. Wisdom is needed to discern the right course of action, but often this wisdom is required at once, and the decision must be made immediately.[136] Wisdom is part of eschatological discipleship because it is essential for answering the question, "What time is it?," and the implied follow-up, "Now what must I do?" In order to act wisely, O'Donovan insists, "We must consider the time we occupy, formed by what we have learned to love, following what has been achieved for us, yet hearing and making answer now, in this new and instant moment."[137] Eschatological discipleship, therefore, involves the cultivation of wisdom so that, in the moment of decision, we instinctively understand the best course of action in reliance on the Spirit for guidance.

Definition of *Eschatological Discipleship*

Now that we have explored in more detail four of the key terms that will be present throughout this book, we are ready to provide a preliminary definition of eschatological discipleship. In short, *eschatological discipleship is spiritual formation that seeks to instill wisdom regarding the contemporary setting in which Christians find themselves (in contrast to rival conceptions of time and progress) and that calls for contextualized obedience as a demonstration of the Christian belief that the biblical account of the world's past, present, and future is true.*

As one can see from this definition, *discipleship* is explained as "spiritual formation" leading to "contextualized obedience." A *worldview* is what helps us evaluate our "contemporary setting" and leads us to discern our times. *Eschatology* refers to "the contemporary setting," as opposed to "rival conceptions of time and progress," and also refers to the truth of the gospel and the future of the world. *Wisdom* is what formation seeks to "instill" in order to help us make the right decisions in our cultural context in light of Scripture. In the following chapters, we walk through the Scriptures to see where we find this understanding of eschatological discipleship, particularly the eschatological grounding of ethical choices.

---

136. Smith, *Imagining the Kingdom*, 80. In speaking of deliberation, we must take care to avoid the fallacy of thinking we reflect and decide our way into every action. As James K. A. Smith writes, "Our being-in-the-world is characterized by inclinations that propel us to all sorts of action 'without thinking,'" which is why eschatological discipleship is vital; it is the instilling of wisdom *so that* the inclinations that propel us into action have been shaped by Scripture and the great drama in which we find ourselves.

137. O'Donovan, *Finding and Seeking*, 145.

PART 2

Biblical Foundations for Eschatological Discipleship

CHAPTER 2

Old Testament Precedent for Eschatological Discipleship

In the previous chapter I introduced a definition of *eschatological discipleship*: spiritual formation that seeks to instill wisdom regarding the contemporary setting in which Christians find themselves (in contrast to rival conceptions of time and progress) and calls for contextualized obedience that demonstrates the Christian belief that the biblical account of the world's past, present, and future is true. As God's redeemed people, we look backward to Christ's atoning work and forward to his return as we seek to be faithful in the present. Discipleship is eschatological because questions such as "What time is it?" and "Where is history going?" impact a disciple's worldview, and as seen in the previous chapter, a dialectical interplay exists between worldview beliefs and practices.

In this chapter we begin to examine the biblical foundation for seeing this eschatological component in the formation of disciples. We start with a brief overview of Old Testament precedent for this kind of spiritual formation—examples of Israelite faithfulness in light of God's promise, the wisdom literature's role in the people's moral formation, and the role of faith while enduring the exile.

Old Testament Precedent

Broadly speaking, the entire story line of the Old Testament points to an eschatological vision of obedience. The formation of Israel is predicated on the fulfillment of God's promise to give his chosen people a special land and through their obedience bless all the nations of the world.[1] Specific

1. On Israel's stewardship of the knowledge of God, see Christopher J. H. Wright, *The Mission of God: Unlocking the Bible's Grand Narrative* (Downers Grove, IL: InterVarsity Press, 2006), 92–93. Israel's obedience was based not only on God's grace in historical acts of deliverance in the past but also on God's promise to use Israel in revealing his grace to the nations so that all peoples might worship God alone. Israel was called to obey in light of God's past faithfulness and in light of their promised future.

examples of eschatological hope are scattered throughout the narrative (Abraham's willingness to move to another land in faith;[2] Joseph's instructions to his descendants to carry his bones out of Egypt;[3] the Israelites' journey to the Promised Land;[4] Joshua's leadership in light of God's promise[5]), but God's eschatological promise in general is not the focus of attention here. Instead, we are searching for specific Old Testament examples of Israelites taking into account their contemporary settings and then, in wisdom, choosing the best course of action in light of God's future promise. The following section will examine several Old Testament examples of people who understood the times in which they lived.

The Sons of Issachar

The first example is undoubtedly the most obscure. The early chapters of 1 Chronicles contain genealogies and lists of warriors who "came over to David before his final anointing and who played a primary role in his eventual elevation to the kingship."[6] A reference to the sons of Issachar is found in this list of names. These were men who understood the times and, therefore, knew what Israel should do (1 Chron 12:32). Bible interpreters should not read too much into the brief, seemingly unrelated remarks found in the author's genealogies and record keeping. Still, it is intriguing that the author considered it necessary to describe these men as having a keen understanding of the times in which they lived and, as a result, knowing what actions Israel should take.

What were the times they understood? From a political standpoint the sons of Issachar knew the future was with David, the shepherd boy turned warrior, who had already been anointed king of Israel but who had yet to ascend to his throne. Because they understood the times, they "cast their lot with David rather than Saul."[7] They were in a time between the times. The rightful king had been anointed, but he was not visibly enthroned. We can

2. Genesis 12; 15; and 17.

3. Gen 50:25; Exod 13:19; Josh 24:32; and Heb 11:22.

4. Carl Ellis Jr., *Free at Last? The Gospel in African-American Experience* (Downers Grove, IL: IVP, 2006), 23–24, 220. Ellis believes one of the reasons God turned Israel back from the Promised Land is because they needed "a reconstruction of their culture. They needed to see things from God's point of view." Seen in this light, the wilderness wandering was God's way of helping them look at their history, their present situation, and their destiny, which he defines as "a people's sense of the direction and ultimate fulfillment of their history" (ibid).

5. Joshua 1.

6. J. Barton Payne, *1 & 2 Chronicles*, Expositor's Bible Commentary, ed. Frank E. Gaebelein (Grand Rapids: Zondervan, 1988), 4:373–74.

7. Ibid., 378.

discern a parallel in the New Testament conception of living in the already/not-yet nature of God's kingdom.[8] Contemporary Christians also live in a time between the times; like David, Jesus has already been marked out as the Messiah of Israel and the true Lord of the world, and yet his reign is not at this time public and visible for all to see.

In the following chapters we will examine in more detail the New Testament concept of eschatology. For now, noting the connection between understanding the times and knowing what Israel should do is sufficient. In other words, a proper understanding of the time in which they lived was essential for the sons of Issachar to obtain the wisdom needed to know what Israel should do. Their obedience was contextual. God not only gave them the Torah to obey; he also expected them to discern the proper application of the Torah in the context in which they found themselves. *For the sons of Issachar, eschatological discipleship is seen in the way they plotted their reality on the time line of biblical history so they could use wisdom in leading others to discover the right course of action.*

The Wisdom Literature

Another plot point in the Old Testament comes from a section of Scripture many view as timeless—the wisdom literature, which consists of Job, Psalms, Proverbs, Ecclesiastes, and Song of Songs. Many of the sayings in these books are proverbial, general truths that transcend their original context. However, to relegate wisdom literature to the category of timeless maxims or quaint moralism would be a mistake. The purpose of the wisdom literature is formative. Although the proverbs are often considered to be timeless, they were given to shape Israel into the kind of people who would make good and wise decisions in particular times and places. The genre may be timeless, but the expected application is always timely.

In the Old Testament, wisdom is not merely something to be loved and admired but to be acted upon, and this action must take place with sufficient thought given to the context—the meaning of the moment. Old Testament heroes like Joseph, Daniel, and Solomon are characterized as full of wisdom (Gen 41:39; 1 Kgs 3:28; Dan 1:17–20), but in each of these

8. Russell D. Moore, *The Kingdom of Christ: The New Evangelical Perspective* (Wheaton, IL: Crossway, 2004), 25–28; and George Eldon Ladd, *Theology of the New Testament* (Grand Rapids: Eerdmans, 1993), 54–132. The terminology of "already/not yet," which refers to the kingdom having "already" arrived in the person of Jesus and awaiting a not-yet consummation is the heart of George Eldon Ladd's proposal in *Theology of the New Testament*. Russell Moore traces the historical outworking of evangelicalism's consensus on the concept of this "inaugurated eschatology" (Moore, *Kingdom of Christ*).

cases, "the quality of 'wisdom' itself receives its meaning from the particularities of each story."[9] In other words, wisdom is demonstrated as obedience within particular contexts; indeed, the reality of particular contexts is why wisdom is necessary in the first place.

Ecclesiastes contains a poem on the mystery of time (3:1–15) and the difficulty of interpreting life without understanding the meaning and significance of time.[10] A later section in Ecclesiastes (8:5ff) refers to wisdom as knowing the proper time and procedure for action in light of the king's authority and what may lie in the future. O'Donovan comments,

> The proverb describes a paradox: the law-abiding man who has no evil in his mind must be the wise man who has "time and judgment" in his mind (i.e., "knowing how to discern the right moment"), precisely in order to respond to an evil which already threatens to overwhelm him. The *innocence* of the gaze which bows before the lovely order of a law-governed world becomes, without being lost, the *cunning* of a practical discernment that negotiates peril at every turn, having no view of the remote future.[11]

We see here a picture of wisdom that requires a discerning of the time, a theme also found in the psalms, especially Psalm 90, which calls us to "number the days" in order to know wisdom.[12] The psalmist's point is not that we need to know the exact number of days we are given but that we should receive each day as a gift, and in conceiving of time as a gift, our hearts will be inclined to wisdom.

The idea of "wisdom as a path," which runs throughout the wisdom literature, is another indication that wisdom implies order and direction.

---

9. Athena E. Gorospe, "Old Testament Narratives and Ethics: A Journey in Understanding," *Conversations at the Edges of Things; Reflections for the Church in Honor of John Goldingay* (ed. Francis Bridger and James T. Butler; Eugene, Ore.: Wipf and Stock, 2012), 35.

10. Craig G. Bartholomew, *Ecclesiastes*, Baker Commentary on the Old Testament: Wisdom and Psalms (ed. Tremper Longman III; Grand Rapids: Baker Academic, 2009), 170. Bartholomew states, "To know [the created] order, humans would require a sense of the origin and *telos* of creation, but in Qohelet's autonomous perspective it is precisely this they lack. God has constituted them with this need, but they lack such a sense of duration of time. The result is that they cannot discern his order, and everything is rendered enigmatic."

11. O'Donovan, *Self, World, and Time*, 120.

12. John Goldingay, *Psalms 90–150*, Psalms, Baker Commentary on the Old Testament: Wisdom and Psalms (ed. Tremper Longman III; Grand Rapids: Baker Academic, 2008), 3:31. Goldingay writes, "The way [the people] experience life can make them face questions. The psalm asks that it may do that, and thus encourage them to apply a wise mind to their understanding of life and God."

We look for "a path" as a way of seeking "direction that will emerge within the complex of circumstances."[13]

The formative purpose of the wisdom literature is evident in the way the New Testament authors sought wisdom in applying biblical truth to contemporary settings. As we will see in the next chapter, in the stories of Jesus and other New Testament examples, we catch a glimpse of how first-century Jews and the early Christians viewed the wisdom genre. They saw this literature as divine instruction in need of contextual application. As Craig Bartholomew points out, "The church found itself in a new act in the drama of Scripture and was thus faced with many novel situations requiring wisdom."[14] In summary, *eschatological discipleship is seen in the way God's instruction formed the Israelites into a people who understood how to live in harmony with God's ultimate purposes for his people and the world.*

Jeremiah's Instruction to the Exiles

Another important scene in the Old Testament drama comes during the exile and the prophets who spoke truth to God's people during this time of trial. Before examining the instructions given to the exiles, we should note how the prophetic task itself is eschatological in nature. The prophets were called to address God's people on God's behalf, calling them to repentance and pointing forward in time to the moment when Israel's mission would be fulfilled for all creation and all nations. The prophets were the interpreters of Israel's history, chastising God's people for their abandonment of their unique calling while simultaneously comforting God's people with the news that God will gather his people and finally bring comprehensive salvation to the ends of the earth.[15]

Of particular relevance for our present purposes is the prophet Jeremiah's response to the reality of God's people being taken from their homeland (Jeremiah 27–29). In his letter Jeremiah encourages God's people to interpret their circumstances within the sovereign plan of God and his unfailing purposes for Israel and thus seek the welfare of the city. This interpretation does not lead to a rosy or naïve view of the situation (Jeremiah criticizes the incurable optimism of the false prophets who will not face reality), but it maintains confidence in God's good plans for the people.

13. O'Donovan, *Finding and Seeking*, 220.
14. Bartholomew and O'Dowd, *Old Testament Wisdom Literature*, 292.
15. Goheen, *Introducing Christian Mission Today*, 47–49.

Notice how Jeremiah's leadership (expressed in commands) is tied to his prior statements about God's overarching plan and Israel's greater story. Derek Kidner summarizes this remarkable letter, observing,

> Notice the starting point, that God has *sent* these exiles to Babylon. At the very least, then, they should accept the situation; but God has little use for grudging attitudes. What emerges in the call to them in verses 5-7 is gloriously positive: a liberation from the paralyzing sullenness of inertia and self-pity, into doing, for a start, what comes to hand and makes for growth, but above all what makes for peace.[16]

This section of Scripture is important because it shows us how discipleship involves understanding the times, and because the apostle Peter later drew upon this theme of exiles and strangers when he exhorted the early Christians to live in holiness, with honor, and in full submission during times of persecution (1 Peter 2). *Eschatological discipleship is seen in the way the people of God, when marginalized and persecuted, interpret their circumstances in light of God's ultimate promise of deliverance and reclaim their identity as having been "sent" into exile to work for the flourishing of civilization.*

These are only three Old Testament examples of obedience involving an incisive understanding of the times. In the next chapter we turn our attention to Jesus's parabolic teaching and the commissioning texts in Matthew and Luke.

16. Derek Kidner, *The Message of Jeremiah* (Downers Grove, IL: InterVarsity Press, 1987), 100.

CHAPTER 3

Eschatological Discipleship in the Gospels and Acts

> In our study of eschatological discipleship in the New Testament, we begin with an examination of Christ's commandment to "make disciples" in light of the portrait of discipleship in the Gospel of Matthew. We will also consider the commissioning texts in Luke and Acts, where the emphasis lies on Christ's followers as "witnesses" to his gospel. Bringing these elements together—the task given to the disciples, as well as the portrait of discipleship in the Gospels and Acts, we will see how Christian obedience is grounded in Christian eschatology.

The Great Commission

Few passages of Scripture are as essential to understanding the mission of the church as the Great Commission text that closes the Gospel of Matthew (Matt 28:16–20). In recent years this text has become prominent in the thinking of missionaries targeting unreached people groups and missional literature that recasts the church itself as a missionary organization.[1] As we examine the Great Commission, we will look first at the significance of Jesus himself giving this command and then seek to place the Great Commission in its eschatological context (within the biblical canon) and its literary context (within the Gospel of Matthew).

The Great Commissioner

At the heart of the Great Commission is the authority inherent in the great *Commissioner*—Jesus Christ himself. Though some may begin their

1. An example of the emphasis on people groups is John Piper, *Let the Nations Be Glad: The Supremacy of God in Missions* (Grand Rapids: Baker, 2003). An example of the missional understanding of the church is Jason C. Dukes, *Live Sent: You Are a Letter* (Birmingham, Ala.: New Hope Publishers, 2011).

quote of the commission with verse 19 ("Therefore, go and make disciples," NLT), the text in Matthew points back to the previous declaration that Christ has been given all authority in heaven and on earth (Matt 28:18). The Great Commission is a responsibility given to the church, yet it is grounded in the authority of the risen Jesus, the Sender. Seeking to implement the desires of Jesus, the risen King, is not optional for Christians. In obeying Christ's words, Christians demonstrate our submission to the authority of God.[2]

Therefore, on the one hand, Christians are called to fulfill the Great Commission because of the authority of Jesus Christ over his missionary people. On the other hand, Christians are called to fulfill this Commission because of the authority of Jesus over all the peoples of the world. In other words, we do not engage in mission simply because *our* Lord has authority over *us*. Rather, we engage in mission because *the* Lord has authority over *all*. The authority of Christ is put on display through the obedience of his people, and the news of his reign is to be extended throughout the entire world so that all people everywhere will recognize the risen King Jesus as universal Lord and Savior.

Goheen places the Great Commission against the backdrop of Daniel 7:14, a messianic prophecy that references a figure who is given all authority, glory, and power, and who is worshipped by all nations and peoples of every language. This invincible kingdom of the Messiah's global dominion is the setting in which the risen Jesus commissions his disciples to call all people to bow their knees to him as Lord.[3] The Great Commission, then, is a statement of the authority of Jesus who, himself sent by God, now sends his people.

The Great Commission's Eschatological Backdrop

We can see the eschatological foundation of the Great Commission by how it is bookended by two statements that point to particular moments in time. First, the statement of Christ's cosmic authority precedes the Commission (Matt 28:18). It is implicitly connected to Christ's redemptive work on the cross and his victorious resurrection, as indicated by Peter's statement at Pentecost that God has made this Jesus both Lord and Christ (Acts 2:36). Immediately following the Commission is the promise of Christ's

2. Wright, *Mission of God*, 51.

3. Michael Goheen, *A Light to the Nations: The Missional Church and the Biblical Story* (Grand Rapids: Baker Academic, 2011), 117.

presence, assured not in a generic, timeless sense but within time—"to the end of the age" (Matt 28:20). Both the statement that precedes the Commission and the statement that follows assume a biblical view of history. The world is *going somewhere.*[4]

Why is this eschatological dimension so important? After all, the task seems simple enough. We might wonder, What has missiology to do with eschatology? The key is in understanding the comprehensive obedience to which Christ calls his followers. How does a disciple know how to obey the living Christ in various contexts? To form followers of Jesus who know what obedience looks like in different cultures and nations is impossible unless these followers are formed, at least in some measure, by the Christian understanding of history and time. Goheen and Bartholomew argue for a worldview aspect of discipleship when they write, "The urgent question is how the church can live faithfully under the comprehensive authority of God's Word, embodying his all-encompassing renewal, and at the same time live within cultures in which other all-embracing worldviews and powers hold sway."[5] The only way for the Great Commission to be fulfilled is for disciples to take the gospel to the nations, a gospel that cannot and must not be diluted or lost among competing worldviews.

The Eschatological Gospel. One must view the Great Commission's command to "make disciples" as eschatological in nature, in part because the gospel at the heart of the Commission is itself eschatological. As Newbigin reminds us, "The gospel is good news of the kingdom, and the kingdom is an eschatological concept. A true understanding of the last things is the first essential."[6] The gospel we proclaim cannot be reduced to a spiritualized, universal message of God's unchanging love but is instead the good news of salvation that arrives in and through historical events.

Eschatology matters because the gospel of the kingdom concerns the in-breaking reign of God, which will be consummated at the end of time. Moltmann is correct when he states, "The eschatological outlook is characteristic of all Christian proclamation, of every Christian existence and of the whole Church."[7] The story line in which the gospel announcement

---

4. Lesslie Newbigin, *Signs Amid the Rubble: The Purposes of God in Human History* (ed. Geoffrey Wainwright; Grand Rapids: Eerdmans, 2003), 8. Newbigin contrasts circular interpretations of history with biblical history, which he describes as "linear." A biblical understanding "interprets history as a real process in which real events happen, events that is to say which have significance for God Himself."

5. Bartholomew and Goheen, *Living at the Crossroads*, 58.

6. Newbigin, *Foolishness*, 134.

7. Moltmann, *Theology of Hope*, 16.

of Jesus Christ finds its meaning begins with God's good world, a world shattered by humanity's fall into sin, redeemed through Jesus's sacrifice, and will one day be restored fully when Christ returns. The gospel is about events that have occurred in history, and these events imply an overarching story of the world.

The gospel we are commanded to take to the nations is the announcement of Jesus Christ crucified and raised, and this announcement is undeniably eschatological. Thus, O'Donovan insists, "Christian ethics depends upon the resurrection of Jesus Christ from the dead," because the resurrection's meaning is "God's final and decisive word" on humanity.[8]

The Imperative of Teaching. A second reason the command to "make disciples" must be viewed eschatologically is because of the specific command to teach disciples to obey all that Christ has commanded them. The imperative "make disciples" is surrounded by three participles: going, baptizing, and teaching. Craig Keener makes clear that when we place "teaching" within the broader context of Matthew's Gospel, we are able to see this teaching as "making the kind of disciples Jesus made, to carry on his mission of proclaiming and demonstrating his kingdom or rulership."[9]

This teaching element, when set in the context of an unbeliever's transfer from the kingdom of darkness into the kingdom of light, implies learning the ways of the kingdom. Darrell Guder explains,

> Those who hear the good news and want to become citizens of the reign of God will need teaching. The church as holy nation has a culture, an accepted way of doing things, a specialized vocabulary to talk about life under the reign of God. The church should not expect new people in its midst to know these things automatically. Becoming a citizen of the reign of God does not come naturally. It is different from just being civil or being a good person. It requires a new loyalty to a new ruler. It demands that we acquire the new habits of a new culture. New people need to become "naturalized" citizens of the reign of God, and teaching is part of the naturalization process.[10]

---

8. Oliver O'Donovan, *Resurrection and Moral Order: An Outline for Evangelical Ethics* (Grand Rapids: Eerdmans, 1994), 13.

9. Craig Keener, *A Commentary on the Gospel of Matthew* (Grand Rapids: Eerdmans, 1999), 718.

10. Darrell Guder, *Missional Church: A Vision for the Sending of the Church in North America* (Grand Rapids: Eerdmans, 1998), 137.

The Great Commission's teaching is geared toward obedience; it is not simply telling someone to obey but rather teaching them to obey, which is the language of apprenticeship, and it implies that discipleship takes place in the world, not just the church service.[11] Again, the contextual nature of obedience is in view here, for teaching to obey cannot refer simply to telling the stories of the Bible or learning the Bible's specific commands. Rather, it implies that obedience must be modeled, that disciples are taught to obey within a cultural context.

The Church as Eschatological Community. A third reason we should see an eschatological component to the Great Commission's command to "make disciples" is because it envisions the church as an eschatological community. It is no coincidence that the command to make disciples is sandwiched between Christ's claim to have all authority in heaven and on earth and Christ's assurance of his presence even to the end of the age.

This eschatological focus is consistent with other New Testament references to the church as firstfruits or a colony of heaven, such as Phil 3:20, where the apostle Paul compares the church to soldiers in a foreign land, a community both heavenly and earthly, with citizenship in a future coming city.[12] Michael Bird explains:

> The church is the *new community* called out from the world into what is the beginning of the *new age*. The resurrection of Jesus and the gift of the Spirit mean that God's new world has begun, the future has partially invaded the present, the seeds of the new creation have already begun budding in the old garden, and God's victory on the cross is now beginning to claim back territory in a world enslaved by sin. The first Christians saw themselves as the vanguard of a new redeemed humanity that God was creating in Jesus Christ. For this reason, we can regard the church as an eschatological community.[13]

If "the Church can be rightly understood only in eschatological perspective,"[14] as Newbigin argues, then the church's commissioning must also be understood within that same perspective.

---

11. Bosch, *Transforming Mission*, 68.
12. Paul S. Minear, *Images of the Church in the New Testament* (Louisville, KY: Westminster/John Knox Press, 1960; republished, Grand Rapids: Eerdmans, 2004), 61.
13. Michael Bird, *Evangelical Theology* (Grand Rapids: Zondervan, 2013), 728.
14. Newbigin, *Household of God*, 135.

The Command to Obey as Contextual. A fourth reason discipleship in the Great Commission should be viewed as eschatological is in the command to obey, a command that is necessarily contextual. Our obedience to Christ's commands and our discerning the times and the best course of action requires wisdom. On the one hand, disciple making requires contextualization at the evangelism stage, as the Christian seeks to "exegete" (fully understand) his or her ministry context in order to offer a compelling presentation of the gospel.[15] On the other hand, disciple making requires contextualization at the obedience stage, as the Christian seeks "to discern God's purpose and be obedient to it among all the ambiguities and perplexities of life."[16]

The church lives between the time of Christ's first and second comings and, therefore, finds itself in the middle of an age to which it must not conform. The church's faithful presence in the world is a witness to another kingdom, which is why Christians are "*in* the world and *for* the world, but not *of* the world."[17] Obedience is contextual because the mission is eschatological, which means believers' obedience must be marked by the horizon of Christ's second coming.

"Making Disciples" in the Gospel of Matthew

Matthew's understanding of discipleship is described thematically within his Gospel. As seen above, a strong connection exists between the command to make disciples and the reality of the kingdom of God, as evidenced by the way in which the announcement of Jesus's authority precedes and grounds the Great Commission. The kingdom of God is at the heart of Jesus's ministry and teaching, and the Gospel of Matthew shows that submission to Christ's authority is at the heart of what it means to be a disciple.

Discipleship is no less than recognizing the presence of the kingdom and trading in one's personal agendas for the kingdom agenda of Jesus Christ. This concept is viewed in the scenes where Jesus calls people to follow him (Matt 4:18–22; 9:9–13; 10:1–15; 19:16–30), lays out the cost of discipleship (Matt 8:18–22; 10:16–25; 10:34–39; 16:24–28), and decries the

---

15. Gary Tyra, *A Missional Orthodoxy: Theology and Ministry in a Post-Christian Context* (Downers Grove, IL: IVP, 2013), 35. Tyra calls this a "missional approach to ministry."

16. Newbigin, *Foolishness*, 60.

17. Allison, *Sojourners*, 153.

hypocrites who use the façade of religious observance to mask their personal agendas (12:1–14; 15:1–20; 16:1–12; 23:1–36).[18]

In Matthew 10:5–15, when Jesus sends out his disciples, he connects his own mission to that of his followers. From this we see that discipleship includes a life that witnesses to the way of Jesus and his kingdom. Emmanuel Jacob summarizes the point clearly:

> Discipleship is undoubtedly the way of learning, and of knowing. It is also about being and doing. It has to do with understanding Jesus' words and obeying them just as he acted in obedience to the divine word. To be a disciple means to teach by word and example to observe everything that Jesus had commanded (28:19). Love is at the heart of this "everything" (19:19; 22:39). Love for God flows out into relationships; it will help Christians not to betray one another (24:10–12) and to support one another (10:40–42; 25:31–46). Love for one another will encourage Christians to endure difficulties, and show itself in acts of mercy (5:7).[19]

Additionally, recognizing the connection between the kingdom of God and discipleship exposes the false dichotomy between seeking justice and doing evangelism. Matthew shows Jesus demonstrating again and again his concern for those who are physically suffering, not merely as an example of a greater spiritual deliverance that awaits them but as a vivid portrait of what it looks like when the reign of God breaks into history (Matt 8:1–17; 9:1–8, 18–34; 12:9–28; 14:34–36; 15:21–28; 17:14–21; 20:29–34). The disciple whose heart models that of Jesus will also yearn for kingdom wholeness to be a reality in everyday life and will work toward that end.

In other words, the proclamation of the gospel of Christ's lordship in heaven should be matched by the demonstration of Christ's lordship on earth. To reduce the Great Commission to evangelism or the Great Commandment to mere social involvement runs the risk of putting asunder what Jesus intended to stay together. Neighbor love without evangelism is not really love at all, while evangelism without love for neighbor fails to incorporate the full-orbed view of discipleship portrayed throughout Matthew's Gospel.

---

18. Emmanuel Jacob, "Discipleship and Mission: A Perspective on the Gospel of Matthew," *International Review of Mission* 91, no. 360 (2002): 106. In his helpful essay Jacob points out additional ways in which a kingdom life is fleshed out.

19. Ibid., 107.

What does Jesus specifically teach about discipleship throughout Matthew's Gospel? It is reasonable to assume that the phrase "teaching them to observe everything I have commanded you" (Matt 28:20) summoned up recollections of Jesus's great discourses recorded in this Gospel (Matthew 5–7; 10; 13; 18; 23–25). Taken together, these five discourses focus primarily on the cost of discipleship as seen in the stringent standards of the messianic community as well as the eschatological anticipation of Christ's coming kingdom.[20]

The Sermon on the Mount (Matthew 5–7), for example, begins with a series of blessings that illustrate the reversal of fortunes now that God's kingdom has broken into the new age. O'Donovan encourages reading the Sermon as a demonstration of the "newly pressing eschatological horizon" providing the context for all lives and tasks when he writes,

> The text begins with a series of blessings that illustrate the climactic reversals that are to change the face of history; it continues with examples of the radicalization of the law in the dawning new age; it teaches about the purpose and context of religious exercises; it explores the pointlessness of anxiety; it displays through a wide variety of applications the law of equal returns; and finally it reflects on alternative outcomes of human lives that respond to moral teaching in different ways.[21]

Ben Witherington concurs, describing Jesus's ethics as "eschatological in character" and giving the Sermon the label of "eschatological wisdom speech." He writes, "This material is, in the main, to be seen not as law, not even as new law, but rather as wisdom—Jesus' wisdom about how his disciples should live their lives."[22] Similarly, N. T. Wright claims that in this sermon, Jesus is calling his followers to "eschatological authenticity," practicing now the habits of the heart that have their goal, their *telos*, in the coming of God's kingdom.[23]

This eschatological backdrop is not only evident in the didactic, straightforward teaching of Jesus. The major discourses of Matthew include

20. Craig Keener, "Matthew's Missiology: Making Disciples of the Nations," *Asian Journal of Pentecostal Studies* 12, no. 1 (January 2009): 15.

21. O'Donovan, *Self, World, and Time*, 63.

22. Ben Witherington III, *The Individual Witnesses*, The Indelible Image: The Theological and Ethical Thought World of the New Testament (Downers Grove, IL: IVP Academic, 2009), 1:129.

23. Wright, *After You Believe*, 107–8, says, "The authenticity that really matters is living in accordance with the genuine human being God is calling you to become."

a number of parables. The next section will examine the eschatological themes found in the Matthean parables—themes that provide insight into Jesus's vision of discipleship.

Eschatological Discipleship in the Matthean Parables of Jesus

The reason it is important to examine the parables of Jesus in the discussion of eschatological discipleship is because the parables give us, in miniature form, insight into the great story of the world and our roles as actors in it.[24] According to Kevin Vanhoozer, Jesus told stories, because he wanted "to change his disciples' worldview, beliefs, values, and practices alike, reframing how we think about ourselves and even how we experience God, the world, and ourselves." He goes on, "To abide in the doctrine of Christ means, at least in part, keeping this eschatological framework uppermost in one's mind. To abide in the doctrine of Christ is to remember that the reign of God has come into the world, unexpectedly, in Jesus' person and work, and to let this headline news color and shape one's everyday experience."[25] Thus, the fact that Jesus taught in parables indicates that he was interested in giving his disciples more than facts to add to their cognitive collection of knowledge. He gave them stories because narrative is one of the most important elements of discerning how best to obey.[26]

Once we understand the formative power of stories and how they relate to the bigger story of the world and our place in it, we see why the parables help in understanding the Great Commission. The portraits of discipleship found in the stories of Jesus reveal what Jesus expects of his followers who understand their place in the great story of the world. A brief analysis of some of the parables included in the Gospel of Matthew reveals a consistent

---

24. Albert Schweitzer, *The Quest of the Historical Jesus* (Mineola, NY: Dover Publications, 2005). The question of eschatology in Jesus's ministry usually leads to issues surrounding his view of the imminent end of the world. A century ago, Albert Schweitzer rescued the historical Jesus from the anti-apocalyptic, timeless moral ethics of nineteenth-century liberals, only then to bind him again by declaring his ethic to be "interim" and no longer immediately relevant because of Jesus's mistaken belief that the end of the world was near. A better way forward is to recognize with Schweitzer the thoroughly eschatological vision of Jesus without mistaking some of Christ's statements as referring to the imminent end of the space-time universe. Additionally, see the critique from Wright, *Jesus and the Victory of God*, 202–9.

25. Vanhoozer, *Faith Speaking Understanding*, 45.

26. Gorospe, "Old Testament Narratives and Ethics," 34. Summarizing the work of moral philosopher Martha Nussbaum, Gorospe explains how narratives aid in ethical deliberation by their particularities, specific situations, characters, and relationships. She notes, "In reading and responding to a narrative, one is led to respond to the specific features of one's situation rather than to apply a general principle that fits all situations. This results in greater flexibility, in responses that are contextual and resourceful, and in sensitivity to the non-repeatable elements of a given situation."

emphasis on the disciple's need to understand the current eschatological moment and then live accordingly.

The Wise and Foolish Builders. Instead of treating each of the Matthean parables individually, I will focus on only a handful of these stories as we explore the common, eschatological themes in Jesus's storytelling. The first full-length parable included in Matthew's Gospel comes at the end of Jesus's Sermon on the Mount (Matthew 5–7). The story (Matt 7:24–27) concerns two builders, one who is wise and builds his house on the rock and the other who is foolish and builds his house on the sand. When the storm comes, the wise man's house remains standing, while the foolish man's house is utterly destroyed. The immediate context for this story is the Sermon on the Mount, which draws to a close with a number of forceful images that stress the importance of right living as the fruit of genuine faith rather than a simple confession of Jesus's lordship (Matt 7:13–23). Words do not prove the sincerity of faith; rather, fruit is what counts.

As he concludes his sermon, Jesus begins the parable by comparing the wise man to "everyone who hears these words of mine and *acts on* them" (Matt 7:24; emphasis added). Martin Luther captured the point of this parable when he wrote, "The doctrine is good and a precious thing, but it is not being preached for the sake of being heard but for the sake of action and its application to life."[27] Here, Jesus's vision for discipleship highlights listening *and* doing, not merely passive hearing and inconsequential belief that fails to lead to action.

Concerning discipleship, it is not obedience in general that is demanded but obedience to Jesus himself. D. A. Carson summarizes Jesus's goal in contrasting the two builders, "A wise person represents those who put Jesus' words into practice; they too are building to withstand anything. Those who pretend to have faith, who have a merely intellectual commitment, or who enjoy Jesus in small doses are foolish builders."[28] It should be no surprise to the reader of Matthew's Gospel to see how quickly the narrative moves from this parable to the crowd's amazement at Jesus's inherent authority (Matt 7:28–29). With these words Jesus is authoritatively putting forth his teaching in a way that implies eschatological consequences for those who reject

27. Martin Luther, *The Sermon on the Mount (Sermons) and the Magnificat*, Luther's Works (vol. 21; St. Louis, MO: Concordia, 1956), 281.

28. Carson, *Matthew*, 194.

his words.[29] The "wisdom" described here (*phronimos*) is displayed in the life of the disciple who puts into practice the words of Jesus.

Various interpretations exist regarding the storms that come against the houses built by the wise and foolish men. A rich historical tradition associates the storms in the parable with the typical "storms of life" encountered by all people everywhere. Within this tradition the moral of the story is that the only way to survive life's trials is to be founded on the rock of Jesus's teaching. John Chrysostom[30] and Augustine[31] take this position, and more recently so has Arland Hultgren, who points to the imagery of storms in Jewish tradition (Ps 6:10–12; 107:28–29; 2 Bar 53:3–12) as evidence for the "trials-of-life" interpretation. Hultgren marshals further evidence from Matthew by pointing to calamities brought against the disciples of Jesus, the prediction of persecution, and other forms of abuse that will cause many to fall away (Matt 24:10; 5:10–12; 10:16–22).[32] He concludes, "The one who truly hears and puts into practice the teachings of Jesus has Jesus' own promise that he will not be overcome in times of calamity. The onslaughts that can come upon a person—whether those that test one's faith or relationships to God—will not prevail wherever a person is a hearer and doer of the teachings of Jesus."[33]

Despite the long tradition of interpreting the storm in this manner, an eschatological reading is preferable. The storm in view is likely that of divine judgment. Michael Knowles sees an allusion to the flood of Noah. He argues that the surrounding context of the parable (which mentions the Day of the Lord in Matt 7:13–23) tilts the evidence in favor of an eschatological reading.[34] Klyne Snodgrass concludes the same because the word "wise" often carries an eschatological nuance. He notes, "The wise person is one who is aware of the eschatological hour and lives accordingly."[35] Dale Allison offers additional evidence from the Old and New Testaments (Isa 28:2;

---

29. Michael P. Knowles, "Everyone Who Hears These Words of Mine," in *The Challenge of Jesus' Parables*, McMaster New Testament Series (ed. Richard N. Longenecker; Grand Rapids: Eerdmans, 2000), 290.

30. John Chrysostom, *Homily* 24.3, cited September 28, 2015, http://www.newadvent.org/fathers/200124.htm.

31. Augustine of Hippo, *Sermon on the Mount*. 2.24.87, cited September 28, 2015, http:// www.ewtn.com/library/PATRISTC/PNI6-1.TXT., 2.24.87.

32. Arland Hultgren, *The Parables of Jesus: A Commentary* (Grand Rapids: Eerdmans, 2000), 134.

33. Ibid., 135.

34. Knowles, "Everyone Who Hears," 289.

35. Klyne Snodgrass, *Stories with Intent: A Comprehensive Guide to the Parables of Jesus* (Grand Rapids: Eerdmans, 2008), 335.

Matt 24:37–39) in favor of an eschatological reading.[36] The contrast between the wise and foolish builders is the climactic finale to Jesus's sermon because it demonstrates the seriousness of what is at stake. Discipleship matters because of the far-reaching implications that transcend this present life's trials and calamities and extend to the life to come.

Further, a historical dimension exists to the judgment threatened in this passage. Knowles believes Jesus's choice of imagery is built on the Jewish conception that the temple was founded on the rock. Thus, "building a house" (using the Hebrew noun *beth*) can refer to God's own house (the temple).[37] N. T. Wright grounds this eschatological vision in the context of Jesus's warnings about the temple when he writes, "The real new Temple, the real house-on-the-rock, will consist of the community that builds its life upon Jesus' words. All other attempts to create a new Israel, a new Temple (remember that Herod's Temple was still being completed in Jesus' lifetime), a pure or revolutionary community, would be like building a house on the sand. When the wind and storms came, it would fall with a great crash."[38]

To make a definitive case that Jesus's parable was a coded warning against the current temple situation is difficult. Such an interpretation is not out of the realm of possibility, of course, but perhaps it is more circumspect to affirm the parable's general teaching of coming eschatological judgment, with "wisdom" in this case being described as living properly in light of eternity.

The Foolish Bridesmaids. Jumping from the end of Jesus's first extended discourse in Matthew to the middle of his last may seem odd, but a thematic link exists between these two parables. Just as the two builders are contrasted in terms of wisdom and foolishness, the bridesmaids in Matthew 25:1–13 are also contrasted in the same manner. The story at hand concerns wise and foolish bridesmaids awaiting the bridegroom. Some of the maidens run out of oil for their lamps. While they are away, they miss the bridegroom's arrival.

Like other parables in Matthew's Gospel, the parable of the foolish bridesmaids is a story that drives home the importance of remaining vigilant to the last moment. The disciple of Christ is not the one who

36. Dale C. Allison, *The Sermon on the Mount: Inspiring the Moral Imagination* (New York: Crossroad, 1999), 170–71.

37. Knowles, "Everyone Who Hears," 290.

38. N. T. Wright, *The Challenge of Jesus: Rediscovering Who Jesus Was and Is* (Downers Grove, IL: InterVarsity Press, 1999), 47.

self-identifies as a Christian but the one who is prepared for Christ's coming. In the same way the two houses in the wise and foolish builders looked alike, even though they were built on different foundations, so also the bridesmaids are all together in the first part of this story as they await the bridegroom. One of the lessons here is that discipleship cannot be summed up in appearances but rather in the exercise of wisdom that leads one to live in light of the kingdom of God. In both cases judgment exposes foolishness, both the faulty foundation of the foolish builder and the lack of preparation from the foolish bridesmaids. Snodgrass concludes:

> The parable underscores that wisdom means understanding the eschatological outlook of Jesus' teaching and then living in a way that fits with the expectation of vindication and the full coming of God's kingdom. I think this parable should be understood as Jesus urging his disciples to live with such wisdom. If the original concern was for his Jewish contemporaries to have a similar wisdom about his own ministry, the practical effect is not much different, and the church has only extended the message. *The important point is that wisdom is eschatologically defined. Wisdom and readiness are virtual synonyms.*[39]

Like the wise and foolish builders, the parable of the bridesmaids reiterates the message that discipleship is formed and described within the context of eschatological preparation.

The Parables of the Treasure and the Pearl. The theme of eschatology and the theme of costly discipleship are often intertwined. Sometimes these parables bump up against each other, with these twin themes back-to-back. The two parables known as the hidden treasure and the pearl (Matt 13:44–46) come immediately after Jesus's explanation of the parable of the wheat and the tares (Matt 13:36–45), a story that contains a sharp message about the coming day of judgment.

We should note that even if Jesus's teaching on eschatology often paints an ominous outlook in light of judgment, other parables highlight the value of the kingdom and the joyful celebration that news of its coming should produce. In fact, the joyful abandonment of one's life for the sake of the kingdom should be considered a proper eschatological response, the positive response to the good news of the coming kingdom, just as other

39. Snodgrass, *Stories with Intent*, 518 (emphasis in original).

parables emphasize the serious response one should have toward the judgment that accompanies its arrival. The parables of the hidden treasure and the pearl focus on the need to celebrate the good news of the kingdom, no matter the cost.[40] Carson writes, "The extravagance of the parable dramatizes the supreme importance of the kingdom."[41]

The interpretation of these brief parables bolsters our understanding of eschatological discipleship. On the one hand, an emphasis is placed on the infinite worth of the kingdom of heaven, a worth that far exceeds the cost of discipleship.[42] On the other hand, the joy of discovering the treasure also exists, a joy that prompts the finder to sell everything in order to acquire it. John Donahue comments, "The joy of receiving God's forgiveness proclaimed by Jesus releases the hearer to respond without counting the cost of the response."[43] No matter which element is emphasized, the portrait of discipleship is clear. The person who understands the eschatological moment and recognizes the value of God's kingdom will joyfully renounce his or her rights, possessions, priorities, or comforts in order to obtain the life of the kingdom. Costly discipleship is required, but the disciple's sacrifice is not pictured as the gritting of one's teeth amid an acceptance of a grueling set of circumstances. Instead, this discipleship is about joyfully giving all to gain all in return.[44]

Laborers in the Vineyard. The parable of the laborers in the vineyard (Matt 20:1–16) highlights the grace that undergirds the cost of discipleship. In the story multiple groups of workers begin taking their place in the field at different hours throughout the day. When the day is finished, the vineyard owner gives all of the workers the same amount of compensation, an action that leads to grumbling on the part of those who bore the brunt of the day's work. The master challenges the grumblers by appealing to his right to be generous.

At first glance this parable appears to have little to do with eschatology and even less to do with discipleship. However, a closer look reveals the connection between the life of a disciple and the life of the master. If the

---

40. Ibid., 246.

41. Carson, *Matthew*, 320.

42. Ibid.

43. John R. Donahue, *The Gospel in Parable* (Minneapolis, MN: Fortress Press, 1988), 69.

44. Brad Young, *The Parables: Jewish Tradition and Christian Interpretation* (Peabody, MA: Hendrickson, 1998), 221. Brad Young helpfully summarizes the parables as picturing "the kingdom's unimaginable worth—a value beyond all human comprehension. The kingdom takes precedence over the supporting theme of the cost demanded from disciples following Jesus. Joyfully seeking the kingdom will provide for every need. For Jesus, the kingdom is everything." It could be added rightfully that, for the disciple, Jesus is everything. The kingdom and the King are inseparable.

master of the house is generous and gracious, then these same characteristics should be true of all who serve him. As Michael Knowles writes, "To expand another metaphor, the kingdom is characterized by the character of the King: God's reign, which obedient discipleship acknowledges, is characterized in its entirety by God's own graciousness and generosity."[45] In other words, costly discipleship is demanded from a generous, unexpectedly gracious master. The reversal of expectations in the surprising conclusion of the story reiterates the graciousness of God that stands at the heart of his kingdom. All disciples are to see themselves as the eleventh-hour workers who are generously offered grace that surpasses any notion of merit.[46]

Other Parables with an Eschatological Focus. Time and space do not permit engaging in an extended treatment of other important parables in Matthew. The following parables do not all make the same primary point. Still, these stories are scattered throughout with eschatological significance.[47] Consider the parable of the talents (Matt 25:14–30), which concerns a king who is absent and whose servants must invest his resources. The traditional interpretation of this parable focuses on the truth that a

45. Knowles, "Everyone Who Hears," 304.

46. Hultgren, *Parables of Jesus*, 43.

47. Several of Jesus's parables are eschatological in the sense that they hint toward a future expansion for the Gentiles. For example, the parable of the mustard seed (Matt 13:31-32; Mark 4:30-32; Luke 13:18-19) may include a veiled reference to Ezek 13:17 and the eventual arrival of Gentiles in the kingdom. Likewise, the parable of the two sons (Matt 21:28-32), one who initially refused the father's order and then obeyed, and one who initially accepted the father's command but failed to follow through, was first applied to the sinful among Israel (tax collectors and prostitutes), who were accepting Jesus's call to repentance ahead of the Pharisees and religious elites. Not surprisingly, many interpreters have extended the original application parable to the situation of the early church, in which Gentiles were accepting the gospel before the Jews. See Carson, *Matthew*, 450.

Toward the end of his ministry, Jesus's parables become increasingly clear that there is a direction toward expansion. Consider the wicked tenants (Luke 20:9-19; Mark 12:1-12; Matt 21:33-46), included in all three Synoptic Gospels, which clearly indicates that the vineyard would be taken away from the religious leaders and given to those who would bear fruit, or the parable of the wedding feast (Luke 14:7-14; Matt 22:1-14), which is perhaps the most explicit in its interpretation of a future kingdom with people from all walks of life. The wedding feast imagery is so multinational that certain interpreters have claimed that much of it must not be from the original Jesus since, by definition, these scholars see Jesus as focused solely on Israel. See, for example, Robert W. Funk, Bernard Brandon Scott, and James R. Butts, eds., *The Parables of Jesus, Red Letter Edition*, Jesus Seminar Series (Sonoma, CA: Polebridge Press, 1988), 43. C. H. Dodd, though claiming the two evangelists have altered the stories for their own purposes, comes to the opposite conclusion as the Jesus Seminar. He sees Luke's version as being most explicit about the extension of the gospel to the Gentiles (because of the messengers being sent in two waves, once to the city and then later to the farther fields and hedges). Since Matthew adds the scene of the man caught without his wedding garment, Dodd concludes that the evangelist wanted to "guard against the reception of the Gentiles into the Church on too easy terms." C. H. Dodd, *The Parables of the Kingdom* (London, Nisbett and Co.: Charles Scribner's Sons, 1956), 121-22. Ironically, the efforts of Oesterly and the Jesus Seminar to rid the parable of problematic "allegorizations" and the assumptions of Dodd regarding the evangelists' alterations actually offer additional support to the notion that the clearest reading of the parable contains the vision of the church's mission to the Gentiles.

disciple must be a good steward of the gifts of God in the present while waiting for the Master's return. Brad Young recognizes stewardship as the primary point of the parable, and yet he also admits that "eschatological force pervades the rich imagery of the plot of the parable."[48] The context, after all, includes waiting for the returning king. The disciples commended as "good and faithful servants" are those who live with eschatological anticipation, choosing to invest in ways that maximize the king's resources. Once again, even though the primary point is stewardship, discipleship is seen through the lens of eschatological anticipation.

Other parables in the Gospel of Matthew make similar points. Jesus's analogy of putting new wine into old wineskins (Matt 9:17) is traditionally understood as a reference to the overlap of eras, referring to the coming kingdom, which will no longer be contained by the exclusivist tendencies of God's chosen people who have lost their saltiness and who have failed to be a light to the nations. God's work through Jesus represents the in-breaking of the kingdom of God; all actions should be commensurate with the new reality.

Likewise, Jesus speaks of a faithful servant whose anticipation for his master's return leads him to alter his priorities (Matt 24:42–51). In these analogies the specific shape of discipleship as put forth in the Matthean parables comes into focus. O'Donovan claims that hope transforms the immediate horizon by demanding watchfulness, a willingness to wait attentively "attending wholly and with concentration focused on what is *not yet* happening, so that whatever *is* happening is handled with a mind supremely bent on something else."[49] It is not a generic faithfulness to God's commands but rather a specific faithfulness formed by the disciple's understanding of what time it is and what the future holds. The vision of the future affects the disciple's actions in the present.

In a related manner the parable of the unmerciful servant (Matt 18:23–35) concerns a man who is forgiven an outrageously large debt he owes the king, only to turn around and demand a tiny amount from one of his own debtors. The focus of this parable clearly is forgiveness and the disciple's responsibility to forgive in accordance with the forgiveness one has received. Even here though, the context of this parable brings eschatology back into focus. The story is prompted by Peter's question to Jesus about

48. Young, *Parables*, 97.
49. O'Donovan, *Finding and Seeking*, 154–55.

how many times he is obligated to forgive someone who wrongs him (Matt 18:21–22). Jesus's reply of "seventy times seven" is not a rhetorical flourish but a reference to the end of exile, the "seventy times seven" years prophesied in Daniel (9:24–27) before God's deliverance will take effect. When considering the significance of Jesus's answer, the parable of the unmerciful servant reveals an eschatological dimension. A disciple forgives not only because he has been forgiven but also because of *what time it is*.[50] In the eschatological day of jubilee, debts are released and debtors are freed from their burdens. The kingdom changes everything.

The themes of eschatological awareness and joyful abandonment to God's kingdom purposes converge in the parables examined above. The Olivet Discourse (Matthew 23–25), where Matthew devotes the largest amount of space to Jesus's eschatological teaching, contains the parable of the sheep and the goats (Matt 25:31–46), which provides another example of how a disciple's life must demonstrate the veracity of his or her confession. Eschatology and fruitfulness come together in one parable. Though we have not treated every parable in the Gospel of Matthew in detail, we can see from these examples how eschatology and discipleship are interconnected, and this eschatological discipleship informs the vision of "making disciples" from Jesus's Great Commission.

The Commissioning Texts in Luke-Acts

The Great Commission (Matt 28:18-20) is often considered the primary and most important scene of Jesus's commissioning of his disciples, but we should not overlook the commissioning scenes found in Luke-Acts. Each scene has its own qualities and emphases. In order to have a proper understanding of Jesus's intentions, we must take each account on its own terms. Luke includes two scenes of commission for Jesus's disciples after the resurrection: Luke 24:44-49 and Acts 1:4-8.[51]

---

50. N. T. Wright, *Evil and the Justice of God* (Downers Grove, IL: InterVarsity Press, 2006), 155.

51. The case could be made for a greater number of Lucan commissioning scenes, such as the calling of the disciples (Luke 5:1-11), the commissioning of the twelve (Luke 9:1-6), the sending out of the seventy (Luke 10:1-20), or the calling and commissioning of Paul (Acts 9:1-8, recounted in Acts 22:6-21 and Acts 26:12-23). For our present purposes we will focus on the tasks given to all of the disciples after Christ's resurrection, since the placement of these two scenes (at the end of Luke's Gospel and the beginning of Acts) indicates their significance in the narrative flow of Luke's work.

Luke's Commissioning Texts in Context

The prominent feature that stands out in Luke's commissioning texts is the emphasis on being "witnesses." This emphasis on being a witness in Luke 24:48 comes at the end of a lengthy book that includes parabolic material, miracle stories, didactic sermons, and so forth. Likewise, the emphasis on witnesses in Acts 1:8 comes at the beginning of a narrative that includes apostolic sermons, more miracle stories, and a historical time line of how this witness went forth to the ends of the earth. If we fail to consider Luke's description of "witnesses" within the overall framework in which these texts are placed, we are likely to take our contemporary understanding of mission and "witness" and read it back into these texts. In other words, we are likely to slap the label of Luke's terminology of "witness" onto whatever activities in which we are already engaged.

To avoid this anachronistic tendency, these two commissioning scenes should be set in context. They are the pivotal point on which the two narratives hang, the hinge on which the door to the Gospel of Luke closes and the door to Acts opens.[52] The Gospel of Luke and the Acts of the Apostles are linked by this emphasis on witness. The apostles who witnessed Christ's death and resurrection now testify to these saving events.[53] They are to live in light of what Christ has done, and their mission is a participation in spreading his kingdom.

Luke 24. The commissioning text at the end of Luke builds on the themes introduced in his Gospel and expanded in Acts. The activities Jesus predicts for his disciples (preaching, ministry in his name, repentance, forgiveness, the nations) are already defined, at least in some measure, by their meaning within the ministry of Jesus himself. By returning to these same themes as Jesus commissions his disciples, Luke implies that the disciples

52. Mikeal C. Parsons and Richard I. Pervo, *Rethinking the Unity of Luke and Acts* (Minneapolis: Fortress Press, 1993), 18. Some disagreement still ensues among scholars regarding the unity of Luke-Acts as a literary work, even when Lucan authorship for both books is presupposed. For example, Mikeal Parsons and Richard Pervo challenge the idea that Lucan authorship means these books should be considered one work. They recommend that scholars disregard the term *Luke-Acts* and, instead, speak of Luke *and* Acts in order to communicate the fact that they are dealing with a Gospel and its sequel and to make clear that the books have different narratives, literary aspects, and theological concerns. For the present purposes it is unnecessary to take a position on the unity and diversity of these two books. The use of the descriptor *Luke-Acts* is shorthand for communicating that these two books originate from the same author, in line with the way scholars speak of the Petrine epistles (1 and 2 Peter) or the Pastoral Epistles (1 and 2 Timothy). Describing Luke and Acts in this way does not detract from the unique and individual purposes of each work on its own but merely reminds of their common author and allows one to proceed with confidence in seeking to understand the two main commissioning texts within each narrative.

53. I. Howard Marshall, *The Gospel of Luke*, New International Greek Testament Commentary (Grand Rapids: Eerdmans, 1978), 906.

will carry on the ministry Jesus started. From a salvation-historical perspective, we should not see this ongoing ministry as a straight line from Jesus to the disciples but rather as a line that has gone through the cross and resurrection, the event that secures the salvation of the disciples and compels their missionary activity.[54]

Jesus's commissioning of the disciples looks backward (to the promise of God unfolded in the Old Testament) and forward (repentance and forgiveness will go to all nations). Luke focuses on the disciples' identity as witnesses to the eschatological fulfillment of Old Testament prophecy in the person and work of Jesus Christ and in the continued ministry of the disciples, who will preach repentance and forgiveness of sins to the nations. The disciples are witnesses to God's work *in the past*, and they are called to be part of his gathering of peoples *in the future*. Two features deserve further elaboration.

First, we see how the commissioning scene in Luke places repentance and forgiveness at the heart of the message being proclaimed. "Repentance and forgiveness of sins" is shorthand for "the gospel" in Luke's view. This feature does not mean the gospel can be reduced to individual forgiveness (after all, the reference to "forgiveness" follows the proclamation of Christ's saving work as the fulfillment of Israel's story, Luke 24:46), but neither should we underplay the close connection between forgiveness and the heart of the gospel. In other places in Luke's Gospel, his summary of Jesus's good news is described as "forgiveness" (1:77; 4:18). Luke likely has both an expansive and individual understanding of "forgiveness of sins" in his account of the commissioning.

The expansive understanding focuses on "repentance and forgiveness of sins" in the context of Christ's proclamation of the end of Israel's exile.[55] The individual understanding keeps in mind the newfound establishment of a personal relationship with God because of the removal of the sin barrier.[56] Both understandings are in view here and should not be pitted against each other. The themes of repentance and forgiveness are present in the other Gospels, but they receive more attention in Luke because of the way he provides stories from Jesus's ministry that illustrate these themes in concrete ways.

---

54. Arthur A. Just Jr., *Luke 9:51–24:53*, Concordia Commentary: A Theological Exposition of Sacred Scripture (St. Louis: Concordia Publishing House, 1997), 1051.

55. Wright, *Challenge of Jesus*, 69–70.

56. Darrell L. Bock, *Luke* (Grand Rapids: Baker Books, 1996), 1940.

Second, we note the prominence given to the disciples' identity as witnesses. While the commissions in the other Synoptic Gospels stress the task of the disciples (Matthew—disciple making, Mark—preaching), Luke focuses on the identity of the disciples as witnesses sent in the power of the Spirit. We will examine this feature in greater detail below.

Acts 1. The commissioning text at the beginning of Acts 1:4–8 picks up where the scene in Luke leaves off, elaborating on the nature of being a witness to the nations by focusing on the geographical expansion of the disciples' ministry and the need for the empowering work of the Holy Spirit. Just as the commissioning text at the end of Luke's Gospel builds on the themes present in the story line, the commissioning text that opens Acts sets the stage for the narrative to come, corroborating the facts recorded in the Gospel and describing the expansion of the witness of the apostles to Jesus.

Acts tells the story of the original eyewitnesses to Jesus's resurrection and the progress of their mission of leading others to repent and find forgiveness of sins in his name. Just as Luke sought to show how the ministry of Jesus fulfilled the promises of the Old Testament, in Acts the evangelist offers scriptural substantiation of the apostles' ministry.[57]

Additionally, Acts tracks the progression of the witnesses' success. The prediction of Acts 1:8 begins to come to initial fulfillment as the book continues. John Stott argues that the commissioning scene serves as a "table of contents" for the book since the first seven chapters focus on events in Jerusalem. Chapter 8 records the disciples' work in Judea and Samaria, and the rest of the book follows the missionary expeditions of Paul on his way to Rome.[58] The universal thrust of God's mission to the nations is predicted in the commissioning scene and is then embodied in the work of the disciples as they fulfill God's plan.

The focus of Acts 1:8 on being witnesses presupposes the importance of the apostolic proclamation of a particular message. It is no surprise, then, to see how much space is given in Acts to the words of the apostles—in sermons, in miracle stories, and before governors. The book does not merely record the witness of the apostles in their deeds but gives great attention to their witness in words.[59] In connection with the opening scene in which Jesus gives his followers this identity, all of the main characters in

57. Donald Juel, *Luke-Acts: The Promise of History* (Atlanta: John Knox Press, 1983), 56.

58. John R. W. Stott, *The Message of Acts: The Spirit, the Church, and the World*, Bible Speaks Today (Downers Grove, IL: InterVarsity Press, 1990), 43.

59. Marshall, *Luke: Historian and Theologian*, 159.

Acts are described as "witnesses" (1:8, 22; 2:32; 3:15; 5:32; 10:39-41; 13:31; 22:15, 20; 26:16).[60] As witnesses of what they have seen, the disciples testify to the death, resurrection, teaching, and work of Christ. Luke includes their speeches as examples of this testimony to God's saving activity.[61]

We can see the significance of these two commissioning accounts by considering their placement in the narrative flow of Luke's work, as well as the connection between these accounts and their immediate literary context. Now we turn to a detailed study of the word *witnesses* in order to discover what Luke intended his readers to understand by his use of this term and how this understanding should become part of our vision for eschatological discipleship.

The Meaning of the Word *Witnesses*

In both of Luke's commissioning scenes, Jesus is first seen making a statement and a prediction regarding the disciples' identity, not a command of the disciples' activity. Second, we recognize the importance given to the name in which the disciples' message will be proclaimed. Third, the message of the disciples includes an intrinsic call for a response. Fourth, we note the corporate identity given to Christ's disciples in these commissioning scenes. Fifth, we observe how these commissionings are connected to the prophecies of the Old Testament that foresee an expansion of God's work to unbelieving Gentiles. Finally, these commissioning scenes imply an obligation on the part of the disciples that cannot be fulfilled apart from receiving the gift of the Holy Spirit.

An Identity, Not Just a Task. In both scenes Jesus speaks of the disciples in terms of present reality ("you are my witnesses") and future identity ("you will be my witnesses"). First, we should note the emphasis in both accounts on Jesus's claiming authority over their identities and activities, *my* witnesses.[62]

---

60. Luke Timothy Johnson, *The Gospel of Luke*, Sacra Pagina Series (Collegeville, MN: Liturgical Press, 1991), 3:403.

61. Bock, *Luke*, 1941-42.

62. The Greek here is ambiguous. The phrase could refer to the fact that the witnesses belong to the Lord (possessive genitive)—"you are the witnesses who belong to me"—or to the fact that the witnesses speak of the Lord in line with their identity (objective genitive)—"you are the witnesses that speak of me." That the Greek is left deliberately ambiguous as a way of implying both meanings is possible, and readers can safely assume that both meanings are true. However, the significance given in Luke 24:44-48 to bearing witness to all that has been fulfilled in the Old Testament, as well as the expansion of the apostles' witnessing *speech* to Jesus, is an indicator that the latter (objective genitive) understanding is the primary one in view here. In this I am largely in agreement with David G. Peterson, *The Acts of the Apostles*, Pillar New Testament Commentary (ed. D. A. Carson; Grand Rapids: Eerdmans, 2009), 80.

Second, in both cases the emphasis falls on the identity of the disciples as witnesses, not the task of witnessing. The focus on the disciples' identity does not negate the task of witnessing, of course, but it does serve as a reminder that the activity of witnessing is birthed from the disciples' identity as witnesses. The prediction of Jesus assumes the task of witnessing, but its focus on the disciples' identity indicates a comprehensive understanding of who the disciples *are*, not just what they *do*. The disciples do not become witnesses because they engage in the activity of witnessing; rather, they engage in the activity of witnessing because they are already witnesses.[63]

"You will be my witnesses" is a promise that indicates a comprehensive identity that becomes the defining factor of the individual and the church, covering all aspects of life. Therefore, witnessing cannot be reduced to one aspect of a Christian's activity but should be seen as the foundational aspect of a Christian's identity. Believers speak of Christ because they are *of* Christ. They witness because he has declared them to be his witnesses. The indicative precedes the imperative.[64]

A Message in Jesus's Name. Second, note the importance of Christ's authority in undergirding the message and mission of the witnesses. Just as the Great Commission in the Gospel of Matthew (28:18–20) began with a statement of Christ's receiving all authority in heaven and on earth, Luke's commissioning scene also indicates the authority of Christ, although the focus in the Lucan texts is on the gospel going out in Jesus's name. The name of Jesus is the locus of authority in the Lucan commissioning scene. In Acts this element is not emphasized in the commissioning scene itself but in the rest of the narrative, where the theme of Jesus's name carrying power and authority becomes a major point of the story.[65]

The focus on Jesus's name reveals something not only about Christ but also about the witnesses. By proclaiming a message of forgiveness of sins in Jesus's name, the disciples demonstrate the authority behind their activity. They are witnesses to the miracles of Jesus, especially his sacrificial death and victorious resurrection. The events at the heart of the gospel are at the

---

63. Goheen, *Light to the Nations*, 127, writes, "We would be mistaken if we were to think of Jesus' call to witness as merely one more assignment added to an otherwise full agenda for the people of God. Witness is not one more task among others: *Witness defines the role of this community in this era of God's story and thus defines its very identity*. Its eschatological role at this point in history is to make salvation known first to Israel and then to the Gentiles" (emphasis in original).

64. Ibid., 128.

65. Acts 2:38; 3:6, 16; 4:7, 10, 12, 17–18, 30; 5:28, 40; 8:12, 16; 9:14–16, 21, 27–28; 10:43, 48; 15:14, 26; 16:18; 19:5, 13, 17; 21:13; 22:16; and 26:9.

heart of their proclamation. The sermons in Acts reveal how the apostles walked their hearers through the story of Christ's work. Likewise, they are witnesses to the character of Jesus in the way they pattern their ministry after his miracles and show his compassion to those in need. In addition, they are witnesses to their own Christian experience.[66] The apostle Paul, for example, recounts his conversion experience on two occasions in Acts (22:6–21 and 26:12–23).

A Message that Calls for a Response. The Lucan commissioning scene sums up the message of the apostles by referring to "repentance" and "forgiveness of sins" being proclaimed to all nations. The reference to repentance and the reference to all nations indicate the intrinsic call for a response that accompanies the proclamation of forgiveness in Jesus's name. One of the distinctive elements in Acts is Luke's tendency to use "repentance" as his preferred term to sum up the response required by those who hear the gospel (see Acts 2:38; 3:19; 5:31; 8:22; 11:18; 13:24; 17:30; 19:4; 20:21; 26:20). In order to gain a proper understanding of the nature of this response, we should examine "repentance" within its Jewish context.

The Greek word for repentance implies "agreeing,"[67] and in one sense repentance is agreeing with God regarding one's sin. However, the word in its Hebrew roots goes further and involves a "turning"[68] of direction. Combining these related meanings, repentance is seen as a change of thinking that leads to a change of direction, based on trust in the proclamation of the good news. The connection between "forgiveness of sins" and "repentance" indicates that the "change of direction" implies a turning away from one's own efforts to find forgiveness apart from Christ. The forgiveness at the heart of the gospel is proclaimed in Jesus's name. Therefore, repentance indicates both a turning from sin and a trading-in of one's own kingdom agenda for the agenda of seeing Christ's name hallowed on earth as in heaven. Further implied in Luke's summary term of *repentance* is turning toward God in faith. Trust in God's promise is presupposed in Luke's label of repentance.[69]

Corporately speaking, then, the repentance being proclaimed refers to the call of Jesus for all people from all nations to turn from their idolatry

---

66. Peterson, *Acts*, 81.

67. Darrell Bock, *A Theology of Luke and Acts: God's Promised Program, Realized for All Nations*, Biblical Theology of the New Testament (ed. Andreas J. Köstenberger; Grand Rapids: Zondervan, 2012), 132.

68. Ibid.

69. Ibid.

and personal agendas and to accept the kingdom agenda of Jesus Christ. Individually speaking, this repentance is expressed in a turning-away from sin and turning toward God in faith for salvation. The message of forgiveness of sins that will be proclaimed to the nations includes an intrinsic call for repentance that includes faith in God's promises.

Witnesses in the Corporate Sense. Next we should note that the idea of witnesses is corporate in Luke and Acts. It concerns the identity of a missionary church, a body of believers united by their mission of proclaiming forgiveness of sins and embodying a new way of life before a watching world. As such, though the activity of "witness" implies a strong priority on the verbal proclamation of the message in Jesus's name, this activity cannot be divorced from the congregation's identity as a corporate witness. These commissioning scenes do not envision, at least not in the first instance, individual Christians as witnesses but rather the church as a witnessing body.[70]

The key point to remember is that Jesus is commissioning a community. The individual disciples are commissioned in relation to their corporate identities, not merely as individual witnesses. Western readers may tend to read these passages in light of the autonomous individual, envisioning the commissioning scenes as tasks assigned to individual Christians. However, a proper focus on the corporate dimension of these accounts helps us see the commissioning in light of the identity Jesus bestows upon a community. Jesus does not send a Christian to the nations but rather a church. By seeking and saving the lost in his ministry, he has formed a new people, the true Israel, who will finally fulfill God's purposes in the world, in light of God's own work in fulfilling the promise he made to Abraham. In fulfillment of his work in Israel, Jesus sends a community to the world.[71]

The communal witness of the church is foreshadowed and promised in the Old Testament, and it sees its arrival as the Holy Spirit descends to fulfill God's promise in the New Testament. To interpret the commissioning texts as applying only to individuals is to miss the rich, eschatological

70. Richard N. Longenecker, *Acts*, Expositor's Bible Commentary (ed. Frank E. Gaebelein; Grand Rapids: Zondervan, 1981), 9:256. Longenecker helpfully summarizes the missionary identity of the church seen in Acts: "The Christian church, according to Acts, is a missionary church that responds obediently to Jesus' commission, acts on Jesus' behalf in the extension of his ministry, focuses its proclamation of the kingdom of God in its witness to Jesus, is guided and empowered by the self-same Spirit that directed and supported Jesus' ministry, and follows a program whose guidelines for outreach have been set by Jesus Himself."

71. Goheen, *Light to the Nations*, 115.

overtones throughout the Scriptures that envision a community serving as the salt of the earth and light of the world.

The terminology of witnesses likely echoes the Lord's words to Israel in Isaiah 43:10–12. We should not miss the high Christology present in Jesus's words to his disciples. By adopting the same words of YHWH to Israel, "You are my witnesses," Jesus is associating himself with God, and he is associating his followers with Israel. The implication is that Jesus is the embodiment of YHWH, and his followers are the true Israel who will finally fulfill the task given to God's people. Witness flows from knowing Jesus.[72]

We find an eschatological dimension in the corporate nature of the "witnesses." Acts 1:8 focuses on the geographical expansion to the ends of the earth, not the eschatological promise of Christ's being with the disciples to "the end of the age" (Matt 28:20). Still, a strong element of eschatology is present in Acts 1:4–8, since Christ's last words in Acts are preceded by a question from the disciples regarding the timetable of the kingdom's restoration to Israel. Their desire to know the timing of God's kingdom coming in its fullness is rooted in Jewish eschatology. When Jesus brushes off their question, he does not do so because it has no validity but rather because he desires to focus on what the disciples are to be (and therefore do) in the meantime.[73] Indeed, they will be an eschatological people, not because they know the signs and the times but because they are indwelled by the Spirit who empowers their witness to the ends of the earth.

From Old Testament Prophecy to the Ends of the Earth. We saw above how the Lucan focus on witnesses builds on the Old Testament, particularly the words of YHWH in Isaiah 43, but the commissioning text in Acts stresses the geographical expansion of this witness. The beginning of the mission takes place in Jerusalem, the center of redemptive history, because of its significance for Israel and now its identity as the city where the Messiah was crucified and raised. However, a further reason exists why Jerusalem is the starting point, the fulfillment of ancient prophecy. In the Old Testament one reads that "instruction will go out of Zion and the word of the LORD from Jerusalem" (Isa 2:3). The commissioning scene in Acts

72. Wright, *Mission of God*, 65–66, comments on this connection: "Israel knew the identity of the true and living God, YHWH; therefore, they were entrusted with bearing witness to that in a world of nations and their gods. The disciples now know the true identity of the crucified and risen Jesus; therefore they are entrusted with bearing witness to that to the ends of the earth. The church's mission flows from the identity of God and his Christ. When you know who God is, when you know who Jesus is, witnessing mission is the unavoidable outcome."

73. Stott, *Message of Acts*, 43–44.

builds on this promise by giving the details of this "going out" of the message—from Jerusalem, to Judea, to Samaria, and the ends of the earth (Acts 1:8). The point is that all national boundaries have been demolished, and the message of the gospel is to go forth to all.

Though this commissioning took some time to be worked out in the early church (one thinks of the issues raised by inclusion of Gentile believers, leading to the formation of the Jerusalem Council in Acts 15), sustained consideration of this commission would link the words of Christ to the promise of multiple Old Testament prophecies. The Word of the Lord (now defined as the gospel of Jesus Christ, not the law of Moses) is to go to all nations (Isa 42:6; 49:6; Acts 13:47). The lordship of Christ extends to all people and can no longer be limited to a Jewish message. Jerusalem may be Ground Zero, but the ends of the earth are in view, just as the prophets foresaw.[74]

Though we recognize the importance of Jerusalem in the Old Testament as well as the prediction of the gospel being taken to the nations, we should not make too strong of a distinction between the centripetal mission of the Old Testament (come and see) with the centrifugal mission of the New (go and tell). The purpose of going and telling is that people might form the family of God. The impetus to "go out" is never divorced from the desire to "bring in" to the fold.[75] The mission of the church is to take the gospel to all peoples, in line with the Old Testament prophecies and in fulfillment of Christ's prediction.

Both an Obligation and a Gift. Strictly speaking, the commissioning scenes in Luke and Acts do not include a command from Christ but instead a prediction. In line with Luke's emphasis on the importance of the person and role of the Holy Spirit, the command of Christ in Luke 24 is not to go into the world to make disciples but rather to go to Jerusalem and wait for the coming of the Spirit.

The fact that Jesus's only command before his ascension is to "go and wait" rather than "go and tell" underscores the importance of the Holy Spirit's role in enabling the disciples to live up to the identity Jesus has given them. To miss this point is to overestimate the work Christians can do in our own power and to miss the necessity of the Spirit in the work of taking the gospel to the nations. To miss this point is also to forget how dependent

74. Bock, *Theology of Luke and Acts*, 133; see also Peterson, *Acts*, 111.

75. Goheen, *Light to the Nations*, 129.

we are on the Spirit for wisdom and guidance through various cultural challenges, wisdom that is a key component of eschatological discipleship.[76]

While it is true that these commissioning scenes are a prediction, not a command, the fact that Christ gives the disciples the title "witnesses" assumes they will, in fact, *behave* in line with this identity. A sense of obligation accompanies the prediction. Imagine a royal family in which a father tells his son, "You will be king one day." This prediction focuses on identity, but it naturally includes certain activities and tasks that will be expected of someone with such an identity, not the least of which includes *ruling*. In a similar manner, though the commissioning texts in Luke focus on the identity of witnesses, we shouldn't miss the fact that Christ expected his followers to engage in activities that demonstrate and prove their identity.

As we turn from the disciples' identity to their task, however, we must keep in mind the power needed for such activity, power that comes from the Spirit. The identity of witnesses leads to the activity of witnessing, only because this activity is undergirded by the power of the Holy Spirit. The obligation comes with a gift.

The necessity of the Spirit's power and presence does not come out of nowhere but is also part of the Old Testament promises. For example, Ezekiel 36:25 focuses on the forgiveness God will grant his people while the next verse promises a new heart and God's Spirit who will indwell the believer and cause him or her to follow God's ways. Along with the promise of forgiveness of sins in Luke 24:47 comes the promise of the Holy Spirit (v. 49) who enables a relationship with Christ and empowers witnesses to fulfill their mission. Not surprisingly, then, in Peter's sermon at Pentecost, he moves effortlessly from proclaiming forgiveness in Jesus (Acts 2:38) to proclaiming the promise of the Spirit (Acts 2:38–39). The promise of God in the Old Testament was that his people would be given new hearts and be empowered for ministry through the person and work of the Spirit.

In summary, we see that the two primary commissioning texts in Luke-Acts (Luke 24:46–49 and Acts 1:4–8) draw attention to the idea of "witness." In the exploration of the word "witnesses" in these texts, we see that God's people are first constituted as a witnessing body to God's eschatological

76. Chan, *Pentecostal Theology*, 110, speaks of the Spirit's role in helping Christians be oriented to the future as we interpret the present, "The Spirit who inspires hope and points us to the 'beyond' of history does so without abandoning history but leads us *through* history to feel the birth pangs of the new age which in fact has already begun when the Spirit inaugurated the 'last days. . . .' The Spirit who drives us forward to a hope beyond history also drives us back into history, challenging us to take our historical existence with utmost seriousness."

action in Christ and that God's people are then expected to live in light of that declaration through the power of the Spirit until the gospel has been spread to the nations.

Summary

In our exploration of these two Gospels and Acts, we have seen how the Matthean and Lucan commissioning texts are grounded in their overarching story of Jesus and his people. Luke's focus on the disciples' identity as "witnesses" complements Matthew's emphasis on what the disciples will do (baptizing and teaching). In both cases the portrait of a disciple from Jesus's teaching (in didactic and parabolic forms) helps us see what discipleship looks like. In the Gospels and Acts, *eschatological discipleship is seen in the way the people of God, constituted by faith in the crucified and risen Jesus, live according to Spirit-guided wisdom that makes them ever aware of the eschatological moment of urgency and helps them reorient their lives as the community of faith (whose identity is "witness") that embodies the mission of God.*

CHAPTER 4

Eschatological Discipleship in the Letters of Paul

> Discipleship emphasizes the importance of holy living, seeking to glorify God with our choices and exalt Jesus as Savior and Lord. However, the stated or implicit rationale for growing in godliness is deficient if it does not take into consideration the eschatological basis for obeying Jesus. As we have seen, according to the New Testament, holiness is not a timeless moral code but rather a timely moral witness grounded in the eschatological reality of Christ's resurrection and return. In this chapter we will examine how the apostle Paul consistently appealed to the Jewish understanding of world history (now reworked and recentered on the resurrection of the Messiah) as he exhorted the early Christians to walk in holiness.

First, we analyze several of Paul's exhortations to the early Christians in light of Christ's resurrection, the dawning of the new creation, and the coming consummation of all things. The focus of the first section is on how eschatology *motivates* Christian obedience.

Second, we analyze Paul's view of the church and the kingdom and how his ethical vision is shaped by his eschatology and perspective on history—now centered on Christ's cross, his resurrection, and return. The focus of the second section is on how eschatology *shapes* Christian obedience.

Paul's Appeals to Holiness Are Eschatologically Motivated

In this first section we will see how Paul consistently exhorted the early Christians to lives of holiness in light of Christ's resurrection, the dawning of the new creation, and the coming consummation of all things. In other words, Paul calls for obedience because of "what time it is." We will briefly examine several key passages in support of this understanding of Paul's ethical vision.

Why Eschatology Matters for Understanding Paul

The reason it is important to keep Paul's eschatological ethic in mind is that too often eschatological reflection is seen as counterproductive and perhaps even a hindrance to ethical exhortation. Some believe that eschatology, since it focuses on the future, naturally draws attention away from the present. The problem of divorcing eschatology from ethics is reinforced by common methods in systematic theology. Because eschatological truths are often relegated to the back of systematic textbooks, it is easy to categorize and label eschatology as speculation about the future in light of Scripture rather than to see how the scriptural vision of the future infuses all present witness.

Richard Gaffin notices this tendency, particularly with regard to the Spirit and his work. Some theologians explain the Spirit's work of sanctification without referencing eschatology, but Gaffin believes this structure of traditional dogmatics "masks the outlook basic not only to Paul but the entire New Testament that the Messiah's coming is one (eschatological) coming which unfolds in two episodes, one already and one still to come, that the 'age to come' is not only future but present."[1] Gaffin worries that these traditional approaches are detrimental to the understanding of Paul's theology because they sever the organic connection between Christ's resurrection and our own and cover the "eschatological quality of the believer's present soteriological experience."[2]

Though some may see eschatology as a distraction from ethics, Richard Hays believes we cannot make sense of Paul's moral vision unless we understand his new creation ethics. He writes, "Paul's moral vision is intelligible only when his apocalyptic perspective is kept clearly in mind," which means "the church is to find its identity and vocation by recognizing its role within the cosmic drama of God's reconciliation of the world to himself."[3] If understanding Paul's eschatology is essential for understanding his ethical exhortations, we must consider how Paul viewed himself and his times within the framework of God's plan for the world.

N. T. Wright suggests that if one were to ask Paul, "What time is it?," the apostle would answer from a Jewish perspective, which had been radically reshaped around Jesus. Wright notes, "A new time is opening up, a new day

1. Richard B. Gaffin Jr., *Resurrection and Redemption: A Study in Paul's Soteriology,* 2nd ed. (Phillipsburg, NJ: P&R, 1987), 90.

2. Ibid., 91.

3. Hays, *Moral Vision*, 19.

is dawning. Through these events the cold, hard grip of the 'present evil age' has been broken, and humans from every quarter are summoned to belong to 'the age to come,' the eschatological springtime which is already present in the Messiah and, through his spirit, in and through his people."[4] Eschatology helps us see how the church fits into this picture. Hays describes the strategic role God has for his people within this context, "The old age is passing away, the new age has appeared in Christ, and the church stands at the juncture between them."[5] Before examining the actual content of Paul's exhortations to this church at the crossroads of the ages, we need to see how Paul envisioned his own ministry within this eschatological context.

The Eschatological Context for Paul's Ministry. Paul was driven by a sense of urgency to preach the gospel (1 Cor 9:16) and take the gospel to the Gentile nations. Much of Paul's ministry focused on teaching and mentoring people who would lead the churches to biblical faithfulness. As a missionary helping form missionary churches, Paul recognized how the kingdom of God impacts one's view of teaching and ministry. The motivation for Paul's ministry was the arrival of God's kingdom within the present evil age. What gave urgency to this task was the need to instruct people on how to live within their particular context. It is not an exaggeration to see all of Paul's ethical instruction as connected to eschatology since by definition it is helping Christians live in the time between Christ's resurrection and his second coming.[6]

Paul's approach was not to give detailed instructions of timeless wisdom in order to edify and educate the early churches. Instead his desire was for them to develop a Christian mind in order that they may discern, through wisdom and scriptural reflection, in reliance on the Spirit, the heart of Christian character and how it is applied in different contexts. As Wright argues, "From this there flows an ethic which is not so much about listing rules to keep (though they will be there in case the characters, not yet fully formed, are tempted to go astray again) but rather about teaching people to think as day-dwellers in a still darkened world."[7] Paul's focus is on discernment, not merely rule keeping.

---

4. Wright, *Paul and the Faithfulness of God*, 555.

5. Hays, *Moral Vision*, 20.

6. L. J. Kreitzer, "Eschatology," in *Dictionary of Paul and His Letters* (ed. Gerald F. Hawthorne, Ralph P. Martin, and Daniel G. Reid; Downers Grove, IL: 1993), 266.

7. Wright, *Faithfulness of God*, 1124.

Furthermore, the primary impetus for Paul's particular mission to the Gentiles was eschatology since Paul believed the plan of God to bring Gentiles into the kingdom had now been revealed. In Galatians 1:15–16, when Paul defends his apostleship, he draws on language from Isaiah's portrait of the suffering servant set apart for God's purposes.[8] In the "fullness of time" (Gal 4:4–7 ESV), God's creational purposes have come to their climax, and through the incorporation of Gentiles into God's worldwide family, all of creation is moving closer to becoming what it was always intended to be.[9] In the Thessalonian correspondence Paul links his Gentile mission to the death and resurrection of Jesus, which began the "last days" as foretold by the prophets.[10] In Colossians he uses the terminology of a mystery once hidden and now revealed (Col 1:25–29), and then in Ephesians 3 we see how this mystery is defined. Eckhard Schnabel summarizes,

> The mystery that has been revealed to Paul and is part and parcel of the gospel of God's grace is the inclusion of the pagans in God's salvation, who are thus incorporated along with Jewish believers into the body of Christ, that is, into the church. . . . As Paul uses the word, *mystery* generally refers to God's decisive action in the sending of Jesus Christ, the crucified and risen Savior and Lord, as the fulfillment of God's plan of salvation.[11]

This plan of salvation includes Paul's mission to the Gentiles, and thus it is accurate to say that Paul understood himself to be "an eschatological emissary" to the world.[12] It is no wonder that, given this self-understanding, Paul spoke of himself as "forgetting what is behind and reaching forward to what is ahead" (Phil 3:13–14), a description of his pursuit of faithful service on the race track to the finish line. What undergirds Paul's missionary work, and all the work of faithful Christians in the world, is the hope

---

8. Andreas J. Köstenberger and Peter T. O'Brien, *Salvation to the Ends of the Earth: A Biblical Theology of Missions*, New Studies in Biblical Theology (ed. D. A. Carson; Downers Grove, IL: InterVarsity, 2001), 166.

9. Tim Harris, "Pauline Theology," in *All Things to All Cultures: Paul among Jews, Greeks, and Romans* (ed. Mark Harding and Alanna Nobbs; Grand Rapids: Eerdmans, 2013), 369.

10. Eckhard J. Schnabel, *Paul the Missionary: Realities, Strategies and Methods* (Downers Grove, IL: InterVarsity Press, 2008), 201.

11. Ibid., 147.

12. Köstenberger and O'Brien, *Salvation to the Ends of the Earth*, 172.

that their exertion matters—that it will count for good in eternity. Because Christians hope, they press on.[13]

This brief survey of some of Paul's writings gives a flavor for how Paul's eschatology provided context for his ministry. Next we will see how this eschatology shaped the content of his teaching. Our focus will be on those texts where the exhortations of Paul are explicitly motivated by eschatology; that is, the *reason* Paul gives for obedience is directly connected to "what time it is," according to the eschatological clock.

Exhortations Explicitly Motivated by Eschatology

Three of the most important passages in which Paul grounds his moral exhortation in eschatological realities are 1 Thessalonians 5:1–11; Romans 13:11–14; and 1 Corinthians 15:34. We will focus our attention on these three passages and interact with other passages as needed.

1 Thessalonians 5:1–11: Children Who Belong to the Day

Paul's letters to the Thessalonians deal extensively with issues related to Christ's return, but the passage that most clearly ties eschatology to ethics is 1 Thessalonians 5. This epistle begins with a summary of Paul's preaching (1 Thess 1:9–10), which focused on Jesus's resurrection from the dead, the expectation that he would come again and rescue his people from the wrath of God. The rest of the letter shows how the gospel of hope enables the Thessalonian Christians to live as an alternative society, a contrasting community that stands out by replacing the Greco-Roman values of their society with values grounded in God's redemptive work through Jesus Christ.[14] Paul emphasized the church's hope of resurrection (1 Thessalonians 4) in contrast to ways of grief that are worldly, but then he turned from reassuring the Thessalonians (1 Thess 3:12–13; 4:13–18; 5:23–24) to exhorting them to live in light of this hope (1 Thess 5:1–11). The Christian hope is not an excuse for passivity but rather an exhortation toward pursuing the day when the Lord will come. The Christian hope is the motivation for living in light of the promised future.[15]

---

13. Summarizing Augustine's take on this passage in *In Epistulam Iohannis*, Homily 4, Passage 6, cited September 28, 2015, http://www.ewtn.com/library/PATRISTC/PNI7-8.TXT; and O'Donovan, *Finding and Seeking*, 124. O'Donovan comments, "We may be 'intent' on what lies ahead for us only if we are 'extended' to the future that is ultimately to come into being," cited September 25, 2015.

14. Murray J. Smith, "The Thessalonian Correspondence," in *All Things to All Cultures: Paul among Jews, Greeks, and Romans* (ed. Mark Harding and Alanna Nobbs; Grand Rapids: Eerdmans, 2013), 298.

15. F. F. Bruce, *1 & 2 Thessalonians*, Word Biblical Commentary (vol. 45; Nashville: Word, 1982), 115.

Paul utters his command to live in holiness within the framework of "day and night." Believers in Jesus are "children of light" and "children of the day" in contrast to those who "belong to the night or the darkness" (1 Thess 5:5). As children of the day, the fledgling community of faith is to understand "what time it is," prepare for the imminence of Christ's return, and build up the church in anticipation for the day Christ returns for his bride (1 Thess 5:9-11). F. F. Bruce comments, "The day had not arrived, but believers in Christ were children of day already, by a form of realized eschatology. The day, in fact, had cast its radiance ahead with the life and ministry of the historical Jesus and the accomplishment of his saving work; when it arrived in its full splendor, they would enter into their inheritance of glory and be manifested as children of day."[16]

Was Paul's emphasis on the nearness and imminence of Christ's return mistaken? Was this type of ethical exhortation therefore misplaced? We will answer this question as we look at the next passage, one that is remarkably similar in its metaphorical usage of light and darkness, Rom 13:11-14.

Romans 13:11-14: Away with the Deeds of Darkness

Like the Thessalonian passage, Rom 13:11-14 comes at a crucial point in a letter in which Paul has already connected eschatology to ethics. Because of the reality of their union with the crucified and risen Christ (Rom 6:2-11), believers are to participate in Christ's resurrection and live in a way that reflects the age to come.[17] Considering themselves alive to God through their union with the risen Jesus (6:11), Christians are to be clothed with the resurrected Christ and are to live as if salvation has already come in its fullness (13:11-14).[18]

What is fascinating about Paul's exhortation here is how he already assumes his readers know "what time it is, how it is now the moment for you to wake from sleep" (Rom 13:11 NRSV).[19] This type of language implies that Paul's exhortation comprehends all the other commands in this letter, brings them together with a sense of urgency, a sense of pressing forward

---

16. Ibid., 111.

17. J. R. Daniel Kirk, *Unlocking Romans: Resurrection and the Justification of God* (Grand Rapids: Eerdmans, 2008), 197.

18. Ibid., 215.

19. Solomon Andria, *Romans: Africa Bible Commentary Series*, New Testament editor, Samuel Ngewa (Grand Rapids: Zondervan, 2012), 245. Paul is not implying that his readers are unsaved, having never been "wakened" by the Spirit. As Andria writes, "[Paul] is not implying that all those he is writing to are spiritually asleep; rather, he is urging them all to stay alert."

to the end.[20] Paul uses the word *kairos*, which indicates a special moment, not just chronological time. This reality is what leads him to expect the Christians "to be up before day breaks fully; this theme, with its echoes of the Easter morning stories, resonates through the early Christian sense of new creation, new life bursting through the wintry crust of the old world. It is, he insists, time to wake up."[21] Paul assumes his readers know what time it is and will live accordingly.

The "night" and "day" contrast of Romans 13 echoes back to the beginning of this section in 12:1-2, where Paul encouraged Christians to have their minds renewed so they live in light of the eschatological situation brought by Christ. The earlier text encouraged the Christians to live in light of the past; since Christ died and was raised, the old age is done away with, and the new one has arrived. Scholars and teachers have often spoken of these kinds of exhortations as imperatives that are linked back to indicatives; that is, commands that are linked to what God has done for us in the past. Not surprisingly, in Romans 12, Paul follows this imperative/indicative paradigm by grounding his exhortation and appeal in what Christ has done in the past. However, here in chapter 13, Paul is encouraging his readers to see the present in light of the future. Once again he exhorts the people, but this time not on the basis of Christ's past work but on the basis of Christ's promised future.[22]

Paul's statement that "the day is near" (Rom 13:12) indicates the sense of urgency in his appeal. Thomas Schreiner claims, "All the imperatives in this text flow from the nearness of the *eschaton*. Because the end is imminent, the people of God should respond with appropriate behavior. Thus one cannot deny that the imminence of the end was one basis for ethics in Pauline thought."[23] Does this mean Paul was wrong since Christ did not return in the first century? No. Paul's emphasis is grounded in the *certainty* of the end and the possibility that this end could be soon. Being morally ready for Christ's return is living in light of the blessed hope, no matter when that will take place.[24]

---

20. Thomas R. Schreiner, *Romans*, Baker Exegetical Commentary on the New Testament (Grand Rapids: Baker Academic, 1998), 697.

21. N. T. Wright, *Romans*, New Interpreter's Bible Commentary, Acts-Introduction to Epistolary Literature-Romans-1 Corinthians (Nashville: Abingdon Press, 2002), 10:728.

22. Douglas J. Moo, *The Epistle to the Romans*, New International Commentary on the New Testament (Grand Rapids: Eerdmans, 1996), 818. Similarly, Wright, *Romans*, 727-28.

23. Schreiner, *Romans*, 698.

24. Ibid., and Moo, *Romans*, 822.

Because of the reality of Christ's second coming and the consummation of the hope of the believer, ethical choices are invested with eternal significance. As Doug Moo explains, "Christians are not only to 'become what we are'; we are also to 'become what we one day will be.'"[25] The application of this text for contemporary readers is simple. We are to know "what time it is" (Rom 13:11), urgently pursue holiness as we live "honorably" as people of the day (13:12–13 NRSV), and display the glory of Jesus Christ, whom we represent (13:14).[26]

1 Corinthians 15:34: Your Body Matters Because of the Resurrection

The verse, 1 Corinthians 15:34, includes a puzzling reference that comes in the middle of Paul's lengthy exposition of the significance of Christ's resurrection. He suddenly exhorts his readers to stop sinning and have a "sober . . . mind" (1 Cor 15:34 NRSV). Interpreters have had difficulty understanding the placement of this sudden exhortation, perhaps because it comes just a few verses after another difficult mention—the baptism of the dead (1 Cor 15:29).

Overlooking this passage is unfortunate since, as Gordon Fee suggests, it is "one of the more significant texts pointing to a genuine relationship between what one believes about the future and how one behaves in the present." He goes on to say, "We should be living in this world as those whose confidence in the final vindication of Christ through our own resurrection determines the present."[27] Schnabel echoes a similar refrain when he notes that the reality of Jesus's resurrection in the past and the believer's resurrection in the future implies that what a person does with his or her body in the present is not irrelevant.[28]

The reference at the end of the verse (the "shame" of acting as if one has no knowledge of God) points back to 1 Corinthians 6:5, where Paul claims it is shameful for believers to pursue lawsuits against one another in light of their future role as judges in God's new world.[29] Interestingly enough, the link between shameful uses of one's body and shameful actions in the body of Christ are both connected to the future reality of resurrection and

25. Moo, *Romans*, 818.

26. Wright, *Romans*, 729.

27. Gordon D. Fee, *The First Epistle to the Corinthians*, New International Commentary on the New Testament (Grand Rapids: Eerdmans, 1987), 775.

28. Schnabel, *Paul the Missionary*, 193.

29. Mark Taylor, *1 Corinthians*, New American Commentary (Nashville: B&H, 2014), 400.

the reality of the new earth. Therefore, to claim the hope of resurrection is to submit oneself to the ethics of the new world, which is why so many throughout history who have downplayed or denied the bodily resurrection (either of Jesus in the past or of believers in the future) through a sloppy spiritualization or through outright unbelief have often exhibited relaxed attitudes toward the Christian ethical vision.[30]

In summary, Paul called the early Christians to holiness by predicating his exhortations on God's eschatological timetable and the people's eschatological future. As N. T. Wright argues, "Christian life in the present, with its responsibilities and particular callings, is to be understood and shaped in relation to the final goal for which we have been made and redeemed."[31] The new age is present already but only partially. The expectation of Christ's return and the consummation of all things create a moral seriousness in which Christians are called to live in light of the final judgment.[32]

Paul's Vision of Holiness Is Eschatologically Shaped

Many of Paul's exhortations to the early church are grounded in the church's hope for Christ's return. Eschatology—living in the time between the times of Christ's first and second comings—motivates a believer's obedience. In the next section we see how eschatology shapes our obedience. The reality of the future new heavens and new earth influence and shape what obedience looks like; we live as citizens of God's kingdom, and we expect the shape of our obedience to be cruciform, in conformity with Christ.

The arrival of God's kingdom is central to Paul's vision of ethics for God's people. As Gregg Allison suggests, "The church as eschatological is a sign of the future-made-present in and through Jesus Christ."[33] The reason the church is the presence of the future is because of its location in time in relation to God's kingdom. Apart from a proper understanding of God's kingdom, ethics are distilled into timeless morals that lose the urgency and significance of their cosmic import. Michael Bird explains the importance of apocalyptic theology (or eschatology) in understanding the shape of how one goes about the theological task of discerning ethical living in accord with the kingdom of God when he writes:

30. Fee, *First Epistle to the Corinthians*, 775.

31. Wright, *After You Believe*, ix.

32. S. C. Mott, "Ethics," in *Dictionary of Paul and His Letters* (ed. Gerald F. Hawthorne, Ralph P. Martin, and Daniel G. Reid; Downers Grove, IL: 1993), 272.

33. Allison, *Sojourners and Strangers*, 153.

> Apocalyptic theology flows through Christian doctrine like blood in the veins of our body. Our worldview and worship are inspired by the invasion of heavenly forces upon the earth and the eventual redemption of our bodies in a new cosmos. Our present identity and mission are determined by who Jesus is and who he will be revealed to be at the end of history. The gospel we announce is fundamentally a declaration of victory to those who do not even believe there is a battle going on. The triumph of the Lamb over the powers and principalities of this world authorizes us to bring redemption to the men and women who live under the tyranny of death, sin, evil, and injustice.[34]

The kingdom of God is what gives significance to the church's mission, but it is also what gives shape to the church's unique ethical perspective. Too often Christians tend to see the New Testament commands as simple rules given by God for humanity's own good, as if they are disconnected from the wider picture of the world God has made and the future God has promised. Only when we see our Christian life within the matrix of relationships that are true of someone who has found life in Christ, the Messiah with whom we share death and resurrection, will we see the fuller picture of how ethics fit into the story of redemption.[35]

Writing specifically about Ephesians, but in a way that applies to any of Paul's letters, Timothy Gombis claims that one of Paul's intentions is to keep believers from a tame, overly individualistic vision of salvation, and so he seeks to expand their imaginative horizons until they are able "to inhabit a new story, to take on a new and renewed set of practices, to see ourselves as part of a radically different and outrageously life-giving story of God redeeming the world in Jesus Christ."[36] Because of the kingdom of God brought and inaugurated by Jesus at his first coming, God's kingdom people are to see themselves as belonging to a new age—an eschatological people under the reign of a risen Lord. As Bird writes,

> The resurrection of Jesus and the gift of the Spirit mean that God's new world has begun, the future has partially invaded the present, the seeds of the new creation have already begun

34. Bird, *Evangelical Theology*, 809.

35. Walsh and Keesmaat, *Colossians Remixed*, 157.

36. Timothy G. Gombis, *The Drama of Ephesians: Participating in the Triumph of God* (Downers Grove, IL: IVP Academic, 2010), 23.

> budding in the old garden, and God's victory on the cross is now beginning to claim back territory in a world enslaved by sin. The first Christians saw themselves as the vanguard of a new redeemed humanity that God was creating in Jesus Christ.[37]

Where does the apostle Paul connect the reality of God's kingdom to believers' present state of obedience? This connection can be seen clearly in Philippians 3:20 and then again in Colossians 3.

Philippians 3:20: Colonies of Heaven

In Philippians 3:20, just after calling his readers to imitate his example of obedience, the apostle Paul reminds them that their citizenship is in heaven, the place from which Christ the Savior will return. Paul Minear sees this passage as describing the church as "an encampment of soldiers in a foreign land who retain their citizenship in the capital city."[38] The reason they are to imitate the apostle and have the proper attitude to this world and the people in it is because of the heavenly city to which they belong.[39]

As in other passages (Rom 13:11–12; 1 Cor 15:54–58; Gal 6:9; 1 Thess 5:4–6), some of which have been examined, Paul is again connecting eschatological hope to ethical demands. This time, however, he is showing how obedience is not only motivated by the return of Christ but is also *shaped* by the present kingdom citizenship of these people.

Unfortunately, some interpreters see citizenship language and rush to an illegitimate conclusion. For example, J. A. Motyer interprets the citizenship language in a way that emphasizes believers' distance from the King and their longing for his return when he writes, "We belong to a far-off homeland and wait for the King of that land to come and fetch us."[40] Motyer is correct in his assertion that we are to long for the constant presence of the King, which is of course the essential truth of heaven. Where his interpretation is lacking is in his vision of the King's coming to "fetch us" from this present world and return us back to our "heavenly homeland." This interpretation misses the true meaning of Paul's usage of the citizenship metaphor.

---

37. Bird, *Evangelical Theology*, 728.

38. Minear, *Images of the Church*, 61.

39. Moisés Silva, *Philippians*, Baker Exegetical Commentary on the New Testament (Grand Rapids: Baker Academic, 1992, 2005), 183–84.

40. J. A. Motyer, *The Message of Philippians*, Bible Speaks Today (Downers Grove, IL: InterVarsity Press, 1984), 198.

The word Paul uses for "citizenship" or "commonwealth" was historically used to describe "a colony of foreigners or relocated veterans whose purpose was to secure the conquered country for the conquering country by spreading abroad that country's way of doing things, its customs, its culture, its laws, and so on."[41] In Paul's day Rome was the empire spreading its dominion and culture across the Mediterranean world. Philippi was a Roman colony, and the citizens there were expected to bring the culture of the city to resemble and acknowledge the authority of Caesar. Philippi was an outpost of Rome, and the Christians were to live as an outpost of heaven.[42]

Placing this text in its historical milieu keeps us from misinterpreting Paul's intent. Instead of thinking that the early Christians were told to remember that this is not their home, and one day Jesus will come back to rescue them from the earth, Paul is instructing his readers in this manner, "You are a colony of heaven, tasked with representing and spreading the dominion of Jesus across the world through your cruciform obedience, waiting with anticipation when he will return to this world and manifest his reign for all to see." In this way the kingdom reality of Christ's past work and future return shapes the kind of ethical wisdom the early Christians must use in contextualizing their obedience.

Colossians 3: Seek What Is Above

Another easily misinterpreted passage is Colossians 3:1-11, in which Paul reminds his readers that they are to seek what is above since they have been "raised with Christ." In these words the past and future converge on the present, with Paul grounding the Colossians' obedience—both in their union with Christ (having died and raised with him) and his future return (you will be revealed with Christ in glory). The primary focus of this passage concerns the power of union with Christ in the everyday ethical choices of believers and their fulfillment of societal roles (Col 3:18-4:1; Eph 5:22-6:9).[43]

The frequent misinterpretation of Paul's command to "seek the things above" (Col 3:1 CSB) is due to a lingering dualism in which "above" means

41. Gerald F. Hawthorne, *Philippians*, Word Biblical Commentary (Nashville: Thomas Nelson, 1983), 43:170.

42. Gordon D. Fee, *Paul's Letter to the Philippians*, New International Commentary on the New Testament (Grand Rapids: Eerdmans, 1995), 379.

43. Ian K. Smith, "The Later Pauline Letters," in *All Things to All Cultures: Paul among Jews, Greeks, and Romans* (ed. Mark Harding and Alanna Nobbs; Grand Rapids: Eerdmans, 2013), 322.

"disembodied, immaterial heaven" and "below" means "this material world." To the contrary, Paul's ethical exhortation here is shaped by the resurrection, and the resurrection is, by definition, bodily. Whatever "seeking what is above" means, it cannot mean focusing on a heavenly world at the expense of this material universe. As Walsh and Keesmaat point out, "[S]eeking that which is above is a matter not of becoming heavenly minded but of allowing the liberating rule of Christ to transform every dimension of your life."[44] The following list of sins and virtues (Col 3:5–11; 5:12–17) bears out this earthly dimension of obedience and its ecclesial context. According to the heavenly reality, the Colossian ethic of living holds together past, present, and future. Jesus's resurrection in the past requires ethical living in the present, and the shape of this new life in Christ is seen in the believer's hope for bodily resurrection.[45]

Obedience Shaped as Suffering

Just as the kingdom of God and its present and future reality give shape to the Christian's vision of obedience, so also the reality of Christ's suffering in the past gives shape to the kind of obedience expected today. Because we participate with Christ in his death and resurrection, we should not be surprised when current phases of ministry and obedience involve discipleship with a cost, a cup of suffering. Jason Hood comments, "From the cross to enthronement, life in Christ leads to a Christ-shaped life now and in the age to come. Believers begin to become what they already are in Christ: the true humans they were originally destined to be."[46] Eschatologically shaped ethics leave no room for triumphalism since the vision of God's kingdom includes a slain lamb on the throne (Rev 5:6).

This "becoming like Christ" takes place within the context of a cosmic battle between good and evil, the forces of darkness and the kingdom of light. Placing our growth in holiness and exhortations to Christian morality within the context of spiritual warfare helps prepare us for the suffering that often accompanies war. Here, then, is the eschatological challenge of ethics in the words of Mott: "Christ is King. God has exalted him. Not every knee, however, has yet bowed to him (Phil 2:9–11). The present time for Paul is situated between the initial triumph of Christ over the powers

44. Walsh and Keesmaat, *Colossians Remixed*, 154.
45. Kirk, *Unlocking Romans*, 215.
46. Hood, *Imitating God in Christ*, 100.

hostile to God and Christ's securing from them full and final obedience and submission. . . . Life is a battlefield of the divine and the demonic."[47]

In this cosmic battlefield Christians pursue holiness with an expectation of both suffering and joy, suffering because we model the sufferings of the Savior and joy because we rest in the reality of his resurrection. The eschatologically shaped life means the reality of the cross and resurrection must be ever before us, allowing us to hold joy and suffering in a tight and unavoidable paradox. The church experiences both joy and suffering, recognizing that suffering harkens back to Christ's example in the past and joy beckons us forward to Christ's return in the future when all things will be made right, no matter how bleak the situation may seem in the present.[48] The result of these experiences is the gradual "Christification" of the believer, as the believer shares in the fellowship of Christ's sufferings in anticipation of experiencing the power of his resurrection (Phil 3:10).[49]

No stranger to suffering, the apostle Paul expected to face personal trials, and he saw suffering as inevitable for those involved in missionary work.[50] The uniqueness of Paul is seen in his outlook on life, where his trials and ordeals are not seen as foes but rather as God's means of refining his character, fortifying the church, and binding him to Christ.[51] Don Howell notes, "Paul's sufferings *authenticate* him as God's servant, *identify* him with the crucified and risen Christ and *edify* the church."[52] Furthermore, this suffering is to be expected. As Michael Goheen points out,

> Human societies and cultures cohere on the basis of foundational beliefs and a shared story rooted in idolatry. When a dissenting group within that culture challenges the public doctrine and reigning story, the powers quite naturally lash back; they cannot allow those beliefs to be challenged beyond a certain point if the cultural community is to hold together. Being different, resisting the idolatry of the dominant story, will mean suffering for Christians.[53]

---

47. Mott, "Ethics," 272.
48. Hays, *Moral Vision*, 26.
49. Hood, *Imitating God in Christ*, 104.
50. Schnabel, *Paul the Missionary*, 143.
51. Don N. Howell Jr., "Paul's Theology of Suffering," in *Paul's Missionary Methods in His Time and Ours* (ed. Robert Plummer and John Mark Terry; Downers Grove, IL: IVP Academic, 2012), 106.
52. Ibid., 101.
53. Goheen, *Introducing Christian Mission Today*, 261.

Obedience, therefore, is not merely shaped by the eventual triumph of the kingdom of God but is also cruciform in the present, formed by the reality of Jesus's suffering sacrifice in the past and fully prepared for the power of resurrection in the future.

Further Reflections on Paul's Eschatological Ethic

Like the parables of Jesus, Paul's letters often connect ethical exhortation to eschatological reality, most prominently in his Thessalonian correspondence, but also in Romans 12–13 and 2 Corinthians 5:1–10. For Paul, eschatology not only provides the context for our obedience; it is also the motivation for our obedience. Believers are children of light who belong to the day that is dawning; we put aside the evil deeds of the night (1 Thess 5:1–11; Rom 13:12 ff). As N. T. Wright suggests, "Paul's vision of Christian virtue . . . is all about developing the habits of the daytime heart in a world still full of darkness."[54] Our belief in Christ's purpose for the future of the world is what gives us power to overcome anxiety and weakness (Phil 4:4–9), to "stand firm" on the rock of resurrection reality (1 Cor 15:58) with confidence that God's new world will come according to his promise (Rom 8:18).

Commenting on the relationship between hope and endurance, O'Donovan writes, "This brings us back from the ultimate horizon of the future to the immediate future directly before our feet, a space illumined by hope in the promise and open for freedom to move into, even if it is no larger than a space for patience, which is an exercise of freedom."[55] What role does hope play in the actions of a disciple? It is one of assurance. We hope in what we do not see (Rom 8:24), and this hope leads to expectancy and endurance.

Just as the parables defined discipleship in terms of wisdom and recognizing "what time it is," so also Paul's ethical exhortations to the New Testament churches deal with the fulfillment of God's will "in the diverse situations of everyday life,"[56] an eschatological discipleship that depends on Spirit-given wisdom. Summing up Paul's vision of obedience, Moltmann writes:

54. Wright, *After You Believe*, 137.

55. O'Donovan, *Finding and Seeking*, 152.

56. E. J. Schnabel, "Wisdom," in *Dictionary of Paul and His Letters* (ed. Gerald F. Hawthorne, Ralph P. Martin, and Daniel G. Reid; Downers Grove, IL: IVP, 1993), 972.

> The imperative of the Pauline call to new obedience is accordingly not to be understood merely as a summons to demonstrate the indicative of the new being in Christ, but it has also its eschatological presupposition in the future that has been promised and is to be expected—the coming of the Lord to judge and to reign. Hence it ought not to be rendered merely by saying: "Become what you are!," but emphatically also by saying: "Become what you will be!"[57]

The apostle Paul's exhortation to be "what we will be" implies that we are to be the people of faith, hope, and love. The embodiment of these virtues is consonant with an eschatologically aware perspective on life. As O'Donovan writes, "Faith in Christ the foundation of Christian existence, love its social embodiment, hope its ground of endurance."[58] The way these three virtues impact the believer's decision making is at the level of everyday Christian life. Faith focuses on God as the believer's sustainer; love embraces "the world in its reality as the field of action;" and hope discerns "the space of opportune time into which our resistance to adversity and our service to God and neighbor may be ventured."[59] Paul's ethical exhortations are grounded in the great story of the world, unfolded in the Scriptures and brought to its climax by Jesus Christ.

Summary

In this chapter we have seen how the apostle Paul's eschatological hope motivated and shaped his ethical reflection. The reality of Christ's future resurrection and his present reign as King of the world gave urgency to Paul's missionary task and shaped his mission to the Gentiles. Paul frequently relied on explicit eschatological statements as he exhorted the early Christians to faithful obedience to Jesus. As a shaping force for ethical reflection, Paul encouraged the early churches to see themselves as outposts of heaven, citizens of God's kingdom on earth, where the future reality of God's kingdom helps Christians discern the proper ethical choices in the present. Additionally, Paul expected Christian obedience to be cruciform in nature, where suffering is not brushed aside in a sloppy overrealized

57. Moltmann, *Theology of Hope*, 162.

58. O'Donovan, *Self, World, and Time*, 99.

59. O'Donovan, *Self, World, and Time*, 100; and Wright, *After You Believe*, 137. Similarly, Wright sees faith, hope, and love as forming "the fundamental character of the person who is anticipating in the present, by patient and careful moral discipline, the goal of genuine humanity which is set before us."

eschatology but is instead one of the refining characteristics of Christian discipleship, one that reminds believers of their death with Christ on the cross and propels them forward in hope for Christ's resurrection. In the life and letters of Paul, it is seen that *eschatological discipleship is obedience to Jesus Christ that is motivated by his climactic work in the past and is rooted in hope for his consummating work in the future.*

PART 3

Christianity in Light of Rival Eschatologies

CHAPTER 5

Introduction to Rival Eschatologies

When the gospel of Jesus Christ is announced in a culture, a missionary encounter takes place between the gospel and the foundational beliefs of a cultural community.[1] Michael Goheen sees three aspects to a missionary encounter: (1) the challenging of a culture's foundational beliefs with the comprehensive biblical story, (2) the challenging of the idolatrous cultural story with the gospel as a counterstory, and (3) the calling for conversion by Christians whose lives and words invite others to live in light of the gospel. The confrontational aspect of a missionary encounter is not always a contest between doctrines (for example, "Jesus is the Son of God" versus "Jesus was only a prophet"). Additionally, it is a confrontation between *time lines*, or *calendars*, or better put, the underlying, often unstated vision of history and the future that influences one's life and choices—in other words, eschatology.

In chapter 2, we saw that eschatological beliefs are not unique to Christians. People who adhere to other religious faiths or no religious faith at all live according to some sort of vision for humanity's future, and this vision is part of what gives meaning and significance to their lives. Just as the term *worldview* can apply to Christianity or to other religions (for example, the naturalist worldview), eschatology can also apply to other belief systems and visions of the future.

Because we have defined eschatology in its broadest sense, without its distinctively Christian contours, we can now contrast Christian eschatology with rival eschatological perspectives. This ability to see the difference between a Christian eschatology and rival conceptions of time and the future is one of the goals of eschatological discipleship, which we have

1. Goheen, *Introducing Christian Mission Today*, 298.

defined as *spiritual formation that seeks to instill wisdom regarding the contemporary setting in which Christians find themselves (in contrast to rival conceptions of time and progress) and that calls for contextualized obedience as a demonstration of the Christian belief that the biblical account of the world's past, present, and future is true.*

Asking, "What Time Is It?"

When giving consideration to the contemporary setting of North America, we should ask the question "What time is it?" from a Christian perspective and set the answer in contrast to other responses to that same question from people in the world. The missionary task is not merely to ask, "What time is it?" and have in mind a Christian perspective (we live in the "time between the times"—Christ's first and second comings), but to discern how our friends and neighbors answer that question from within their own worldviews. Once we understand the answers, implied and explicit, that our friends and neighbors give to the "What time is it?" question, we are better equipped to present the true, biblical account of our world.

Discerning our current cultural moment takes place as we see ourselves in light of the major salvific moments of Christianity—both what Christ has done in the past and what he will return to do in the future. As Christians we read our times today in light of the biblical answer to "What time is it?" in order to be faithful disciples who proclaim and embody the good news of Jesus Christ. In this we are pursuing what Lesslie Newbigin called "missionary obedience," Christian faithfulness that challenges false eschatologies as the gospel is proclaimed.[2]

Discerning the Times

The danger of failing to discern our current times correctly is that we will succumb to the world's vision of reality in ways we would never foresee. The difficulty of reading our current times is magnified not only by what we *do* see in their times but also in what we *don't.* Oliver O'Donovan comments,

> Our own age is the hardest of all ages to understand. It is composed of a mass of popular ideas and perceptions, often difficult to document though they are as familiar as the air we breathe, which acknowledge no duty to be consistent with each other.

2. Newbigin, *Household of God*, 153–54.

> They may be derived from the thoughts of great thinkers, but when they are, they have lost most of what subtlety and discrimination they once had. They ration and restrict our access to thought about life and action in ways we must look hard in order to recognize.[3]

O'Donovan's counsel points out the difficulty of understanding one's own worldview, let alone someone else's, especially considering the puzzling inconsistencies that often arise between one's behavior and beliefs. Do these inconsistencies make our general speech about eschatology and worldview impossible? No, for as was noted in chapter 2, speaking of worldviews as "ideal types" are common ways of understanding the world, types that spin off into endless variations among people in practice.

The same ideal is evident in the eschatological component of a worldview. Believers should expect to find variations of eschatological outlook among the people with whom we interact, but we should also expect to see the broad contours of a general eschatological framing come to light. A missionary to India would expect to find people whose eschatology is "circular" and consistent with the Hindu conception of time, even if individuals in India have a variety of beliefs and practices regarding their view of the future. Such a missionary would be expected to discern the rival eschatology and gently challenge it with the biblical view of world history and the future.

In a similar way, for those of us who seek to live according to God's mission in Western cultures, we should be equipped to confront false conceptions of time in our own societies. Contemporary worldviews prevalent in North America contain a vision of the future that is not only persuasive but is also *presupposed*. The time line or calendar of world history that underlies belief and practice is often implicit and assumed, not always explicit and declared. Because history and the future can be viewed in different ways, eschatological discipleship calls for the exercise of wisdom in discerning these rival visions and countering them with the true story of the world as outlined in the biblical narrative.

---

3. O'Donovan, *Self, World, and Time*, 1.

A Summary of This Section

In the following chapters, we build on the definition of and biblical examples of eschatological discipleship by showing how a Christian in North America can ask the worldview question "What time is it?" as a way of discerning and countering rival eschatologies in the twenty-first century. We will examine three worldviews and their particular eschatological visions. We start with the Enlightenment, a view of history that sees society as shedding the supernatural superstitions of the past while on the march of progress toward a future of technological and scientific advancement. Next, we will consider the sexual revolution, a view of history wherein the staid morality of previous generations is rejected in favor of a wide-ranging embrace of any and all consensual sexual pleasure as a mark of liberation and fulfillment. Finally, we will examine consumerism, a view of history in which happiness and success are seen in terms of desire and consumption for products that have been commoditized.

The Relationship between Rival Eschatologies

Before beginning the study of each eschatology, we should consider the possibility that the latter two eschatologies are variations of the first; that is, the sexual revolution applies the Enlightenment eschatology of progress and liberation to sexual ethics, while consumerism applies Enlightenment eschatology to the market and the individual's pursuit of wealth. To make this case, we could demonstrate how these eschatologies lead to overlapping concerns. For example, the consumerist eschatology of commodification is evident in much of the public discourse about sex and marriage and family, while the Enlightenment's eschatology (that puts the autonomous human self at the center of the world) shows up in the consumerist emphasis on identity through consumption. Because these eschatological visions have striking similarities, we will not force an arbitrary distinction as if a person can only hold to one of these views as opposed to the others. Neither should we make the case that all North Americans hold these rival conceptions of time all at once or in the same degree.

Keeping those caveats in mind, I have chosen to single out these three visions for closer analysis (even with their commonalities) in order to show how they affect belief and behavior in different spheres of society. Our aim is to discern what aspect of eschatology is providing the strongest source of motivation for friends and neighbors, who may act according to their view of the future without explicitly commending it. Eschatological discipleship includes the equipping of contemporary Christians to understand and counteract rival eschatologies in light of our identities as God's kingdom people.

CHAPTER 6

Christianity and Enlightenment Eschatology

> We begin with Enlightenment philosophy and its vision of history and the future because this understanding of world history is found in school textbooks, academic journals, and in contemporary discourse. In addition, it is the philosophical tradition in which the sexual revolution and consumerism are rooted.

We will begin by examining the Enlightenment period of history and a few of its greatest thinkers. Next we will see how Enlightenment thought has led to the secular age we now inhabit and how it has shaped our civilization. Then we will look more in-depth at the Enlightenment's eschatology, its view of history and the future and how this viewpoint functions in our society. Finally, we will offer a few ways for Christians to discern Enlightenment eschatology and counter it with a biblical perspective.

Defining the Enlightenment

In the most general of terms, the Enlightenment is the philosophical tradition of the seventeenth and eighteenth centuries that saw human reason as the pinnacle of history and the implementation of science and technology as hastening toward a better future. Although we can debate the roots of Enlightenment thought, as well as its strengths and weaknesses, for present purposes delving into the specifics of every philosopher who helped usher in this new era is unnecessary. Instead it is enough to summarize several distinctives of the Enlightenment view of the world, particularly in relation to time and progress. We begin with an overview of the Enlightenment's historical development and a few of the common characteristics rising from this time period.

Historical Development

Defining the historical time period of the Enlightenment is notoriously difficult, in part because it depends on our view of history as a whole. It is feasible that two or three hundred years from now historians might view our own time as part of the Enlightenment era since people in the West are the inheritors of Enlightenment thought and have succeeded in cultivating a society that is indebted to many key tenets of this philosophy. On the other hand, some would limit the Enlightenment to the one hundred-year span that began with the English Revolution's establishment of a constitutional monarchy (1688) and ended with the French Revolution (1789).[1]

Because of the brevity of our historical overview of the Enlightenment's primary characteristics, we will adopt the narrow view of the Enlightenment's span, while remaining cognizant of the fact that the influence of these philosophers cannot be limited to one particular period of time. Some philosophers preceded that one-hundred-year period (Descartes, Bacon, Spinoza), and their ideas were influential in the philosophy of the day. Furthermore, the United States of America came into existence during the latter years of the Enlightenment century, and the influence of the American project on Western civilization is impossible to discern apart from the Enlightenment philosophy that was such a dominant force in the founding of the nation.[2]

Several important figures in the Enlightenment are John Locke (1632-1704), Voltaire (1694-1778), David Hume (1711-1776), and Immanuel Kant (1724-1804).[3] Each of these men made unique contributions to

1. Peter Gay, *The Enlightenment: An Interpretation*, The Rise of Modern Paganism (New York: Alfred A. Knopf, 1966), 17. Peter Gay finds the narrowly defined century as the best way forward, partly because the French philosopher Montesquieu was born in 1689, and the French-German author Baron d'Holbach died in 1789.

2. George Marsden, *The Twilight of the American Enlightenment: The 1950s and the Crisis of Liberal Belief* (New York: Basic Books, 2014). Marsden makes the case that Enlightenment thought reigned supreme in American history until the 1950s, when public intellectuals continued to put forth Enlightenment ideals while denying the particular Enlightenment foundations.

3. The danger of oversimplification exists in compiling several Enlightenment thinkers into one paragraph and reducing their history into a couple pages of text. One could even contest our use of the word Enlightenment since so many philosophies are flying under that banner. To now speak of other time periods in the plural, rather than the singular, is not uncommon. Consider the increasingly used term *Reformations* in the plural to describe the tumultuous period of history in which multiple Protestant movements formed and spread during the 1500s. See Carter Lindberg, *The European Reformations*, 2nd ed., Eugene, Ore.: Wiley-Blackwell, 2009. Some might believe that speaking of the Enlightenment in general is counterproductive, and we should only speak of Enlightenments happening in different countries at different stages under different philosophers. Nevertheless, for our present purposes, while admitting the complexities involved, I agree with Gay, who argues for one overarching description of this history. "The Enlightenment" as a catch-all description just fits: "There were many philosophies in the eighteenth century, but there was only one Enlightenment. . . . The men of the Enlightenment united on a vastly ambitious program. . . ." Gay, *Enlightenment*, 3.

philosophy, yet Peter Gay sees a common thread at the level of motivation. Theirs was "a dialectical struggle for autonomy" in which they sought to assimilate their Christian and pagan inheritances and then become independent of them.[4]

Immanuel Kant defined the Enlightenment project (and its motto) in one often-cited paragraph:

> Enlightenment is man's emergence from his self-imposed nonage. Nonage is the inability to use one's own understanding without another's guidance. This nonage is self-imposed if its cause lies not in lack of understanding but in indecision and lack of courage to use one's own mind without another's guidance. *Dare to know!* (*Sapere aude.*) "Have the courage to use your own understanding" is therefore the motto of the enlightenment.[5]

The problem as laid out by Kant is that dependent ignorance is "the inability to use one's own understanding without another's guidance." Notice the solution: independent thought—"have the courage to use your own understanding." In laying out the problem and solution this way, Kant is also appealing to virtue. The way of dependent ignorance is cowardly; the way of independent thought is courageous. Kant's plea for intellectual maturity is an example of how the Enlightenment was representative both individually (through the philosophers who were seeking to gain knowledge) and collectively (through peoples who were shaking off the traditional sources of morality and authority and seeking to control their own destiny).

Did the Enlightenment achieve its objectives? Did Kant prevail, and was the problem of guided ignorance overcome? In one respect we could say yes. The philosophers' rebellion reclaimed the paganism of classical antiquity in order to critique Christianity, but then they refashioned that ancient paganism until they were emancipated from both sources of authority.[6] In another respect we may be inclined to say no, partly because the Enlightenment's goal of achieving an objective, universal source of truth and morality (which one can take hold of without guidance) never came to pass. Put the yes and no together, and we see how the Enlightenment

---

4. Gay, *Enlightenment*, xi.
5. Kant, "What Is Enlightenment?," 384, in Gay, *Enlightenment Anthology*.
6. Gay, *Enlightenment*, xi.

project has failed in reaching its primary objective but has succeeded in becoming a major influence on Western civilization.

What of the Enlightenment thinkers themselves? Did they see their cause as "winning the day"? Did they believe they had been successful in "emancipating" the world from superstition and the people from their "self-imposed tutelage"? A skeptical, circumspect take on the times is found in the same essay from Kant (written in 1784). "If someone asks, 'Are we living in an enlightened age today?' the answer would be, 'No,'" but then Kant clarified, "We are living in an Age of Enlightenment."[7] In other words, Kant's society had not reached the stage where it could be considered *enlightened*, but the society was certainly undergoing the *process of enlightenment*. We will return to the Enlightenment philosophers' self-assessment and interpretation of history when we examine in more detail the eschatology of this movement.

Characteristics of Enlightenment Thought

A common thread found in most Enlightenment philosophers is an ambitious goal for rational and independent thinking. Peter Gay defines the Enlightenment as "a program of secularism, humanity, cosmopolitanism, and freedom, above all, freedom in its many forms—freedom from arbitrary power, freedom of speech, freedom of trade, freedom to realize one's talents, freedom of aesthetic response, freedom, in a word, of moral man to make his own way in the world."[8] As one can see from this summary, certain characteristics of human thought dominate discussions about the Enlightenment, and the fact that these commonalities surface in the consideration of these philosophers indicates that we are, indeed, speaking of a specific point in time, with specific and common characteristics, leading to implications for the world today.

The Pursuit of Universal Morality Grounded in Human Reason. Considering the ethics of the Enlightenment, Alasdair MacIntyre describes the fundamental, driving principle behind the movement as "the project of an independent rational justification of morality."[9] The project of the Enlightenment was to transcend (or perhaps, displace) other moralities that rely on a faith that looks beyond this present world and discover instead a critical

---

7. Ibid., 20. Quoting from Immanuel Kant, "Beantwortung der Frage: Was Ist Auflarung?," *Werke*, IV, 174.

8. Gay, *Enlightenment*, 3.

9. MacIntyre, *After Virtue*, 39.

morality that could be ascertained by reason alone. *That* morality would then suffice for the basis of universal civilization.[10] In this we discover the first characteristic of Enlightenment thought, a passionate pursuit of a universal moral standard based in human reason, not in divine revelation.

An Oppositional Posture Toward Traditional Religion. This leads to a second major characteristic of Enlightenment thought, its oppositional posture toward traditional religious belief. To be sure, the Enlightenment thinkers' attempt to displace or transcend the "divinely revealed" source of morality was not an attempt at overthrowing all Christian notions of morality and decency. In fact, some of the Enlightenment philosophers (particularly Hume and Diderot) could be considered morally and ethically conservative—radical in their philosophy, perhaps, but rather staid in their moral conclusions. Many of these philosophers believed that when society was "enlightened," the people would discover a rational and critical vindication of conservative moral rules.[11]

Nevertheless, because the idea of religion (more specifically, divine revelation) as making up the foundation of morality was so strong during their era, Enlightenment thinkers had no choice but to position themselves against religion. There was no other way to make their case for a universal morality that was rationally based than to challenge religion's reliance on divine revelation. Even if, as they expected, many of their society's views of right and wrong turned out to be remarkably similar to Christian ethics, the philosophers wanted to derive those views from elsewhere. They attempted to remove the revelatory foundation of societal ethics while leaving in place much of society's morality.

This oppositional posture toward traditional religious belief was necessary for the struggle toward objectivity. Peter Gay writes, "Myth could be sympathetically understood only after it had been fully conquered, but in the course of its conquest it had to be faced as the enemy. . . . The Enlightenment had to treat religion as superstition and error in order to recognize itself."[12] George Marsden sees this Enlightenment opposition to religion playing out differently in North America. In the American context Protestant churches and leaders retained a privileged place as the predominant religion. The Enlightenment's effect on religion in the United States was not

10. John Gray, *Enlightenment's Wake: Politics and Culture at the Close of the Modern Age* (Abingdon, UK: Routledge Classics, 2007), 185.

11. MacIntyre, *After Virtue*, 47.

12. Gay, *Enlightenment*, 37.

to banish it from polite society but instead to privatize its beliefs so Christianity could not intrude into public activities.[13]

The Rejection of a Shared Teleology for Humanity. When you combine (1) the Enlightenment's pursuit of an independent, revelation-less justification for morality with (2) its oppositional posture toward traditional religion, you arrive at a third characteristic of Enlightenment thought, a shift in the foundation of moral theory that leaves humanity without a shared teleology. No longer is there any basis for making a case for what a human should aim for or be. The self is liberated from its outmoded forms of social organization, but in the act of liberation, the bigger question of what one is free *for* goes unanswered.[14]

This loss of a shared teleology impacts the political environment in Enlightenment-influenced societies. Cultural debates are influenced by underlying Enlightenment assumptions so powerful that people often fail to recognize them as anything other than "self-evident." The political ideals of both the Right and the Left assume, uncritically and without question, the goals of the European Enlightenment project.[15] These characteristics of the Enlightenment are prevalent in today's discourse, to the point these beliefs are considered self-evident. North Americans now inhabit a secular age in which many expect morality to be debated on "this-world" terms, without any appeal to a higher or transcendent authority.

The Enlightenment and Our Secular Age

As we consider the Enlightenment's long shadow across our current moment in time, we will consider two aspects common to Enlightenment philosophy that give us an idea of how the Enlightenment's eschatology will look. First, we see a consistent emphasis on the shedding of inherited religious traditions that appeal to the supernatural. Second, we see the redirecting of faith away from divine revelation and toward human reason, with science becoming the most dependable guide to truth, and the critical method becoming the necessary tool for attaining it. In this section we examine more in-depth the Enlightenment's appeal to reason, its transformation of science, its religious elements, and its impact on Christianity. The goal is to see how contemporary society has been shaped and fashioned into a secular age.

---

13. Marsden, *Twilight of the American Enlightenment*, 106.
14. MacIntyre, *After Virtue*, 60.
15. Gray, *Enlightenment's Wake*, 24.

Enlightenment Reason

One of the dominant characteristics of the Enlightenment, as seen above, is the appeal to reason. Why did this characteristic pit the Enlightenment thinkers against Christianity? After all, Christians promoted the scientific method—Christians who believed the world is designed and, therefore, can be studied. However, the Enlightenment emphasis on reason judged Christianity as having surrendered rational and critical thought to revelation, thus squandering the heritage of ancient thinkers, dismissing the resources of the pagan world and only exploiting those resources when convenient. Christianity's paradoxical failure was most evident in the dismissing of rational thinking in philosophical matters (by appealing primarily to divine revelation), while abusing human rationality in scholastic debate (by trivializing and wasting mental exertion on doctrinal minutia).[16]

Within this environment one can see why the appeal to reason (apart from revelation) was so strong. Charles Taylor describes the appeal,

> Disengaged rationality seems to separate us from our own narrow, egoistic standpoint and make us capable of grasping the whole picture. It is what allows us to become "impartial spectators" of the human scene. The growth of scientific rationality can therefore be experienced as a kind of victory over egoism. We are no longer imprisoned in the self; we are free to pursue the universal good.[17]

Seen in this light, the Enlightenment was part of the drive for liberation, a way of freeing oneself from past constraints and opening new doors of knowledge and wisdom.

Adding to the appeal of rationality's "freedom" was the philosophers' understanding of their own role in this upward journey. The philosophers saw themselves as the heroes leading to freedom and justice. For example, Diderot described the philosopher as the one "who, trampling underfoot prejudice, tradition, venerability, universal assent, authority—in a word, everything that overawes the crowd—dares to think for himself, to ascend to the clearest general principles, to examine them, to discuss them, to admit nothing save on the testimony of his own reason and experience."[18]

16. Gay, *Enlightenment*, 226.

17. Charles Taylor, *Sources of the Self: The Making of Modern Identity* (Boston: Harvard University Press, 1992), 331.

18. Arthur M. Wilson, *Diderot* (New York: Oxford University Press, 1972), 237.

Notice how the philosopher is cast as the hero who breaks free from the enemies standing in the way of reason and then "dares to think for himself" by refusing to believe anything that does not accord with his own reason and experience.

This idea of breaking free from religion, particularly its supernatural elements, in favor of reason was one of the key drivers of the Enlightenment, and the result was a heightened sense of human autonomy. Goheen and Bartholomew sum up the results of Enlightenment thought regarding scientific reason,

> In the Enlightenment view, scientific reason was to be *autonomous*, liberated from a (Christian) faith increasingly dismissed as obscurantist, ignorant, and superstitious. Moreover, scientific reason was to be *instrumental*, employed to control, predict, and shape the world. Finally, scientific reason was to be *universal*, to transcend human culture and history, to discern such laws as are true for all people at all times.[19]

We can already observe the outline of eschatology in the Enlightenment's story of liberation from irrational faith, a story that shows the salvation of humankind through reason, backed up by science as both its driver and justification.

Enlightenment Science

The scientific method takes an increasingly large role in Enlightenment thought. It is not that science becomes the *only* source of knowledge for an Enlightenment-influenced society but that it becomes the "supremely privileged form of knowledge."[20] Other sources of knowledge may find a place, including religious thought and personal experience, but science becomes the judge and jury whenever these other sources collide. In this way science begins to occupy the role that religion once had—offering both revelation of the natural world and saving humanity from sin's consequences.[21]

The Enlightenment worldview's priority on science as a form of knowledge leads to a common assumption of the age, that religious explanations of the world, however emotionally appealing they may be, are inadequate.

19. Bartholomew and Goheen, *Living at the Crossroads*, 93 (emphasis theirs).
20. Gray, *Enlightenment's Wake*, 236.
21. Bartholomew and Goheen, *Living at the Crossroads*, 89.

Science has become the driver that pushes people forward; religion is the obstacle holding people back. From a rationalist perspective, religious faith is nothing more than a coping mechanism for a harsh world, a futile attempt to find meaning and sense in the suffering and mystery of human experience. People who leave their religious faith and adopt a purely materialist view of the world often give credit to science for their "deconversion." They see science as the arbiter of truth. There are no mysteries in the world, only puzzles still unresolved by scientists.

Ironically, this appeal to science as the final arbiter of truth is, at its heart, self-refuting. As John Gray points out, "It is an Enlightenment dogma that the advance of science advances human rationality; but there has never been much to support this article of human faith."[22] Gray is correct to speak of the Enlightenment's view of science as "dogma"—just as much an article of human faith as any fundamental assumption that a religion would put forth. The claim to scientific neutrality must be unmasked, and the idea of science as the privileged form of knowledge must be challenged like any other truth claim.

The Enlightenment and Secularization

A Western assumption common today is that we find ourselves on the road toward greater heights of human knowledge, and this journey continues as we walk farther away from the religious faiths of the past and our reliance on supernatural revelation. The nineteenth-century French philosopher August Comte told the story of human ascent this way. In the first stage people attributed mysterious events to the gods. The second stage was metaphysical, with abstract entities replacing the gods. The third stage is interpreting the outworking of nature in terms of natural laws. At each stage of human development, a supernatural explanation for something is replaced with something else. Jonathan Witt explains how Comte's explanation led to the idea of the "God gap" and why so many people in this secular age turn to rational or anti-supernatural explanations for things that remain unexplainable:

> Humans used to attribute practically every mysterious force in nature to the doings of the gods. They stuffed a god into any and every gap in their knowledge of the natural world, shrugged,

22. Gray, *Enlightenment's Wake*, xv.

> and moved on. Since then, the number of gaps has been shrinking without pause, filled with purely material explanations for everything from lightning bolts to romantic attraction. The moral of this grand story: always hold out for the purely material explanation, even when the evidence seems to point in the other direction.[23]

The assumption that all events can be explained by natural causes is, of course, unproved by science, and yet it continues to hold sway among many in society today, not least among some of the most educated. For example, author Julian Barnes, in his book on death, wonders aloud what it will be like when, in the future, people look at Christian faith the same way this generation views Greek and Roman mythology—a bygone era of superstition which may fascinate people but no longer has any direct impact or claim on their lives.[24] Barnes's confidence that religions are fading away is a good example of this simplistic view of the Enlightenment—the age of reason has ushered in a new time of history in which humanity will cast off the chains of religious superstition.

The real and powerful role of this narrative in today's societal psyche should not be underestimated. It is true that the impact of the Enlightenment can lead, in some cases, to total unbelief. However, in many cases the plausibility of the Christian worldview is challenged but not altogether abandoned. Religiosity continues to be a powerful force in human existence, centuries after the early Enlightenment thinkers issued their challenge, but the nature of this religiosity has changed (as we will see below).

The idea that the Enlightenment has progressed as religion has declined is what Charles Taylor calls a "subtraction theory," and however popular it may be as an explanation of the rise of the Enlightenment, Taylor believes it to be a myth and not a true representation of today's secular society.[25] Taylor argues that secularity has not arrived as a result of the steady erosion of religious faith; instead we might define secularity as a society in which faith is no longer axiomatic. What has changed is not that

---

23. Comte's view is summarized by Jonathan Witt, "The Icon of Materialism: Why Scientism's Cherished Progress Narrative Fails," *Touchstone* (March-April 2015): 41.

24. Barnes, *Nothing to Be Frightened Of*, 60-63.

25. Smith, *How (Not) to Be Secular*, 26. For Taylor, "The secular is not simply a remainder; it is a sum, created by addition, a product of intellectual multiplication . . . it wasn't enough for us to stop believing in the gods; we also had to be able to *imagine* significance within an immanent frame, to imagine modes of existence that did not depend on transcendence."

people don't believe anymore but that wide swaths of people view unbelief as a legitimate option. Therefore, we are not in a zero-sum game where religion fails as reason wins but where both win and lose simultaneously. Religious people entertain doubts their forefathers would never have wondered about, simply because they live in a society where doubt and unbelief are prevalent. Likewise, nonreligious people entertain doubts about their doubts, wonder about transcendence, and are haunted by their losses.[26] As Julian Barnes's book on death begins, "I don't believe in God, and I miss Him."[27]

What does this age of secularity have to do with people's eschatological outlook on the world? Once faith is no longer axiomatic, reason and science often rush in as the objective referees in all sorts of disputes, which has led to a split between facts and values. Values are subjective, and morality is an invention. Meanwhile, science is objective, and the facts are indisputable. Christianity gets reduced to private beliefs and values, where it can flourish as a subculture for people who wish to be into that sort of thing, but it has no basis for speaking to what is happening "on the ground" in the other spheres of human life.[28]

Taylor's overall objection against simplistic subtraction theories is correct, but how the secularization process plays out differs from country to country. Martin Marty sees three paths of secularization in the West, and they differ according to context. "Maximal secularity" is what we find in some European countries where the Christian faith is seen as the enemy of secularization and must be replaced. "Mere secularity" is what we find in the United Kingdom, Canada, and Australia, where the Christian faith is largely marginalized and ignored, allowed to exist but expected to decline. "Controlled secularity" is what is seen in the United States, where the majority of citizens profess faith, but their faith has been altered and privatized to fit the secular vision.[29]

---

26. See Taylor's essay, "Disenchantment-Reenchantment," in Charles Taylor, *Dilemmas and Connections: Selected Essays* (Boston: Harvard University Press, 2011), 287–302.

27. Barnes, *Nothing to Be Frightened Of*, 1.

28. Goheen, *Introducing Christian Mission Today*, 142–50. Goheen shows how Christianity both challenged and, in some measure, accepted this Enlightenment paradigm in considering the church's mission.

29. Martin E. Marty, *The Modern Schism: Three Paths to the Secular* (New York: Harper & Row, 1969); and Goheen, *Introducing Christian Mission Today*, 221–23, which tweaks Marty's thesis by showing how decline is not the only story. There is also the growth of evangelicals and Pentecostals in secular societies.

Enlightenment and Unbelief

Even if, with Taylor, we reject "subtraction stories," we should not underestimate the disorienting and fundamental shift of the Enlightenment concerning belief. To wrestle with the rise of unbelief in Enlightenment cultures is important because, unless we understand its appeal, we will not know how best to respond.

It is commonly assumed that a person who rejects faith in a transcendent being has reached this conclusion solely through the analysis of scientific evidence. However, Charles Taylor believes conversions to unbelief are based less on scientific proof than the converts think. What is really going on is *not* that the convert has suddenly discovered proof that God does not exist or that religion must be false. Instead, the convert has already entered another story, one in which the rationalist picture seems more plausible than religion's appeal to mystery and transcendence. The convert attributes his conversion to "scientific proof," but Taylor wonders, what if the subconscious reason for abandoning faith is that the unbeliever is attracted to the rugged appeal of rationalism—the fierce facing of reality, however stark the picture may be? He writes:

> What made [atheism] more believable was not our "scientific" proofs; it is rather that one whole package: science, plus a picture of our epistemic-moral predicament in which science represents a mature facing of hard reality, beats out another package: religion, plus a rival picture of our epistemic-moral predicament in which religion, say, represents a true humility, and many of the claims of science unwarranted arrogance. But the decisive consideration here was the reading of the moral predicament proposed by "science," which struck home as true to the convert's experience (of a faith which was still childish—and whose faith is not, to one or another degree?), rather than the actual findings of science.[30]

Seen in this light, people who abandon their childhood faith may attribute their conversion to scientific evidence when, in fact, it is the appeal of leaving behind childhood and grasping for maturity, in this case the cold hard realities of a fierce and lonely world. The freedom of being without God is that we are able to fashion reality as we please, to order our life and our

30. Taylor, *Secular Age*, 366.

vision of the world however we think best. Those who reject faith as childish see themselves as progressing past silly superstitions, choosing instead to accept scientific evidence no matter where the conclusions lead.

Believers may have a hard time understanding why anyone would make this switch. It seems like such a poorer story, one that robs fragile humanity and temporal lives of any eternal or lasting significance. However, Taylor describes why this rugged rationalism is attractive, "We are alone in the universe, and this is frightening; but it can also be exhilarating. There is a certain joy in solitude. . . . The thrill at being alone is part sense of freedom, part of the intense poignancy of this fragile moment. . . . All meaning is here, in this small speck."[31]

This attractiveness is on full display in the opening lines of Richard Dawkins's *Unweaving the Rainbow*, a passage often read at humanist funerals:

> We are going to die, and that makes us the lucky ones. Most people are never going to die because they are never going to be born. The potential people who could have been here in my place but who will in fact never see the light of day outnumber the sand grains of Arabia. Certainly those unborn ghosts include greater poets than Keats, scientists greater than Newton. We know this because the set of possible people allowed by our DNA so massively outnumbers the set of actual people. In the teeth of these stupefying odds it is you and I, in our ordinariness, that are here. We privileged few, who won the lottery of birth against all odds, how dare we whine at our inevitable return to that prior state from which the vast majority have never stirred?[32]

Taylor argues that the decisive factor in a conversion from faith to unbelief is the trading of one story for another. Only *then* does evidence enter the picture and confirm the person's slide toward unbelief.[33]

At its heart, then, this journey away from faith may be driven by ethics more than evidence. What proves decisive is not the latest piece of science but the story science tells, as well as the desired self-image of being mature and rational. Now that we begin to see how this story plays itself out, and

31. Ibid., 367.

32. Richard Dawkins, *Unweaving the Rainbow: Science, Delusion, and the Appetite for Wonder* (Geneva, Ill.: Mariner Books, 2000), 1.

33. Taylor, *Secular Age*, 365–66.

how the story gives shape to our vision of the past, present, and future, we can trace the underlying eschatology of this worldview.

The Enlightenment's Eschatology

The Enlightenment has already been considered in general terms—its emphasis on reason and science as the supremely privileged form of knowledge. Now we turn attention to the built-in time line that is part of this worldview. What is the Enlightenment's eschatology? What is the vision of the past and the way forward? One word sums up Enlightenment eschatology, *progress*. In this section we look at the eschatology of some of the early Enlightenment thinkers, explore the key term *progress*, and then consider how it comports with the overall worldview.

The Enlightenment Thinkers' View of the Future

To immediately equate a cheery optimism with Enlightenment thinking is to simplify, and even distort, the original sources. In fact, the original Enlightenment had two sides, with some Enlightenment thinkers (Hume, Kant, and Voltaire) believing their society was on the verge of cultural decline, not ascent. At the same time, most Enlightenment philosophers, many of whom saw the culture in decline, thought of themselves as the potential masters of Europe. They were heartened by a revolt against superstition, and they saw themselves as the men who were courageously "bringing light to others."[34]

Though they were undecided concerning what the future may hold, the Enlightenment philosophers' vision of the past indicates that they believed in the inevitability of human ascendance, *if only* their ideas would take hold. They may have seen their own culture as one of decline, but they saw the past in an even more negative light. "History was a register of crimes, a tale of cruelty and cunning, at best the record of unremitting conflict," writes Peter Gay.[35] If their view of the future was pessimistic, their view of the past was that it was an utter disaster.

---

34. Gay, *Enlightenment*, 20–21.

35. Ibid., 32–33. The philosophers saw world history as divided "between ascetic, superstitious enemies of the flesh, and men who affirmed life, the body, knowledge, and generosity; between mythmakers and realists, priests and philosophers." The theory of progress depended in humanity's willingness to be enlightened (with the philosophers at the vanguard of this illumination), and the fact they continued to write and push their views was an indication that they believed progress was possible, and this progress would result in an escape from the pendulum of philosophy versus belief.

This hope that the past could be overcome is what led to the eschatology of progress and why, even with the doubts of the early philosophers, we can still refer to the theory of progress as one of the foundational tenets of Enlightenment eschatology. John Gray is right to see the early philosophers as shaped by the idea of forward movement—progress in science, technology, education—in escaping the past. He notes, "It is this core project that is shared by all Enlightenment thinkers, however pessimistic or dystopic they may sometimes be as to its historical prospects."[36] One reason their underlying faith in progress was so persistent, even in the presence of discouraging signs of decline, is because their own experiences of personal progress shaped their perceptions. Peter Gay claims their view of progress was "less a theory" and more "an experience," and he points to their own status and professional trajectory as evidence.[37]

Even though the historical record of Enlightenment thought is more complex than seeing an unbroken line of movement toward progress, the resulting ethos of the Enlightenment has birthed a more distinct and optimistic view of progress, at least in the hope of science and technology for escaping from the past. This emphasis on progress (driven by science and technology) becomes the central, defining factor of Enlightenment eschatology.

An Eschatology of Progress

In Immanuel Kant's essay on the Enlightenment, he expresses a degree of skepticism about how much Enlightenment has already taken place (differentiating between "an enlightened age" and "an age of enlightenment"), and yet in his reasoning is embedded the core doctrine of Enlightenment eschatology: progress. Consider this section in which Kant contrasts the church's dogmatism with the enlightenment of humanity:

> But should a society of ministers, say a Church Council . . . have the right to commit itself by oath to a certain unalterable doctrine, in order to secure perpetual guardianship over all its members and through them over the people? I say that this is quite impossible. Such a contract, concluded to keep all further enlightenment from humanity, is simply null and void even if it should be confirmed by the sovereign power, by parliaments,

36. Gray, *Enlightenment's Wake*, 186.
37. Gay, *Enlightenment Anthology*, 24.

> and by the most solemn treaties. An epoch cannot conclude a pact that will commit succeeding ages, prevent them from increasing their significant insights, purging themselves of errors, and generally progressing in enlightenment. That would be a crime against human nature, whose proper destiny lies in such progress.[38]

We can see the eschatological view of progress here, elements that surface in spite of Kant's skepticism regarding the state of his own society. First, he believes the dogmas of the church (which are unalterable) are an obstacle to humanity's enlightenment. Second, he describes these dogmas (and other political treaties and pacts) as relics of the past that prevent humanity's growth in "insights" and correction of "errors." Then, in the clearest example of Enlightenment eschatology, Kant describes the "proper destiny" of "human nature" as "progress."

A clear vision of history and the future is present in Enlightenment philosophy. Gay says the Renaissance was "the first act of a great drama in which the Enlightenment was the last—the great drama of the disenchantment of the European mind."[39] For this reason Enlightenment-influenced people today consider the turning point of world history to be the dawn of the Age of Reason in the seventeenth and eighteenth centuries. United States history is traced back to the founding of the American republic, which took place during the century in which Enlightenment philosophy was most dominant. The "new Jerusalem" postmillennial eschatology of the pilgrims and Puritans who first came to the New World, with their idea of ushering in a new society of progress and peace, had been, by the time of the American Revolution secularized into a tamer, deistic worldview of a distant God and its corresponding eschatological faith in the Enlightenment's discoveries in reason and science.[40] We cannot make sense of the Enlightenment as a whole until we see eschatology at work.

Unfortunately, this confidence in progress as humanity's destiny is a view of the future that often entails a warped view of the past. Once people

---

38. Kant, "What Is Enlightenment?," 387.

39. Gay, *Enlightenment*, 279.

40. Goheen, *Introducing Christian Mission Today*, 148. Goheen links the Puritan belief that the early Americans were living at the dawn of the third era to the later, secularized view of progress, wherein a golden age of humanity comes through human effort. We can observe the founders' vision of history and America's role in some of the almost-messianic statements and imagery on coins and dollar bills. For example, *Novus Ordo Seclorum* is Latin for "new order of the ages."

relegate the past to darkness and position themselves as leading humanity into the light, they tend to distort aspects of history that do not fit the eschatology they espouse.[41] Peter Gay claims that the historians of the Enlightenment "looked into the past as into a mirror and extracted from their history the past they could use."[42] The abuses of Enlightenment historians became so common and prevalent that the term *whiggery* was adopted to describe these more extreme accounts of historical revisionism.[43] O'Donovan describes "whiggery" as a teleological account of history which led to interpreting the past as a self-elaborating progressive narrative. Of course, such interpretation turns out to be selective, "screening out whatever might find no authentification in 'where we have got to.'" He adds, "Where things are going becomes a way of representing what other people are doing, and invests with a spurious dignity a rush for cover in the crowd."[44] Confidence in progress toward a better future is what leads to distortion of what has taken place in the past.

Enlightenment eschatology does not limit itself to matters of science and morals. Rather, it spills out in everyday discourse, relating to various moral and ethical quandaries of one's day. When people say, "Now that we live in the twenty-first century" or "I can't believe this happens in our day and age," they are implicitly endorsing the Enlightenment view of history and assuming that everyone else also is endorsing it. (Otherwise, how does

---

41. Vinoth Ramachandra, *Gods that Fail: Modern Idolatry and Christian Mission* (Downers Grove, IL: IVP, 1996), 30. This revisionist history is part of the legacy of G. W. F. Hegel (1770–1831) who described God not as a personal being but as an evolving process of thought. Vinoth Ramachandra comments, "Hegel's Reason, the deity which guides the course of world history, blends neatly with the idea of Progress which was beginning to seduce the European mind at the turn of the eighteenth and nineteenth centuries. Progress was the notion that history was the tale of continuous and sustained human improvement of which modern Europe was the crowning pinnacle. . . . All human action, including the conflicts and tribulations of history, are endowed with a meaning derived from their appointed place within the dynamic scheme of things."

42. Gay, *Enlightenment*, 32.

43. Herbert Butterfield, *The Whig Interpretation of History* (repr.; New York: W. W. Norton, 1965), criticizes the English Whig historians for telling the story of society as if it were an inevitable progression toward liberty, with the contemporary setting as the pinnacle of human achievement. Self-serving historical revisionism was also a powerful tool wielded by Communist revolutionaries in Romania in the late 1940s. Keith Hitchens, *A Concise History of Romania* (Cambridge, MA: Cambridge University Press, 2014), 249, 251, says the new regime "required historians to demonstrate the correctness of the Marxist-Leninist (and for a time, Stalinist) interpretation of historical development and thereby focus on economic forces and the class struggle. . . . They assigned to historians the task of restoring the national heritage and showing how the Communist regime of Gheorghiu-Dej fitted into the general course of Romanian history and how it was in essence the natural culmination of earlier strivings of 'progressive forces' to promote a true people's democracy and secure social justice."

44. O'Donovan, *Finding and Seeking*, 231–33.

appealing to the calendar make sense, unless one shares a similar view of the past, present, and future and what constitutes progress?)[45]

The Darwinian theory of evolution reinforces the idea of "progress," only in this case science is not the driver but the discoverer of biological progression. The application of evolutionary theory to sociology and morality leads to politicians and world leaders describing themselves as "evolving" on key issues, a "process" whose end is already assured once evolutionary terminology is employed to describe it. The claim of being "on the right side of history" is a demonstration of confidence in one's own views as expected to win out, a confidence that is misplaced, as N. T. Wright points out:

> People in the Western world still assume that whenever there is a crisis it's important to be on the right side of history. Somehow we are supposed to have privileged access to information (a) that history is moving in a particular direction, (b) that we know what that direction is, and (c) that the direction is toward universal liberal democracy on the Western model. . . . Progress is invoked in the two areas where it can be least assumed: the political and the moral.[46]

Appeals to "progress" and labels such as *progressive* assume the right side of human destiny and the way forward into the future.

We will examine in greater detail some of the moral implications of Enlightenment eschatology in the chapter on the sexual revolution. For now we must wrestle with a different question. Is the Enlightenment eschatology of progress itself on the decline?

The Future of Enlightenment Progress

Some thinkers believe the eschatology of the Enlightenment is beginning to strain under the weight of its own pretense. Even though the story of progress seems to be unassailable in the Western mind and appears to withstand world events that would cause one to question the idea that society is moving in an upward trajectory of progress (such as two world wars, chemical warfare, nuclear armament, or societal unrest), there are signs that the Enlightenment eschatology is loosening its grip on the imaginations of

45. Wright, *Simply Good News*, 85.
46. Ibid., 112.

Western peoples. Some thinkers and philosophers believe this particular understanding of history and the future is showing its age and losing its appeal.

Postmodernism may be the biggest critic of Enlightenment eschatology. Philosophers such as Michel Foucault and Jacques Derrida have challenged some of the arrogant assumptions of the Enlightenment's vision of reality. Summarizing the criticism coming from postmodern thought, Goheen and Bartholomew write, "The possibility of achieving universal, objective knowledge—the goal so central to modernity—is considered by many postmodern thinkers to be impossible. . . . The corollary of this skepticism has been a profound suspicion concerning the hidden agendas of so-called neutral modern knowledge. . . . The consequence of this skepticism is an awareness of the inevitable pluralism within knowledge."[47] In this way political and ethical stances are interpreted as a way of grasping for power, not as a discovery of objective right and wrong.

In the field of anthropology, researchers who have accepted some of the postmodern critique of Enlightenment thought have pointed out the inherent appeal to power in much of their discourse concerning time and the theory of progress. Anthropologist Johannes Fabian's important book, *Time and the Other*, shows how anthropology built around Enlightenment philosophy denied "coevalness" to the subjects of its historical inquiry by speaking of cultures as "primitive" or "medieval" or belonging to another time.[48] Fabian exposes such terminology as a power play, as a way of asserting the Western world of rationalism as the pinnacle of human flourishing and judging all other cultures accordingly.[49]

Even if we reject Fabian's postmodern resistance to judging morality as good or bad in different cultures, we can appreciate how his exposing of "typological time" (measured "in terms of socioculturally meaningful events")[50] punctures the balloon of Enlightenment hubris. We are also

47. Bartholomew and Goheen, *Living at the Crossroads*, 110; and Carl Raschke, *The Next Reformation: Why Evangelicals Must Embrace Postmodernity* (Grand Rapids: Baker Academic, 2004), 31. Carl Raschke believes the end of the Enlightenment project is synonymous with the demise of the correspondence theory of truth and the "idolatrous and relativistic proclivities of modernism as a whole."

48. Johannes Fabian, *Time and the Other: How Anthropology Makes Its Object* (New York: Columbia University Press, 1983), 31, says that the denial of "coevalness" is "a persistent and systematic tendency to place the referent(s) of anthropology in a Time other than the present of the producer of anthropological discourse."

49. Ibid., xl, says, "If it is true that Time belongs to the political economy of relations between individuals, classes, and nations, then the construction of anthropology's object through temporal concepts and devices is a political act; there is a 'Politics of Time.'"

50. Ibid., 23.

better equipped to recognize when politicians and world leaders attempt to gain support for specific policies by speaking of opposing peoples or viewpoints as "retrograde," or "backward" or "medieval." The anthropologist's attempt to deny "coevalness" with other cultures whose lifestyles differ from their own is matched by the politician's denial of coevalness with his or her political opponents.

Additional reasons exist as to why the Enlightenment view of progress has become contested in modern days, including poverty, environmental degradation, proliferation of weapons, psychological problems, and social and economic problems.[51] John Gray believes the Enlightenment philosophy and its corresponding eschatology of progress fails on its own premises for being "a kind of rationalist fideism, a humanist variation of Pascal's wager, which nothing in our actual historical experience supports."[52] Gray, himself an atheist, is both a product of Enlightenment rationalism and a critic of it:

> We live today amid the dim ruins of the Enlightenment project, which was the ruling project of the modern period. If, as I believe, the Enlightenment project has proved to be self-destroying, then that fact signals the close of the modern period, of which we are the heirs. Our patrimony is the disenchantment which the Enlightenment has bequeathed to us—a disenchantment all the more profound since it encompasses the central illusions of the Enlightenment itself.[53]

In line with MacIntyre's assessment of the Enlightenment's failure, Gray believes the Enlightenment project failed because human consensus based on universal knowledge never came about; instead, "an ultimate diversity of moral perspectives" was discovered.[54] Furthermore, reason never supplanted religion, and religion never withered away to the margins of society. Instead, religious conflict is at the heart of world conflict.[55]

The resulting collapse has made the ability to reason with one another all the more difficult. Alasdair MacIntyre sees moral debate over good and evil, right and wrong, as resembling "the fragments of a conceptual

---

51. Bartholomew and Goheen, *Living at the Crossroads*, 104–5.
52. Gray, *Enlightenment's Wake*, 100.
53. Ibid., 216.
54. Ibid., 243.
55. Ibid., xvii.

scheme, parts which now lack those contexts from which their significance derived."[56] This has led to the rise of emotivism, which he defines as "the doctrine that all evaluative judgments and more specifically all moral judgments are *nothing but* expressions of preference, expressions of attitude or feeling, insofar as they are moral or evaluative in character."[57] In this environment people assume the worst of their opponents. They no longer attempt to appeal to unassailable criteria or compelling reasons to make the case for one policy over another, which leads to deep suspicion that something other than reason itself is motivating their activism. "If I lack any good reasons to invoke against you, it must seem that I lack any good reasons," MacIntyre explains. "Hence it seems that underlying my own position there must be some non-rational decision to adopt that position."[58] A nefarious motivation or irrational prejudice must be guiding one's opponent since there is no longer any way to base a particular point of view on a moral axis that is commonly accepted.[59]

Even secular philosopher Jürgen Habermas worries about the steady corrosion of cultural solidarity brought about by Enlightenment thought. He writes, "Liberal societal structures are dependent on the solidarity of their citizens. And if the secularization of society goes 'off the rails', the sources of this solidarity may dry up altogether." Then, in a surprising move for someone committed to naturalism, Habermas acknowledges the limits of secular theory and opens the door for religion to reclaim its place at the table when he writes, "I shall suggest that we should understand cultural and societal secularization as a double learning process that compels both the traditions of the Enlightenment and the religious doctrines to reflect on their own respective limits."[60] To imagine the early Enlightenment thinkers countenancing such a view is difficult, which is why it may be time to consider that we are in the "twilight" of the Enlightenment, according to the memorable image provided by George Marsden,[61] or perhaps it is on the verge of "a post-Enlightenment culture," described by Gray as the era when

56. MacIntyre, *After Virtue*, 2.

57. Ibid., 12.

58. Ibid., 8.

59. Gray, *Enlightenment's Wake*, 222. Gray describes moral discourse as a jumble of moral judgments that are "assimilated to preferences" and as deeply "incoherent," due to the inability to agree on what is good for humanity or what virtues are necessary for moral reasoning to proceed.

60. Jürgen Habermas, "Pre-political Foundations of the Democratic Constitutional State?," in *Dialectics of Secularization* (San Francisco, CA: Ignatius Press, 2006), 22–23.

61. Marsden, *Twilight of the American Enlightenment*.

"the rationalist religions of humanity are almost as archaic, as alien and as remote as the traditional transcendental faiths."[62]

From Gray's perspective, the Enlightenment is deflating from the inside. It is collapsing in on itself with its central claims notwithstanding the scrutiny of its own test of knowledge. If Gray is right, why does the Enlightenment eschatology of progress continue to be so powerful? His answer is that society will cling to the exhausted eschatological myth of the Enlightenment "more from fear of the consequences of giving it up than from genuine conviction."[63] In other words, as noted in chapter 2 concerning Hiebert's analysis of a worldview being contested, it is emotionally unsettling for our deepest and unexamined assumptions about life to be put to the test. Most people would rather maintain their worldview assumptions, even if they worry that evidence may be mounting against them, than to dismiss them for an untested replacement.

As appealing as it may be for the Christian to cheer on the collapse of the Enlightenment's hubris, seen most clearly in its eschatology of progress, it's too early to consider contemporary culture as "post-Enlightenment." Some would make the case that the postmodern turn is simply an ultimate form of modernity.[64] We should not underestimate the resilience of the belief in progress, particularly at the societal level where it seems faith in humanity's upward trajectory continues unabated. Perhaps philosophers like Gray and MacIntyre see that the Enlightenment train has engine problems and is breaking down, but for the passengers in the train, forward movement continues (albeit in starts and stops) and few people question the ability of the engine to get the train to its destination.

A Missionary Encounter with Enlightenment Eschatology

The gospel confronts the Enlightenment's rival eschatology by proclaiming a different view of history. Christians claim that the turning point of the ages was not the dawn of reason in the sixteenth century but the dawning of new creation in the first. We do not believe the world is heading toward a

---

62. Gray, *Enlightenment's Wake*, 152.

63. Ibid., xiv.

64. Goheen and Bartholomew, *Living at the Crossroads*, 113; and Timothy Keller, *Preaching: Communicating Faith in an Age of Skepticism* (New York: Viking, 2015). Goheen and Bartholomew say, "It is very important to note that, from a Christian perspective, the roots of modernity, though attacked by many of these postmodern philosophers, have never been altogether abandoned by them. The ideal of human autonomy, for example, tends to remain as firmly entrenched as ever." Pastor Tim Keller takes this approach. His manual on preaching includes a chapter titled "Preaching to the Late Modern Mind."

secularist utopia in which naturalism reigns supreme but toward a restored cosmos in which every knee bows to King Jesus.[65] Eschatological discipleship includes the equipping of believers to see through and counter the Enlightenment's eschatology with the truth about the world—a "missionary encounter" with an Enlightenment-influenced society. Below are a few suggestions for how best to confront this rival eschatology.

Challenge "Progressive" Narratives in the Culture

First, we must go to the heart of the conflict with Enlightenment eschatology. As Newbigin suggests, we must unmask the central tenet of the Enlightenment and reclaim the public nature of Christian truth. "We cannot forever postpone the question: What is the real truth about the world?" Once we ask this question, we are brought into conflict with "the central citadel of our culture"—the Enlightenment doctrine that "the real world, the reality with which we have to do, is a world that is to be understood in terms of efficient causes and not of final causes, a world that is not governed by an intelligible purpose, and thus a world in which the answer to the question of what is good has to be left to the private opinion of each individual and cannot be included in the body of accepted facts that control public life."[66]

According to Newbigin, believers cannot help but challenge this Enlightenment eschatology because it is a fundamentally different perspective on human life and human destiny.[67] If we succumb to this eschatology, it will not be by denying openly the significance of the resurrection but by privatizing its meaning, reducing the public implications of the event, and limiting Christianity to matters related to personal piety or personal

---

65. Ramachandra, *Gods that Fail*, 112. Sri Lankan theologian Vinoth Ramachandra goes so far as to reclaim the use of the word "demonology" to explain a society's enslavement to an idolatrous vision of progress. "When human beings give to any aspect of God's creation (for instance, sexuality and/or fertility) or to the works of their hands (e.g. science, the nation-state, the market mechanism) the worship that is due to the Creator alone, they call up invisible forces that eventually dominate them. When what is meant to be a servant is treated as a master, it quickly becomes a tyrant. This is seen in every human project: once a project acquires a certain size and becomes invested with human dreams of 'progress' or of 'liberation,' it attains a life of its own, dragging human beings and societies in its wake. . . . Such demons always demand human sacrifices, whether in the name of 'patriotism,' 'revolution,' or 'scientific progress.' So the cult of idolatry leads to the sacrifice of the weak and apparently useless members of society (from fetuses to other ethnic groups, to the infirm or the mentally handicapped), to the destruction of the earth's eco-systems and the abdication of human responsibility for the planet."

66. Newbigin, *Foolishness to the Greeks*, 79.

67. Ronald Wright, *A Short History of Progress* (Toronto, Canada: House of Anansi Press, 1994), 4. Wright refers to the Enlightenment's vision of progress and its faith in human ability to better the world as a "secular religion."

salvation.[68] Christians in a secular age must confront the Enlightenment's myth of progress with the public truth of Christ's resurrection.

Second, Christians can challenge the myth of progress by exposing the mythical assumption that religion is on a journey of steady and inevitable decline and that secular identity will continue to grow. The "decline of religiosity" narrative is demonstrably false, and Christians must challenge those who continue to promote such theories in the face of evidence by using the Enlightenment's methods against the Enlightenment's myths. This task can be accomplished in several ways.

One method is to see the dark side of this myth of progress. Instead of viewing the Enlightenment's history of progress as good for humanity, Christopher Lutz offers a stinging indictment, "While these events are commonly read as the history of progress toward individual freedom, they are also moments in the history of the turn to voluntarism that gave birth to the modern culture of emotivism that tyrannizes those traditional moral communities that it does not dissolve."[69] In other words, not all the developments that find their way onto the time line of Enlightenment eschatology are healthy, and the imperialist and colonial tendencies at the height of Enlightenment influence are symptoms of the disease.

Another method of challenging the "religious decline" narrative is demographic reality. For example, Eric Kaufmann does not see the future as belonging to the secular elites, but rather the religious grassroots, and, somewhat ominously, some of the strongest forms of religious faith (including radical Islam). "We have embarked on a particularly turbulent phase of history in which the frailty of secular liberalism will become ever more apparent," he writes. "We see the collapse of the great secular religions of the twentieth century; the growing importance of values in determining fertility; an uneven demographic transition which is reshaping Western populations; the rise of global identity politics: all this in an atmosphere of

68. Goheen, *Introducing Christian Mission Today*, 171. Goheen lays out the ways evangelicals have been shaped by the Enlightenment paradigm. He says, "As the powerful humanist story relegates religion to the private realm (privatism), reduces sin and the gospel to the individual person (individualism), and locates renewing power exclusively inside the person (interiorism), the evangelical church has sometimes simply quietly accepted that place assigned to it." Some Christians have succumbed to the Enlightenment in the opposite way, by making Christianity little more than an aid to the world's social agenda, by reducing sin and the gospel to social structures (social gospel) and by locating renewing power in the political process.

69. Christopher Lutz, *Reading Alasdair MacIntyre's After Virtue* (New York: Bloomsbury Academic, 2012), 48.

multicultural toleration."[70] The rise of radical religion is a sign that religiosity may be growing in devotion and in numbers, not declining.

A third method of challenging the myth of progress is noting the continuing (and growing) relevance of religion in world affairs, despite the ongoing acceptance of secularization theories by intellectual elites.[71] John Gray believes the new atheists have gotten louder in recent years because they are worried that religion is flourishing instead of declining.[72] Sociologist Rodney Stark says, "It is a very religious world, far more religious than it was 50 years ago." He shares statistics that seem surprising if one believes the twenty-first century is an "enlightened" age of progress that necessarily entails the demise of religion. "Of the world population 81 percent claim to belong to an organized religious faith, 74 percent say religion is an important part of their daily lives, and 50 percent have attended a place of worship in the past seven days. Russia has more occult healers than medical doctors, 38 percent of the French believe in astrology, and 35 percent of the Swiss agree, 'Some fortune tellers can foresee the future.' Nearly everyone in Japan has their new car blessed by a Shinto priest."[73] The idea that religion is fading away in favor of a secularist paradise of reason and rationalism is demonstrably false, and it is not progress to cling to such ideas in the face of all evidence; rather it is folly.

Of course, while it may be helpful to show how the "subtraction theory" that sees a corresponding increase of secularity and decrease of religious fervor as false, Christians cannot be content with showing how religiosity is on the rise (as if this concept is a reverse-subtracting theory). However, we can do something more effective, which is to show the failure of the myth of progress, or at least the reasons this myth lets people down.

N. T. Wright goes beyond the statistics that call into question the myth and points instead to the Enlightenment eschatology's lack of emotional resonance and resolution. "The myth of progress fails because it doesn't in fact work," he writes, "because it would never solve evil retrospectively; and

---

70. Eric Kaufmann, *Shall the Religious Inherit the Earth: Demography and Politics in the Twenty-First Century* (London, UK: Profile Books, 2010), ix.

71. Stephen Prothero, *Religious Literacy: What Every American Needs to Know and Doesn't* (New York: HarperCollins, 2007), 43. "Today what needs explaining is not the persistence of religion in modern societies but the emergence of unbelief in Europe and among American leaders in media, law, and higher education."

72. John Gray, "What Scares the New Atheists," accessed August 23, 2015, http://www.theguardian.com/world/2015/mar/03/what-scares-the-new-atheists.

73. Rodney Stark, "A Worldwide Religious Awakening," accessed August 8, 2015, http://www.slate.com/bigideas/what-is-the-future-of-religion/essays-and-opinions/rodney-stark-opinion.

because it underestimates the nature and power of evil itself and thus fails to see the vital importance of the cross, God's *no* to evil, which then opens the door to his *yes* to creation." He then contrasts the Christian story with the Enlightenment myth, turning upside down the eschatological time line, "Only in the Christian story itself—certainly not in the secular stories of modernity—do we find any sense that the problems of this world are solved not by a straightforward upward movement into the light but by the creator God going down into the dark to rescue humankind and the world from its plight."[74]

Like Wright, Christians who seek a missionary encounter in a culture formed by the Enlightenment's eschatology must turn upside down the time line of progress in favor of the story of salvation. We challenge the "progressive" narrative so often assumed by society. At the same time, we must challenge the "declension" narratives that often appear in the church.

Challenge "Declension" Narratives in the Church

As we saw earlier, a person who is fully convinced that the current era is the most privileged, progressive, and advanced in human history will find it unnecessary to reach into the past and retrieve insights that may be useful for contemporary society. The past is something people are escaping *from,* not something they would ever turn *toward.*[75] "Those who identify totally with our times can easily accept a straight theory of progress," Charles Taylor writes. "We have nothing to learn from past epochs; insofar as they were different from ours, we can set them aside as irrelevant."[76] Whatever is found in the past that does not fit with the contemporary *zeitgeist* can be swept away without even the slightest engagement.

Some Christians have embraced the Enlightenment's eschatology of progress and treat the past as something to evolve from, not something from which they could learn. Protestant liberalism's emphasis on reason and the human ability to progress beyond certain moral standards has led to schism in multiple denominations, as "traditionalists" are embattled with "progressives" over the significance of the Christian tradition

---

74. N. T. Wright, *Surprised by Hope: Rethinking Heaven, the Resurrection, and the Mission of the Church* (New York: HarperOne, 2008), 87.

75. John Fea, *Why Study History? Reflecting on the Importance of the Past* (Grand Rapids: Baker Academic, 2013), 45, summarizes the progressive historian's view of history and how the replacement of history with "social studies" transforms the goal of historical reflection from understanding to usefulness, "History must serve present needs or else it is useless and not particularly worthy of study by children."

76. Taylor, *Secular Age*, 745.

and the consensus of the church on dogmas that challenge the Enlightenment eschatology (belief in miracles, for example, or more recently, sexual ethics).

Other Christians reject the Enlightenment's "progressive" interpretation of history while continuing to treat the past in much the same way, as if it has little to offer other than where it is useful in reinforcing their own convictions about how best to follow Christ. Feeling the pressure of increasing alienation from the modern age, and holding tightly to the significance that stems from believing in transcendence, the Christian may be inclined to adopt a narrative of decline and then pine for the "good old days" when belief in God was assumed, not challenged, when the burden of proof was on the shoulders of the irreligious, not the devout. In reaction to the thoroughgoing progressive who adopts an eschatological perspective that shows things have been getting better, the thoroughgoing traditionalist tends to adopt an anti-Enlightenment eschatological perspective (not formed by Scripture) that shows things getting worse.[77]

The problem is, when we react to the Enlightenment trajectory of ascendancy by matching it with a declension narrative just as powerful in its appeal, we are falling for an opposite myth, especially when compared to the truly Christian eschatological viewpoint. The operative word for Christians who adopt a declension narrative is *return*. If one has fallen from a pinnacle, then the solution must be to return to the previous heights. Thus, the Christian searches for a previous era to idealize, an era by which to judge the present. Taylor explains the sentiment, "*They* (the Middle Ages, or the seventeenth century, or the pre-60's America) got it right, and we have to repudiate whatever in modern times deviates from that standard."[78]

The declension narrative is at work in various movements within Christianity. Some Christians may long for the pristine days of the early church and desire to return to the simplicity of those times. However, a cursory reading of the New Testament reveals that the earliest

---

77. G. K. Chesterton, "The Blunders of Our Parties," April 19, 1924, in *The Collected Works of G. K. Chesterton, The Illustrated London News*, 1923-25 (vol. 33; San Francisco, CA: Ignatius Press, 1990), 313. These two visions of history lead the progressive to push for liberation and innovation (to advance progress) and the traditionalist to defend the *status quo* (to impede decline). Chesterton famously compared conservatives and progressives this way, "The business of progressives is to go on making mistakes. The business of the conservatives is to prevent the mistakes being corrected. Even when the revolutionist might himself repent of his revolution, the traditionalist is already defending it as part of his tradition. Thus we have the two great types—the advanced person who rushes into ruin, and the retrospective person who admires the ruins."

78. Taylor, *Secular Age*, 745.

days were not flawless; doctrinal crises, moral quandaries, disciplinary actions, and divisive factions often carried the day. Some may look back to the church fathers. The recent translations and commentaries on these ancient works offer spiritual nourishment, but it is a mistake to think of the centuries of ecumenical councils as a "Golden Age." These were also the years that gave a neo-Platonic vision of the body, downplayed the ordinary Christian life, led to ascetic extremes, and married church and state to the point crusades could be led in the name of the Prince of Peace. Some may look back to the Reformation's recovery of justification by faith or the Puritan era of personal piety, which stirred revivals that shook the landscape of early America. However, all the Reformation heroes are marred in some way or another, for instance, Luther's anti-Semitism, Calvin's egregious treatment of doctrinal disputants, Edwards's acceptance of slavery, and so forth.

In short, no Golden Age of Christianity exists. Taylor quotes Leopold von Ranke's famous phrase "*unmittelbar zu Gott*" applied to the ages of history. Loosely translated, it means all ages are "directly or immediate to God." In other words, these ages "differ because each mode of Christian life has had to climb out of, achieve a certain distance from its own embedding in its time. . . . But far from allowing these modes to be neatly ranked, this is the difference which enables them to give something to each other."[79]

Enlightenment eschatology affects contemporary evangelicalism by leading some to adopt uncritically its myth of progress and leading others to adopt uncritically a desire for a golden age. In contrast to the progressive's rosy view of the present and untested view of the future, Christians may feel like they are always standing in the middle of the road with hands outstretched, saying, "Stop and consider!" as the rushing crowd surges forward to a future that will never fulfill their utopian dreams. However, this conservative tendency should never harden into a perspective that views a past era as necessarily better or worse than one's own. Oliver O'Donovan suggests:

> We must look on the past not only as *history* but as *the history of God's world*, a goodness sustained and upheld to the end. . . . In the goods of earth and heaven we find provision for our present

79. Ibid.

> agency, affording resources for the moment in which we are given to act. The unwisdom which asks why past times were better than these has assumed a false position, that of an aesthetic observer valuing goods or different ages from some supposed time-transcending viewpoint. Our position in time is not capable of judging the present against the past, any more than it can judge the present against the future. It is a moment of deliberation, of making up our mind to act.[80]

Seen in this light, church history is a treasure box, not a map. As Christians, we do not honor our forefathers and mothers by seeking to return to their times; rather, we honor them by receiving their wisdom and learning from their victories and failures. We retrieve from the past the elements and tools needed for faithfulness today. No golden age of Christianity existed in the past, only an unbroken line of broken sinners saved by the grace of God and empowered to transmit the gospel to the next generation.

Overcome the Myth of Progress with the Gospel of Hope

Christians will not be effective in missionary encounters until we feel the full force of the Enlightenment eschatology's appeal—the attractiveness of maintaining hope that the world is getting better, no matter how contrary the circumstances. If it is true that the Enlightenment's eschatology is like a balloon that needs to be punctured (even while it may already be deflating on its own), then Christians must consider what air should be pumped into the balloon. It is one thing to cheer the demise of the myth of progress and another to cast a better vision, one rooted in hope and truth. For Christians to meet Enlightenment hubris with a Christian variation of the same would be a sad irony; instead, our response must be to offer hope.

Christian hope has a distinctive shape. Society often reduces hope to a wish, a human longing for a future that may or may not be certain. The Christian sees hope as rooted in God and his promises.[81] Therefore, the Christian is to be confident, never cocky. We trust not in our own efforts to bring about a particular vision of the future but in God to restore his

---

80. O'Donovan, *Finding and Seeking*, 196.

81. Newbigin, *Household of God*, 122; and Marva Dawn, *A Royal "Waste" of Time: The Splendor of Worshiping God and Being Church for the World* (Grand Rapids: Eerdmans, 1999), 35. "Paradise is the promise of the One whose presence creates it. It is the perfect fulfillment of the genuine hope our world craves."

creation and put the world to rights. Over against the Enlightenment eschatology that narrows our horizon such that "the present mood dictates the prospect of the future,"[82] we embrace a more expansive vision, choosing instead to look through a different window altogether to a future that may seem uncertain and impossible yet nevertheless is assured.

When cultural shifts take us by surprise and the obstacle of Enlightenment eschatology seems insurmountable, we may be tempted to replace hope with something else, either fear of the future or nostalgia for the past. Instead, the Christian must ask, "What time is it?"—firmly rejecting the Enlightenment's false eschatology on the one hand while holding fast to biblical eschatology on the other. Newbigin challenges us to understand the times in which we live and avoid both fearing the future and longing for the past:

> The real question is: *What is God doing in these tremendous events of our time?* How are we to understand them and interpret them to others, so that we and they may play our part in them as co-workers with God? Nostalgia for the past and fear for the future are equally out of place for the Christian. He is required, in the situation in which God places him, to understand the signs of the times in the light of the reality of God's present and coming kingdom, and to give his witness faithfully about the purpose of God for all men.[83]

To fear the future is to worry that the Enlightenment view of progress is correct and that Christians are truly being left behind. To yearn for a golden era in the past is to relapse into Enlightenment eschatology the opposite way, committing the same Whig approach to history that employs a highly selective account of the past in order to justify current actions in the present.

Being a faithful people of hope is far more difficult than taking the easy path of *ressentiment*—the Nietzschean concept warned about by James Davison Hunter. *Ressentiment* is "grounded in a narrative of injury or, at least, perceived injury; a strong belief that one has been or is being wronged. The root of this is the sense of entitlement a group holds," Hunter

---

82. O'Donovan, *Finding and Seeking*, 161.

83. Lesslie Newbigin, "Rapid Social Change and Evangelism," unpublished paper, 1962, 3, quoted in Bartholomew and Goheen, *Living at the Crossroads*, 106.

says. "Over time, the perceived injustice becomes central to the person's and the group's identity."[84] The political landscape in North America is heavily influenced on rights, wrongs, and a mind-set of entitlement, and too often Christians have fallen into this "discourse of negation"—a strategy for cultivating solidarity around a group that is afraid of further injury or that needs to mobilize against the newest threat.[85]

Christian hope is a sword that cuts through the marrow of *ressentiment*, challenging our fear of injustice going unnoticed by reminding us of the future when God will right all wrongs. Hope does not lead to a quiet endurance of abuse, without speaking for the truth; it does, however, keep before us the truth that any loss experienced is only temporary. Further, hope challenges *ressentiment* with cheerful courage. We betray our faith when we are united more by bitterness and grievances than by cheerful confidence in God's good purposes for the world and our love for the people who injure us.

In a society where Christians feel entitled to privilege, *ressentiment* is one of the primary temptations. In other societies, where persecution is rampant and injustice has become an accepted reality of everyday life, the greater temptation for Christians is despair. However, the darkest times are the moments when hope comes into its own and shines as the piercing light that it is. Newbigin challenges us to look back to the resurrection when facing discouragement, for "the way we understand the past is a function of our whole way of meeting the present and the future. The community of faith celebrates the resurrection of Jesus as the ground of assurance that the present and the future are not under the control of blind forces but are open to unlimited possibilities of new life."[86] Hope is what leads us to soldier on, especially in the face of evidence that says the cause is lost. To maintain faith when the signs indicate things are working out as one would like is not hope. To rest assured in the coming victory is hope, even when all seems to be failing, and this is the hope that grabs the attention of a world that knows only false eschatology.

Rediscover the Church as a Community Apologetic

One reason the Enlightenment's eschatology seems plausible to many in today's society is because many institutions and cultural forces make it

---

84. James Davison Hunter, *To Change the World* (New York: Oxford University Press, 2010), 107.
85. Ibid., 108.
86. Newbigin, *Foolishness to the Greeks*, 63.

seem plausible. Consider academic institutions where the majority of professors adhere to something similar to the Enlightenment's myth of progress. When a student walks into an academic environment and absorbs this vision of the past and future, it becomes more plausible than before. The eschatology is assumed, and that is what makes it so powerful.

Understanding how one's social environment impacts one's view of what is plausible, we should not be surprised to see children from evangelical congregations find their faith challenged when they come into contact with an academic atmosphere that assumes the truth of Enlightenment philosophy. Often their Christian faith will not be directly opposed by rival philosophies but more subtly—through what is deemed "plausible" and "forward thinking," according to the Enlightenment's vision of the future. It is not the aggressive atheistic professor, popularized in evangelical films like *God's Not Dead*, who is most likely to persuade young Christian college students. It is more likely to be the subtle yet powerful presence of a community that lives, without question, according to another view of the world and another definition of progress and the past.

What might this truth mean for engaging people who are in the process of abandoning the faith they inherited as children? Commenting on Charles Taylor's belief that rejecting one's faith is due largely to the appeal of rationalism (and what is plausible), not merely philosophical evidence, James K. A. Smith writes,

> If Taylor is right, it seems to suggest that the Christian response to such converts to unbelief is not to have an argument about the data or "evidences" but rather to offer an alternative story that offers a more robust, complex understanding of the Christian faith. The goal of such witness would not be the minimal establishment of some vague theism but the invitation to historic, sacramental Christianity.[87]

The classical approach of apologetics is to present rational proofs for God's existence and then from this point to argue for the uniqueness of Jesus Christ and his resurrection. Classical apologetics is beneficial in its effort to show that Christianity is true.[88] However, if Taylor is correct, then

87. Smith, *How (Not) to Be Secular*, 77.

88. For a concise and helpful overview of five different approaches to apologetics, see Steven Cowan, ed., *Five Views on Apologetics*, Zondervan Counterpoints Series (Grand Rapids: Zondervan, 2000).

people are already likely to accept or reject reasons for belief before they ever hear them because the greater story is already conditioning them to accept or reject "proofs" of God's existence and the truth of Christianity. Consequently, perhaps one of the best ways to engage unbelievers is to invite them to see the community of faith in worship and in action. Lesslie Newbigin spoke of the people of God as a community apologetic, submissive to the Scriptures and challenging the plausibility structures of Enlightenment thought.[89] It is not that the church replaces other, rational strategies and arguments for belief in God but rather that the church becomes the atmosphere, the teller of a better story, a story whose truth begins to work on the heart of nonreligious persons, conditioning them for the moment when the classical apologetics "proofs" are then used by the Holy Spirit to confirm the belief he has already initiated in them.

Walsh and Keesmaat view the community as indispensable in the role of conversion, "When people are first attracted to another worldview it is usually because of the lived lives, the praxis, of the community that holds it. The truth of the worldview must be embodied if it is to be known."[90] Christians should make use of the various tools at our disposal in order to persuade people to follow Jesus, but we must not leave out the world where God's good news comes alive—the people of God who corporately witness to a kingdom that has no end. It may be that the best apologetic for a secular age is a people who are in this world but not of it, who counter the Enlightenment's eschatology with the true story of a new world which began on a Sunday morning outside Jerusalem.

Conclusion

The Enlightenment myth of progress is an eschatological viewpoint that opposes Christian eschatology at various points. It trades divine revelation for human reason; it puts the autonomous individual at the center of the world; it sees science as the privileged form of knowledge that drives the world forward; and it uses the language of the future in order to justify actions in the present. In order for there to be a missionary encounter with an Enlightenment-influenced society, Christians must embrace eschatological discipleship—the process by which we recognize and reject the

89. Lesslie Newbigin, *The Open Secret: An Introduction to the Theology of Mission* (Grand Rapids: Eerdmans, 1995), 304, quoted in Goheen, *Introducing Christian Mission Today*, 246; and idem, *Foolishness to the Greeks*, 58.

90. Walsh and Keesmaat, *Colossians Remixed*, 128.

Enlightenment's rival conception of time and then demonstrate in our corporate witness (through words and deeds) how the reality of resurrection hope vastly supersedes the myth of progress.

CHAPTER 7

Christianity and the Sexual Revolution

As we turn attention to the sexual revolution as a rival eschatology, we must keep in mind that these worldviews are not hermetically sealed off from one another. Indeed, we can see the Enlightenment eschatology of progress at work in the sexual revolution, with technology as one of the drivers and the autonomous individual at the center of existence.

According to James Kalb, at the bottom of the fiercest debates today is a fundamental misunderstanding of the human person. He writes, "This project's goal is best understood as eschatological, or perhaps counter-eschatological, a social world that recognizes no transcendent authority above it, no history behind it except the history of its own coming into being, and no nature of things beneath it that cannot be transformed technologically into what we choose."[1] Kalb overstates his case to say that the sexual revolution is countereschatological because of its dismissal of history. This characteristic is, in fact, one of the clearest signs that eschatology is at work—the same kind of Dark Ages mythology at work in the Enlightenment, only now applied to sexuality.

On the one hand, the sexual revolution is the application of the Enlightenment's rejection of divine revelation (with regard to sex) and the embrace of the autonomous individual's right to self-definition (as opposed to the Aristotelian vision of the human character's development). On the other hand, the sexual revolution's emphasis on individual expression could be interpreted as a backlash against the Enlightenment's privileging of scientific knowledge.

Is the sexual revolution simply the application of Enlightenment philosophy to sexuality, or is it a variation of Romanticism, the philosophical

1. James Kalb, "Technocracy Now," *First Things* (August/September 2015): 25.

movement that rose up to challenge core tenets of Enlightenment reductionism?[2] We have reason to believe the sexual revolution belongs to the Romanticist ethos, not the least of which is society's frequent appeal to the mystical "inner self"—an inner essence walled off from scientific or biological restraints, something that needs to be uniquely expressed through sexual behavior. Isaiah Berlin described the way Romanticism countered the Enlightenment:

> a new and restless spirit, seeking violently to burst through old and cramping forms, a nervous preoccupation with perpetually changing inner states of consciousness, a longing for the unbounded and indefinable, for perpetual movement and change, an effort to return to the forgotten sources of life, a passionate effort at self-assertion both individual and collective, a search after means of expressing an unappeasable yearning for unattainable goals.[3]

Berlin's description fits well with the sexual revolution's emphases. We may conclude, then, that some aspects of the sexual revolution fit snugly within the Enlightenment framework while other aspects resemble the Romantic counterpoint. The relationship between the sexual revolution and the Enlightenment is, therefore, complicated—another reason to consider their eschatological elements separately.

Moving forward, we will explore the eschatology of the sexual revolution first by defining the worldview and, second, by demonstrating the movement's connection to the cultural belief that self-expression is the purpose of life and is the best path to human flourishing. Once we see how the sexual revolution has made inroads by attaching itself to the expressivism of our day, we will examine its eschatological framework and then offer a Christian response.

Defining the Sexual Revolution

Before considering the eschatology of the sexual revolution, we must come to an understanding of this label and how it developed. What are the common themes and assumptions about humanity and happiness reflected

2. Taylor, *Secular Age*, 473–75. Taylor categorizes the Romantic self as the "Expressive self." For a brief overview of Romanticism, see Bartholomew and Goheen, *Christian Philosophy*, 154–56.

3. Isaiah Berlin, *The Crooked Timber of Humanity: Chapters in the History of Ideas* (2nd ed.; Princeton, NJ: Princeton University Press, 2013), 96–97.

by this philosophy? Toward what is the revolution directed? In exploring these questions, we will examine the sexual revolution's historical development and how it came to be associated with matters related to human repression and human fulfillment.

Historical Development of the Sexual Revolution

We have seen how the Enlightenment project of discovering a rational, universal basis for knowledge and morality independent of divine revelation spread throughout Europe and North America. The sexual revolution developed in parallel with the Enlightenment, not surprisingly, since issues related to sexual practice (the rightness and wrongness of certain actions) make up a large part of one's moral framework. In order to grow in maturity and reach their full potential, men and women were once expected to exercise restraint in the management of sexual passions and desires. Denying oneself sexually, in line with the structural and societal boundaries that reinforced sexual norms, was not viewed as "repressive" but rather "dignifying" because this expectation of human strength and self-control in choosing what is best for societal stability not only individual pleasure is what separated humanity from the animal kingdom.[4]

Society's shifting views of sexuality coincided with industrialization. Over time sexuality became less about the global nature of humanity and sex's vitally important role in the propagation of the species and more about the value of sexuality for the individual in relation to family. As family life became more private, so did the meaning given to sex. Sexual behavior was perceived as having less to do with public norms and values and more to do with personal and family existence. Privatization was developing in multiple spheres of life, and the place of sexuality gradually receded into a matter of personal choice and privacy.[5]

By the beginning of the twentieth century, the rise of psychological studies and the practice of psychotherapy led to a new emphasis on one's sexuality as integral to the human person. Sigmund Freud (1856–1939) focused on the libido and its role in the human psyche. The instincts of love and aggression were considered fundamental for understanding the subconscious motivations behind human behavior. According to this view repression of sexuality was necessary for civilized society, but sexual

4. Gerard Fourez, "The Sexual Revolution in Perspective," in *The Sexual Revolution* (ed. Gregory Baum and John Coleman; Edinburgh: T&T Clark, 1984), 5.

5. Ibid., 8.

self-control should be conscious because unconscious repression resulted in various neuroses.[6]

One of Freud's disciples, Wilhelm Reich (1897–1957), wrote an influential book entitled *The Sexual Revolution* (1936),[7] and in it he disagreed with his predecessor on the necessity of sexual repression for the good of society. He advocated a "sexual revolution," something he described as "radical change in the conditions of sexual life" to counter the "disgraceful medieval sexual legislation" that inflicts harm on humanity.[8] Notice how Reich describes laws concerning sexuality as belonging to "medieval" times. Already we can see traces of the sexual revolution's eschatological focus in the book that bears its name.

According to Reich, the problem of unhealthy emotional behavior is sexual repression, with its moralistic and unimaginative restrictions that cause various neuroses in people. The solution, of course, is sexual liberation.[9] It is important for us to examine both of these elements of the sexual revolution's worldview one by one—the "problem" of repression and the "solution" of liberation.

Sexual Morality and Repression

In the Christian worldview sin, the breaking of God's law, is the problem from which humanity needs deliverance. In contrast, for the sexual revolution, it is no longer the breaking of moral codes but rather the rejection of instincts forbidden by those moral codes that constitute humanity's biggest problem. Loneliness and alienation do not come as a result of moral transgression but as a result of self-restriction when morals and instinct collide. "The organism is forced to armor itself against both the instinct and the outside world, to restrict itself. This 'armoring' results in a more or less reduced capacity for living," claims Reich. This "reduced capacity for living" is the rigidity that afflicts the majority of people and has become "by far the most important source of loneliness" in contemporary culture.[10]

According to Reich, moral restrictions are both the cause and the result of sexual dysfunction. The healthy person should not feel compelled

6. Antonio Hortelano, "The Sexual Revolution and the Family," in *The Sexual Revolution* (ed. Gregory Baum and John Coleman; Edinburgh, Scotland: T&T Clark, Edinburgh, 1984), 51.

7. The title in German is *Die Sexualität im Kulturkampf* ("Sexuality in the Culture War").

8. Wilhelm Reich, *The Sexual Revolution: Toward a Self-Regulating Character Structure* (trans. Therese Pol.; New York: Farrar, Straus and Giroux, 1974), preface to the 3rd ed., 1945, xvii.

9. Ibid., 4.

10. Ibid., 4–5.

to live according to a moral code, precisely because the healthy person no longer has impulses that require restraint. Moral standards, intended to restrain human sexuality from excess, actually *fuel* sexual excess and anti-social impulses—activities that would not present a problem if "the basic genital needs [were] gratified."[11]

To be clear, Reich was not against morality per se but only against morality that is compulsory and opposes one's natural instincts. The morality of a "sex-economy," he wrote, is "in full harmony with nature and civilization" and is "life-affirming."[12] Reich uses the word "morality" in two different ways. The "self-evident" morality prohibits rape, murder, etc. (harm to others), and then the "pathological morality" insists on sexual abstinence, monogamy within marriage, etc. (harm to oneself). The establishment of pathological morality is what leads to the destruction of self-evident morality. In other words, the reason so much harm is done to others is because of the old moral code of repression that does so much harm to oneself.[13]

As Roger Scruton points out, Reich's advocacy for sexual liberation goes back, in part, to Freud's idea of sexual repression, "which describes sexual desire as a kind of hydraulic force, which will burst out in surprising places unless 'repressed' by the superego."[14] Scruton shows how this idea altered the significance of sexual behavior; it was now "the release of desires welling up from the 'real me' inside." The tendency toward indulging these desires should not be resisted, because "to release those desires is to produce a harmless, localized pleasure. To repress them is to 'bottle up' urges that become dangerous when contained and not allowed to flow freely."[15]

The jump is short from repression to oppression. Scruton traces the thinking to its current state, "To deny [sexual desires'] release is to *repress* them, and repression of the sexual urge is also oppression of the individual."[16] The movement from repression to oppression helps us understand the political ramifications of the sexual revolution. When the idea of sexual repression and liberation is applied to politics, we begin to see why tolerance as a political ideal is insufficient in the cause of sexual justice.

---

11. Ibid., 6.
12. Ibid., 25.
13. Ibid., 28.
14. Roger Scruton, "Is Sex Necessary? On the Poverty of Progressivism's Fixation on Sexual Liberation," *First Things* (December 2014): 35.
15. Ibid.
16. Ibid.

Contemporary activists for sexual liberation demand neutrality, not merely toleration of sexual minorities. John Gray describes the difference:

> It is wrong for government to discriminate in favor of, or against, any form of life animated by a definite conception of the good. It is wrong for the government to do so . . . because such policy violates an ideal of *equality* demanding equal respect by government for divergent conceptions of the good and the ways of life that embody them. To privilege any form of life in any way over others, or to disfavor in any way any form of life, is unacceptably discriminatory.[17]

Where does this movement lead? To a world in which ultimate questions of morality and what constitutes "the good life" are reduced to the private sphere and banished from public debate. Gray is right when he says, "What the neutrality of radical equality mandates is nothing less than *the legal disestablishment of morality*. As a result, morality becomes in theory a private habit of behavior rather than a common way of life."[18] The sexual revolution intends to bring about the legal disestablishment of morality and, as a result, suffers the loss of a common culture, built on specific conceptions of virtue and goodness.[19]

Sexual Morality and Self-Fulfillment

If the problem is sexual repression, then the solution must be sexual liberation, but what does this liberation look like? Here we begin to see how the Romanticist counterpoint to the Enlightenment reveals a new take on the human pursuit of happiness, one that resembles the Enlightenment in its rejection of a standard divinely revealed, but counters the Enlightenment in its pursuit of transcendence through self-discovery and expression. Whereas ancient civilizations would have seen the purpose of human life as the discovery of divine reality and the alignment of one's self with that transcendent vision, the Romanticist understanding views the purpose of human life as the discovery of one's inner essence and the expression of that essence as necessary for self-fulfillment. Apply the Romanticist vision of the

17. Gray, *Enlightenment's Wake*, 29–30.
18. Ibid.
19. Ibid., 118.

purpose of life to the sexual revolution, and we find self-fulfillment through sexual satisfaction to be a primary way of realizing oneself in this life.

Returning to Reich, we see once again the problem of repression as "sex-negating" moral regulations that are, in the end, "life-negating." This repression is the greatest obstacle to human flourishing. Thus, what is the goal of the sexual revolution? Reich is clear that "the sexual revolution has no more important task than finally to enable human beings to realize their full potentialities and find gratification in life."[20] Notice the emphasis on a human being realizing his or her potential through sexual expression and gratification. If self-fulfillment is the purpose of life, and gratification is necessary for achieving this goal, then orgasm is essential to self-fulfillment. Orgasm becomes "man's only salvation."[21]

Just as Christianity stood in the way of the Enlightenment's pursuit of a universal morality based on human reason (because of its insistence on divine revelation and its rejection of science as the privileged form of knowledge), so now Christianity stands in the way of the sexual revolution's pursuit of human flourishing through sexual fulfillment. According to Reich, religious convictions load people with guilt and shame, keeping them from sexual happiness. This simple goal has been impossible for thousands of years, "denied in the name of religion."[22] To bring about salvation and end this repression, then, the power of religion must be broken, and the appeal to religion as a substitute for sexuality must be seen as the "deadly influence" it is.[23]

Before we examine in more detail the way sexual liberation corresponds to the wider cultural value of self-expression, we must note that belief in self-fulfillment through sexual release does not necessarily lead to rampant promiscuity or excessive sexual behavior. Many people continue to live by traditional moral guidelines (such as monogamy within marriage), even as they accept the sexual revolution's foundational premise that *self-fulfillment is what marriage is all about.*

Once the foundational premise of the sexual revolution—that the purpose of life is self-fulfillment and self-expression (through sexuality)—is accepted, then a marriage—while still traditional on the outside—becomes,

20. Reich, *Sexual Revolution*, 24–25.

21. Eustace Chesser, *Salvation through Sex: The Life and Work of Wilhelm Reich* (New York: William Morrow and Co., 1973), 67.

22. Ibid., 25.

23. Ibid., 78.

at its core, a consumer transaction. The person entering the marriage covenant sees the institution as a way of achieving self-fulfillment, working toward his or her interests. On the surface the commitment appears the same, but underneath, the goal of self-fulfillment has transformed the relationship into "an instrumental and typically temporary good." Self-fulfillment redefines marriage, and in a culture where divorce is common, the permanence of marriage must "continually be open to re-evaluation. If at any point it fails to promote the self-actualization of one spouse or the other, the option of ending the partnership must be available."[24] Thus, the sexual revolution not only impacts sexual practice but also revolutionizes societal expectations regarding morality and marriage.

The Sexual Revolution and Self-Expression

Now that we have summarized the development of thought behind the sexual revolution, we can examine in more depth the fundamental goal of this movement (self-fulfillment) and how it is achieved (self-expression). We will consider how the sexual revolution fits into an overarching Enlightenment emphasis on human autonomy, as well as Romanticism's emphasis on human expression.

Self-Expression in the Age of Authenticity

Charles Taylor describes our secular age as "the age of authenticity." By this he does not mean authenticity as opposed to hypocrisy but rather conformity. He defines the phrase this way:

> I mean the understanding of life which emerges with the Romantic expressivism of the late-eighteenth century, that each one has his or her own way of realizing his or her humanity, and that it is important to identify and live out one's own, as against surrendering to conformity with a model imposed from outside, by society, or the previous generation, or religious or political authority.[25]

24. Rodney Clapp, *The Consuming Passion: Christianity and the Consumer Culture* (Downers Grove, IL: IVP, 2007), 193; and Os Guinness, *The Last Christian on Earth: Uncover the Enemy's Plot to Undermine the Church* (Grand Rapids: Baker Books, 2010), 99. Os Guinness reflects on the result of this development, "The wedding vow 'Till death do us part' has given way to the wedding wish, 'So long as love lasts.' With the expressive revolution triumphant, and sex now linked to pleasure rather than procreation, love seems not to be lasting so long."

25. Taylor, *Secular Age*, 475.

Another good word that gets at the heart of how Taylor uses the word "authenticity" is *nonconformity*. The point of nonconformity is being true to yourself as opposed to whatever "self" to whom others may want you to be true. Note the four areas Taylor mentioned in his definition.

Imposition from Outside. To summarize, we might say that it is the job of each individual to make one's own life. Any identity that comes from outside oneself may squelch originality and authenticity. A person cannot "find oneself," "realize his or her potential," "release one's true self" and so on, unless he or she rejects every model of life that does not come from within oneself. Furthermore, to allow anyone or anything to shape you into something you are not is a betrayal of your identity. An extreme version of this perspective is found in Rhonda Byrne's *The Secret*, an unabashed paean of praise to the unfettered ego, heralded by Oprah Winfrey as one of the previous decade's greatest books.[26]

Imposition from Society. Rejecting societal expectations is necessary; otherwise a person can no longer contribute his or her unique essence to society. A person is not bound by biology, society, morality, or culture but can be whatever he or she feels deep down inside. People are whatever they want to express.[27]

Imposition from the Previous Generation. In some cultures continuity with the past is a sign of wisdom, the ability to draw from the reserves of history in order to make wise choices today. Institutions and the expectations that grow around them are cherished, sometimes to a fault, but they are seen as valuable nonetheless. The Age of Authenticity, however, finds much of its dramatic flair in innovation and experimentation, breaking free from "the way we've always done it" in favor of building a new world that maximizes individual flourishing of expression. People express themselves by venturing out on their own, by blazing their own paths, and by deriding the past generation's expression.

---

26. Rhonda Byrne, *The Secret* (New York: Atria Books, 2006), takes the power of positive thinking to a whole new level. One must expect the universe to conform to his or her demands and then be open to receiving whatever is desired. The book critiques the notion of self-sacrifice and encourages readers to put themselves first and look out for their own interests ahead of everyone else's.

27. Lisa Abend, "In Sweden, Boys Won't Be Boys," *Time*, December 16, 2013, accessed September 18, 2015, http://content.time.com/time/magazine/article/0,9171,2159265,00.html. In the last two decades, casting off societal restraints has been evident most clearly in gender roles and identity. In this case freedom is not in accepting binary definitions of male and female but in expanding the number of options for people to "find" and "express" themselves while simultaneously going to great lengths to avoid stereotypes or expectations. One of the most prominent cases of gender neutrality is Sweden where a new, genderless pronoun has been invented and children are encouraged to pursue activities generally associated with the other gender.

Imposition from Religion and Politics. The church and state are common foes in the battle to express oneself at all costs. Religion imposes order by appealing to divine authority. (Christianity goes so far as to call for self-mortification, the dying to oneself, and living to God that demands the putting of others first, over one's own desires.) Additionally, political authority can limit the freedom of self-expression, which is one reason younger generations tend to be libertarian when it comes to governmental regulation, and simultaneously advocates of big government in areas where progressive forms of self-expression may be at risk.[28]

In these four areas mentioned by Charles Taylor, the Age of Authenticity gives rise to a cultural narrative of individual expression that opposes any kind of conformity. We now turn to the effects this idea of human flourishing has on the different spheres of society, church, and politics.

Sexuality in the Age of Authenticity

The ethos of authenticity and the resistance to these four spheres of outside influence do not lead to anarchy and the overthrow of these sources of authority. Instead, these institutions are subtly shaped by the Age of Authenticity's expectations. In the case of religion, the Age of Authenticity does not necessarily lead to a revolt against religious authority, but instead it recasts religion as a method of enabling the kind of authentic self-expression believed to be most valuable.[29] In other words, the Age of Authenticity is not likely to empty churches; rather, it is likely instead to fill them with people who believe the primary purpose of religious observance is to facilitate "finding oneself" and "chasing one's dreams." Within this frame of mind, sinfulness is no longer falling short of the glory of God but the falling short of one's own potential.[30] Sin is failing to be true to oneself. People choose a church based on how it will help them discover their unique potential and find fulfillment in life. The smorgasbord of spirituality is there for the taking.

---

28. Pew Research Center, "Millennials in Adulthood: Detached from Institutions, Networked with Friends," Next America Series (March 7, 2014), accessed June 3, 2015, http://www.pewsocialtrends.org/2014/03/07/millennials-in-adulthood.

29. Christian Smith and Melinda Lundquist Denton, *Soul Searching: The Religious and Spiritual Lives of American Teenagers* (Oxford, UK: Oxford, 2005), 164. Consider the surveys of American teenagers that show a remarkable commonality of seeing religion as helping people achieve a primary life goal, "To feel good and happy about oneself and one's life."

30. Robert Schuller, *Self-Esteem: The New Reformation* (Waco: Word Books, 1982), 64. Popular pastor Robert Schuller defined sin as "any thought or act that robs myself or another human being of his or her self-esteem."

The Age of Authenticity impacts political authority, not by stirring up anarchists who want to bring down the government but by forming a generation of people who rely on the government to ensure their "rights" and their "freedom" and to protect others from "non-discrimination" in order to foster "respect"—all terms which are good but which, in Taylor's estimation, too often get deployed as "argument-stopping universals, without any consideration of the where and how of their application to the case at hand."[31] In order to enforce neutrality, then, the public discourse moves moral concerns from the realm of debate and into the realm of "rights."

The problem with this movement from debate to rights is, as John Gray points out, that it barters away any impulse toward compromise. "To make a political issue that is deeply morally contested a matter of basic rights is to make it non-negotiable," writes Gray. He adds, "Rights do not allow divisive issues to be settled by a legislative compromise: they permit only unconditional victory or surrender."[32] It is no wonder, then, that *New York Times* columnist Ross Douthat, writing about the inevitability of same-sex marriage, chose the title "The Terms of Our Surrender" to make his point about how traditional Christians will be treated.[33]

When morally contested issues move from the arena of debate to the arena of rights, motivation no longer exists to "live and let live" when people dissent from the legally enshrined orthodoxy. The Age of Authenticity, when applied to the fight against sexual repression and the fight for sexual liberation, justifies the use of political and legal levers to penalize dissenters who express moral disapproval or advocate for certain forms of sexual restraint. "Freedom of choice" becomes absolute, as if every option must be inherently equal and beneficial, but we are left without any real opportunity to discuss what the choices entail or what their consequences may be.

The Age of Sexual Identity

The sexual revolution makes sense to many people in contemporary society because it unites the Enlightenment's focus on individual autonomy and Romanticism's focus on self-expression. The Age of Authenticity, when reworked around sexual self-expression, opens the door for sexuality as the

---

31. Taylor, *Secular Age*, 479.

32. Gray, *Enlightenment's Wake*, 34.

33. Ross Douthat, "The Terms of Our Surrender," *New York Times*, March 1, 2014, accessed September 18, 2015, http://www.nytimes.com/2014/03/02/opinion/sunday/the-terms-of-our-surrender. html?_r=0.

pinnacle of self-expression and one of the foundational components of "the good life."

The seeds of this worldview are present in the earliest Enlightenment philosophers. Charles Taylor recounts the story of how Diderot once presented a dialogue between a Tahitian man and his guest, a European priest.[34] The Tahitian offered his wife and daughters to the priest, who declined due to his moral convictions. In the ensuing conversation, the Tahitian man blasts the morality of Western Christianity and pleads for the naturalness of sexual fulfillment.[35]

The Enlightenment appeal to nature and universal reason, combined with Romanticism's rebellion against the naturalistic bars that trap humanity in a disenchanted cosmos, has led to a reconceived purpose for human life: self-expression. When applied to sexuality, liberation becomes, according to Roger Scruton, "a release of the true self, the inner self, from the shackles of bourgeois society, and the purpose of this release is not some new form of domesticity, since that is merely a new form of enslavement. The purpose is self-expression—and, in particular, the pursuit of pleasure that is self-enhancing, though forbidden by the social norms." The enemy, then, is our past and its moral code that prohibits pleasure since "pleasure is, in itself, morally neutral. The attempt to stamp out any form of it, or any particular means to obtaining it, is therefore a gross violation of individual liberty, and an act of repression."[36]

This "violation" of individual liberty is seen as even more egregious now that people have begun basing their entire identities on sexuality and sexual desires. People who identify with the LGBTQ community consider themselves a "sexual minority," but Antonio Hortelano critiques the implication of defining oneself by sexual desire, noting, "It is one thing to try to free ourselves from sexual taboos or irrational prohibitive obsessions and quite a different thing to be obsessed with the idea that the only important and decisive thing in men's lives is sexuality."[37] Reich's vision of sexual release as an aspect of self-fulfillment that is vitally important has morphed

---

34. Taylor, *Sources of the Self*, 328.

35. Ibid., 329, quote from Diderot, *Supplement au Voyage de Bougainville*, in *Oeuvres Philosophiques* (Paris, France: Garnier, 1964), 476, "I don't know what this thing is you call religion, but I can only think badly of it, since it prevents you from tasting an innocent pleasure, to which nature, the sovereign mistress, invites us all; to give existence to one like you; . . . to do your duty towards a host who has given you a good welcome, and to enrich a nation, by bestowing upon it one subject more."

36. Scruton, "Is Sex Necessary?," 34–35.

37. Hortelano, "Sexual Revolution and the Family," 51–52.

into the idea that sexual desire is one of the most important aspects of self-identity.[38]

The Sexual Revolution's Eschatology

Just as the Enlightenment's eschatology of progress led from the "darkness" of intellectual tutelage to the "light" of moral independence, the sexual revolution's eschatology moves from the "darkness" of sexual repression into the "light" of unhindered sexual liberation. As we examine the eschatological perspective of the sexual revolution, we will see how the Enlightenment notion of progress is applied to sexuality and how the success of the revolution depends on escaping certain moral norms.

The Sexual Revolution's Vision of Progress

The sexual revolution is a story formed by Enlightenment autonomy and told through Romanticist expression. Intellectual "enlightenment" is accompanied by sexual "emancipation."[39] The eschatology at work in this story places the autonomous individual at the center of an epic battle, with forces of illegitimate authority arrayed against any sexual self-expression that does not conform to social norms. The "dark ages" are not the medieval times of ignorance but the centuries full of arcane and inexplicable restrictions placed on human sexuality. "Progress" is made as sexual restrictions are loosened and as criticism of various forms of sexual expression diminish.

While science and technology are the drivers of the Enlightenment eschatology, entertainment takes on the role of propelling society "forward" in matters related to sexuality. Consider, for example, the 1998 film *Pleasantville*, which encapsulates the eschatological vision of the sexual revolution with a beautifully artistic use of black-and-white and color film-making. The film tells the story of a brother and sister who travel back in time to the black-and-white, wholesome world of a 1958 television show. As the narrative progresses, the townspeople begin to awaken to their innermost sexual desires, and as a result they (and objects in town) shift

---

38. Jenell Williams Paris, *The End of Sexual Identity: Why Sex Is Too Important to Define Who We Are* (Downers Grove, IL: InterVarsity 2011), 10. Paris points out the irony of sex being much more than it used to be ("Sexual desire is now considered central to human identity, and sexual self-expression is seen by many to be essential for healthy personhood"), as well as much less than it used to be ("We're told that sex can be mere recreation . . . and sex is used for trivial purposes").

39. Rudolf Siebert, "The Frankfurt School: Enlightenment and Sexuality," in *The Sexual Revolution* (ed. Gregory Baum and John Coleman; Edinburgh, Scotland: T&T Clark, 1984), 27.

from black-and-white to color. The antagonists in the film are the men in power who see the changes as detrimental to society and seek to clamp down on the colorful influences—banning books, censoring music, and reestablishing moral and social norms. At the end of the film, the world is transformed from the antiseptic, wholesome 1950s into the colorful and life-giving expression of sexuality.

Pleasantville is a reverse take on the Christian story of creation, fall, and redemption. Whereas in the biblical story sin leads to a diminished life and spiritual death, in *Pleasantville* sin colors the world and leads to vibrancy and spiritual vitality. In one scene a young woman shows a bright red apple to a young man (yet uncolored) and encourages him to eat it. Partaking of the forbidden fruit brings life; abstaining is to choose to stay dull. The eschatology of the sexual revolution is clear; the light came on (or the color began!) when the repression of the 1950s was overcome by the "free love" of sexual gratification, which is the Enlightenment myth of progress (independence from divine revelation) applied to sexual behavior.

However, not all advocates of the sexual revolution believe in the connection between the Enlightenment vision of progress and the current drive for sexual liberation. For example, postmodern philosopher Michel Foucault counters the idea that the banishment or repression of sex once served an economic purpose of progress. Instead, Foucault sees sex as becoming linked to confession, with sex now releasing its fundamental secrets. "We demand that sex speak the truth," he writes, "and we demand that it tell us our truth, or rather, the deeply buried truth of that truth about ourselves which we think we possess in our immediate consciousness."[40]

Even here, in a passage by someone who eschews the Enlightenment's myth of progress, we see the hope attached to the sexual revolution; our sexuality can tell us something about ourselves deep inside. Once again we are back in the Age of Authenticity, with sexual expression playing a vital role in the discovering of one's true self. Thus, Foucault critiques the Enlightenment's arrogant eschatology even while he hints toward a similar trajectory of sexual fulfillment, only now the hope has become individualized.

One way the eschatology of sexual liberation has spread is by reducing sex to a matter of physical pleasure and severing its intrinsic connection

40. Michel Foucault, "Foucault Text: From The History of Sexuality," in *The Postmodern God: A Theological Reader*, Blackwell Readings in Modern Theology (ed. Graham Ward; Malden, MA: Blackwell, 1997), 131–32.

to procreation.[41] The moral good of contemporary times is not the ancient virtue of self-control or channeling of sexual expression into a relationship that will blossom into the life of the family but the enjoyment of consensual sex apart from traditional moral restraints.[42] Roger Scruton sums up how this eschatological perspective of liberation from repression reinforces the Enlightenment's doctrine of the autonomous individual at the center of human existence: "My pleasures are mine, and if you are forbidding them you are also oppressing me. . . . Self-gratification acquires the glamor and the moral kudos of a heroic struggle. For the 'me' generation, no way of acquiring a moral cause can be more gratifying. You become totally virtuous by being totally selfish."[43] The myth of progress that forms the eschatology of the sexual revolution goes beyond mere self-expression, however. It also leads to the transformation of what is considered beneficial for society. The norms of societal stability and the foundations of society's institutions are shaken by the revolution's upward trajectory.

The Sexual Revolution's Progression beyond Moral Norms

In the sexual revolution's eschatology, progress is not only measured by sidestepping longstanding social and sexual norms but also by society's no longer expecting people to live according to these moral norms. The seeds of this eschatological perspective are present in Reich's initial work, and they are most evident in his critique of monogamy in marriage. At one point Reich shares the example of a 35-year-old female who had been married for 18 years but was in a turbulent marriage with a man having an affair. She was manifesting adverse physical symptoms—such as palpitations, insomnia, irritability, and episodes of depression—but because of her moral standards, she had refused to pursue an adulterous relationship with a friend. Reich diagnoses her with a neurotic illness and attributes her symptoms to her sexual abstinence. After she had sex with her friend, Reich reports that "her neurotic complaints which were due to sexual stasis disappeared a short time later. She was capable of making this decision

41. E. J. Graff, "Retying the Knot," in *Same-Sex Marriage: Pro and Con, A Reader* (ed. Andrew Sullivan; New York: Random House, 2004), 137. The separation of sex from procreation in the public consciousness has led to the widespread acceptance of same-sex marriage, which E. J. Graff acknowledged would make the institution of marriage stand for something different from in the past, "sexual choice, for cutting the link between sex and diapers."

42. Michel Foucault, *The Use of Pleasure*, The History of Sexuality (vol. 2; New York: Vintage Books, 1990). The title of Foucault's work on sexuality demonstrates this shift toward the focus on pleasure.

43. Scruton, "Is Sex Necessary?," 36.

because of my successful attempt to eliminate her moral reservations."[44] In other words, the moral norm of monogamy and faithfulness in marriage must not stand in the way of the "progress" of sexual fulfillment.

As mentioned above, entertainment continues to be one of the primary drivers of societal change in morality—both reflecting and directing public consensus on what progress entails. Vice president Joe Biden was not off base in crediting the popular television comedies like *Will and Grace* (1998-2006) and *Modern Family* (2009-) for the public's rapid embrace of same-sex marriage.[45] Not surprisingly, equating the sexual revolution's "progress" with the subversion of moral norms shows up in historical examinations of pop culture and the books, movies, and television shows that have "pushed boundaries" regarding sexuality. Fred Kaplan sees the uncensored publication of D. H. Lawrence's *Lady Chatterley's Lover*, in 1959, as a landmark event that signaled the end of obscenity laws[46] and the corresponding reception of the birth control pill as a sign that women could now be, in the case of one advertisement, the mythical Greek princess Andromeda, "unfettered" from the chains that link sexual pleasure to procreation.[47]

Jennifer Keishin Armstrong's history of *The Mary Tyler Moore Show* (1970-77), a show hailed by critics as one of television's greatest situation comedies, tells the story of how the show is the bridge from *I Love Lucy* (1951-57) to HBO's *Girls* (2012-17), the latter of which is considered a feminist achievement for its portrayal of women, sex, nudity, and transgression of social taboos. The narrative tension Armstrong uses in telling the story of *Mary Tyler Moore* is how the show subtly challenged the sexual mores of the 1950s and 1960s in favor of looser restrictions in the 1970s.[48] For example, in the 1950s censors would not allow the cast of *I Love Lucy* to use the word *pregnant* on television ("with child" or "expecting" were acceptable

---

44. Reich, *Sexual Revolution*, 73.

45. Carolyn Bankoff, "Joe Biden Is 'Absolutely Comfortable' with Gay Marriage," *New York Magazine* (May 6, 2012), accessed September 25, 2015, http://nymag.com/daily/intelligencer/2012/05/biden-absolutely-comfortable-with-gay-marriage.html. Biden claimed *Will and Grace* "probably did more to educate the American public than almost anything anybody's done so far. And I think—people fear that which is different. Now they're beginning to understand."

46. Fred Kaplan, *1959: The Year Everything Changed* (Hoboken, NJ: John Wiley and Sons), 45-54.

47. Ibid., 229.

48. Jennifer Keishin Armstrong, *Mary and Lou and Rhoda and Ted: And All the Brilliant Minds Who Made the Mary Tyler Moore Show a Classic* (New York: Simon & Schuster, 2013). Peter Biskind's endorsement reads, "Jennifer Keishin Armstrong's deft weave of social history and sharp entertainment reporting explains how this revolutionary show made the world safe for Lena Dunham" (star of *Girls*).

substitutes).[49] In the 1960s shows like *The Dick Van Dyke Show* (1961-66) were required to keep the actors playing husbands and wives in separate beds,[50] but *The Mary Tyler Moore Show* showcased a single woman pursuing a career, and the show occasionally suggested she was sexually active.[51]

Armstrong's account of *Mary Tyler Moore* focuses on the show's understated, yet demonstrable "progressiveness" in matters pertaining to sexuality. The show's spin-off, *Rhoda* (1974-78), delved even further into matters once considered taboo (cohabitation, adultery, divorce),[52] and the Norman Lear sitcom *Maude* (1972-78) introduced the epitome of women's "progress" when the main character went through with an abortion.[53] The end of shows like *Rhoda* and *Maude* came during a social backlash in which religious people and politicians protested the disappearance of a family hour for wholesome entertainment, leading to a resurgence of "safer" entertainment like *Happy Days* (1974-84).[54]

Nevertheless, the sexual revolution is seen ultimately triumphing, as Armstrong concludes the book by hailing contemporary shows like HBO's *Girls,* with its flagrant nudity and coarse language, whose first episode referenced *Mary Tyler Moore.*[55] In this historical account of a classic television show, all the necessary elements of the sexual revolution's eschatology are present. There are "repressive" standards of morality in the past, a courageous group's rejection of moral norms, the "progress" of transgressing boundaries, the heroic fight for "freedom" over against religious opposition, and the success of removing the sexual norms that once guided society so that nothing is really "shocking" anymore.

According to the sexual revolution's eschatology, questioning or countering sexual norms is the way "progress" is achieved, which is perhaps why abstinence education continues to be controversial in public schools. Without any moral standard to which to appeal, parents and teachers who oppose abstinence curriculum do so on the basis of a utilitarian approach (teenagers will have sex anyway, so they might as well make the best of it) or a liberationist mind-set (abstinence is not a virtuous choice of exercising

49. Lucille Ball, *Love Lucy* (New York: G. P. Putnam's Sons), 217.

50. Armstrong, *Mary and Lou and Rhoda and Ted*, 14-15.

51. Ibid., 172-73. Armstrong mentions the show's subtle nods to the character of Mary Richards using birth control or being out all night.

52. Ibid., 221.

53. Ibid., 176.

54. Ibid., 224-33.

55. Ibid., 292.

self-control but rather a pitiful position that damages one's humanity).[56] Absent from the discussion is any teleological purpose for sex beyond temporary self-gratification.

The social unit most responsible for passing moral norms from one generation to another is the family. For this reason "progress," according to the sexual revolution, goes hand in hand with the subversion of the family, redefining the father-mother-child unit around some other union and declaring all family structures essentially to be equal in dignity. In the 1940s and 1950s, Reich saw the family as an obstacle to sexual progress, reproducing itself by "crippling people sexually" and preserving sexual repression, while simultaneously reinforcing the patriarchal structure that keeps men in control of the world.[57] Today the sexual revolution has opened the door to ever-expanding combinations of relationships considered "family,"[58] and fewer children belong to homes where they are raised by their biological mothers and fathers.[59]

Meanwhile, the words of G. K. Chesterton seem more prophetic than ever, "This triangle of truisms, of father, mother, and child, cannot be destroyed; it can only destroy those civilizations which disregard it."[60] The family may be an obstacle to the goals of the sexual revolution, but as a foundational pillar of society, it will remain remarkably resilient, even when society seeks to redefine it.

---

56. Reich, *Sexual Revolution*, 108. Reich described abstinence as "dangerous and absolutely deleterious to health," leading to horrible neuroses that keep people from sexual fulfillment later in life.

57. Ibid., 82.

58. Elizabeth Brake, *Minimizing Marriage: Marriage, Morality, and the Law* (London, UK: Oxford University Press, 2012), 157. Elizabeth Brake proposes the legal recognition of polyamorous relationships as a way of "denormalizing" heterosexual monogamy as the ideal way of life. Her "minimal marriage" refers to individuals having "legal marital relationships with more than one person, reciprocally or asymmetrically, themselves determining the sex and number of parties, the type of relationship involved, and which rights and responsibilities to exchange with each."

59. Gretchen Livingston, "Less than Half of U.S. Kids Today Live in a 'Traditional' Family," Pew Research Center (December 22, 2014), accessed June 3, 2015, http://www.pewresearch.org/fact-tank/2014/12/22/less-than-half-of-u-s-kids-today-live-in-a-traditional-family. According to Pew Research, "Less than half (46%) of U.S. kids younger than 18 years of age are living in a home with two married heterosexual parents in their first marriage. This is a marked change from 1960, when 73 percent of children fit this description, and 1980, when 61 percent did." Pew Research further states, "Less than half of U.S. kids today live in a 'traditional' family."

60. G. K. Chesterton, *The Superstition of Divorce* (New York: John Lane, 1920), 66.

A Missionary Encounter with the Sexual Revolution's Eschatology

How, then, do Christians engage in a missionary encounter with people who believe in the progress offered by the sexual revolution? We cannot merely follow the well-worn political paths of liberals and conservatives, paths that have appeared after decades of political wrangling. Instead, we must faithfully embody the gospel in our own times by discerning between the good and righteous creational design of sexuality and our own misdirected rebellion.[61] This means that we will live at the crossroads of commitment to the biblical story and the world's idolatry, both affirming God's good intentions for sex and disavowing its human distortions. We should expect this posture of affirmation and rejection to challenge both conservative and liberal assumptions of sex.

In what follows, we examine three fruitful ways to challenge the sexual revolution's eschatology with a Christian vision of the future. The first is to put sex in its proper place, over against the oversized hope society places in sexual expression and over against the problematic silence of the church when confronted with its internal complicity. Second, we must ensure that the gospel we proclaim focuses on human satisfaction in Jesus Christ, not on self-gratification that makes religious observance merely a means to self-fulfillment. Third, the church must expose the myth of sexual progress and showcase the fallout from our culture's rebellion against God's good design. Finally, the church must be open to people who have been wounded and affected by the sexual revolution's failure to deliver hope and healing.

Put Sex in Its Place

To "put sex in its place" means Christians will need to take sexual sin *more* seriously than our culture and take sexuality, in general, *less* seriously than our culture. Concerning the first angle, taking sexual sin more seriously, one temptation for Christians confronted with sexual immorality is to relegate discussion of sexual matters to the realm of privacy, thus adopting a Victorian-era silence about such matters. However, this privatization of sexuality exacerbates the problem. When we fail to discuss matters related to marriage, family, sexuality, and divorce, we reinforce the idea that these are personal institutions and private troubles—not something that is the church's business at all. If the church does not take sexual sin among its

61. Bartholomew and Goheen, *Living at the Crossroads*, 136.

members seriously, how can it speak prophetically to the world about God's good design for sexuality?

The silence of the Christian church with regard to sexual sin among its own members communicates the societal myth that sexuality can be casual and free of consequences. By failing to take sexual sin seriously, the church minimizes the significance of sexual choices, as if a person can cultivate a virtuous character despite harboring sin in this one sphere of life. However, the idea that the human person can wall off this aspect of character misses the bigger picture of how discipleship takes place.

Growth in holiness and the pursuit of Christian virtues form Christians into people with God-honoring habits of holiness. Regularly giving into vice is problematic, no matter how much the Age of Authenticity promotes self-expression. As N. T. Wright points out, "The more someone behaves in a way that is damaging to self or to others, the more 'natural' it will both seem and actually be. Spontaneity, left to itself, can begin by excusing bad behavior and end by congratulating vice."[62] In other words, the church today that excuses or minimizes bad behavior will be the church tomorrow that congratulates the same. Silence toward sin will become celebration of sin.

Concerning the second angle, taking sexuality in general *less* seriously than the culture, Christians must counter the prevailing ideology that bases identity on sexual attraction. The Christian view of the person is one of dignity. We must not reduce our human self-understanding and self-expression to sexual urges. Neither should we consent to the often-unstated assumption of society that human flourishing is, in some way, dependent on sexual relationships. Richard Hays argues that the biblical witness undercuts cultural obsession with sexual fulfillment, "Scripture (along with many subsequent generations of faithful Christians) bears witness that lives of freedom, joy, and service are possible without sexual relations. . . . Never within the canonical perspective does sexuality become the basis for defining a person's identity or finding meaning and fulfillment in life."[63]

On the one hand, when the world claims sexual expression is at the heart of what it means to be human, the church must counter this reductionist vision of humanity by appealing to a higher dignity for the human person. On the other hand, when the world reduces sexual expression to

62. Wright, *After You Believe*, 156.
63. Hays, *Moral Vision*, 390–91.

meaningless and casual acts, the church must counter this reductionist view of sex by appealing to the mystery and transcendence of the sexual union between man and woman. Christians cannot embrace the myth of casual sex because we believe the sexual union does not culminate in itself but points beyond the conjugal act to the true spiritual union of Christ and his church. N. T. Wright places the Christian view of sexuality within the grand narrative of Scripture, observing,

> The male/female relationship, woven so centrally into the story of creation in Genesis 1 and 2, is not an accidental or a temporary phenomenon, but is, rather, symbolic of the fact that creation itself carries God-given life and procreative possibility within it. Even to consider the question from this angle poses a sharp contrast to the way in which, in our present culture, sexual activity has become almost completely detached from the whole business of building up communities and relationships, and has degenerated simply into a way of asserting one's right to choose one's own pleasure in one's own way. To put it starkly: instead of being a sacrament, sex has become a toy.[64]

Wright critiques society's cheapening of sexual acts, and so must we, even while we question the elevation of sexual identity to such a position of prominence. To see sexual acts as the most important aspect of human pleasure, the fulfillment of which becomes the basis for human flourishing, is to make an idol out of a good gift of God. The culture makes sexual pleasure an idol and casual sex a right, and so the church has the paradoxical task of undercutting society's exalted hope in sex while also heightening the seriousness of sex's spiritual reality.[65]

Proclaim Fulfillment in Christ, Not in Sexual Expression

In a world deeply influenced by the sexual revolution's eschatology, Christians must contextualize the preaching of the gospel in a way that emphasizes the difference between the sexual revolution's "good news" of self-fulfillment through sexual expression and Christianity's good news

64. Wright, *Simply Christian*, 232.

65. Russell Moore, "Man, Woman, and the Mystery of Christ: An Evangelical Protestant Perspective," *Touchstone: A Journal of Mere Christianity* (March/April 2015): 23, says, "In the Evangelical Christian perspective . . . there is no such thing as a casual sexual encounter at all, when we are speaking in spiritual terms. . . . The sexual act, mysteriously, forms a real and personal union."

of the ultimate fulfilling of all human longings in the person and work of Jesus Christ. Christians have good news to offer in an age where "gospel" is "self-actualization." After all, the idea of discovering and being true to oneself can become exhausting. The sexual revolution's narrative paints a picture of exhilaration in casting off society's restraints and expressing one's inner essence, but the initial euphoria of salvation through self-expression wears off, and the resulting society is plagued with doubt, where people constantly wonder if their "true self" is good enough. Contemporary culture's hymns that praise the freedom of self-expression (for example, "Let It Go" from Disney's *Frozen*) ignore the relational cost of such freedom, a freedom that begins to resemble a prison of loneliness rather than a richly layered life of relationship.

In response to this cultural narrative, we must proclaim the gospel that comes from outside ourselves, no matter how countercultural this may seem. When people in today's culture discover how exhausting it is to try to be "true to themselves," when looking further and further inward eventually shows them they do not have the resources to transform their own lives, the church must be ready to break in with good news that life change is not mustered up from inside but rather granted through grace from outside.[66]

At the same time, the church is to challenge the narrative that happiness is found solely in self-expression. The biblical view of the self is that humans are broken, twisted, and sinful. The self is something that needs redemption, not expression. This redemption takes place within a redeemed community, not as spiritual individuals piecing together their own strategies for personal spirituality and fulfillment but walking together with people who shape and form them into the image of Christ. In the future Christians will need to be clearer than ever regarding the public purpose of marriage,[67] the gift of celibate singleness,[68] and God's good and wise design for sexuality.

---

66. Michael Horton, *Christless Christianity: The Alternative Gospel of the American Church* (Grand Rapids: Baker Books, 2012), 58, says, "Liberals and revivalists both de-emphasize God's transcendence and tend to see God's Word as something that wells up within a person rather than something that comes to a person from outside."

67. Eric Teetsel and Andrew Walker, *Marriage Is* (Nashville: Broadman and Holman, 2015), Kindle Loc 336 of 2136. Teetsel and Walker state, "Where marriage thrives, people flourish; where marriage crumbles, people suffer. Therefore no church can claim to love its neighbor, to be salt and light, to seek the good of the city around it, yet fail to address the state of marriage and the family."

68. Dietrich Bonhoeffer, *Letters and Papers from Prison* (London, UK: Fontana, 1953), 163, said, "[T]he essence of chastity is not the suppression of lust but the total orientation of one's life toward a goal."

Expose the Falsehood of the Sexual Revolution's "Progress"

Because the sexual revolution's eschatological trajectory of progress is false, it will fail to deliver on its promises. Just as the Enlightenment myth of progress has begun to show its cracks and strains, the sexual revolution has begun to do the same.

Recent researchers have been focusing on the breakdown of the nuclear family, and statisticians on the right and the left now question the wisdom of pursuing policies that make this cultural breakdown more acceptable.[69] When no-fault divorce became the norm in American society, many assumed it was better for two parents who do not get along to separate and remain civil than to stay together in a tense home. The statistics, however, now show the opposite. What was promoted under the guise of scientific research and common sense has now been shown to be disastrous.[70] Meanwhile, the glorification of single motherhood, expressed in the idea that this life choice is just as acceptable a choice as any other, has been shown to be false. Some who blasted Vice President Dan Quayle for criticizing the television show's promotion of single motherhood as a vocational choice in *Murphy Brown* (1988–98) have now admitted that Quayle was right. Nothing compares with intact homes with children being raised by their mothers and fathers.[71]

The church will be unable to cultivate a culture of healing and hope amid the false worldview of the sexual revolution until Christians are clear that the utopian ideals of "progress" lead to ruin, not peace. Russell Moore asks the right questions:

> Despite the promise of women's empowerment, the Sexual Revolution has given us the reverse. Is it really an advance for women that the average adolescent male has seen a kaleidoscope of images of women sexually exploited and humiliated

---

69. For an overview of recent research on family structures in the United States, see Robert I. Lerman and W. Bradford Wilcox, *For Richer, For Poorer: How Family Structures Economic Success in America* (Institute for Family Studies), 2015, n.p. [cited 12 September 2015]. Online: http://www.aei.org/wp-content/uploads/2014/10/IFS-ForRicherForPoorer-Final_Web.pdf.

70. Elizabeth Marquardt, *Between Two Worlds: The Inner Lives of Children and Divorce* (New York: Crown Publishers, 2005), 169, 189.

71. Isabel Sawhill, "20 Years Later, It Turns out Dan Quayle was Right about Murphy Brown and Unmarried Moms," *Washington Post* (May 25, 2012), n.p. [cited 23 July 2015]. Online: https://www.washingtonpost.com/opinions/20-years-later-it-turns-out-dan-quayle-was-right-about-murphy-brown-and-unmarried-moms/2012/05/25/gJQAsNCJqU_story.html. Sawhill, of the Brookings Institute, admitted Dan Quayle was right when she saw the increasing number of single-parent homes and their relation to poverty.

> in pornography? Is it really empowerment to have more and more women economically at the mercy of men who leave them and their children, with no legal recourse? The adolescent girl facing the pressure to perform sex acts on her boyfriend, or else lose him, what is this but the brutal patriarchy of a Bronze Age warlord? All of these things empower men to pursue a Darwinian fantasy of the predatory alpha-male in search of nothing but power, prestige, and the next orgasm. That's not exactly a revolution.[72]

Just as we must puncture the Enlightenment myth of progress with the preponderance of evidence that religiosity worldwide is not declining, so also we must showcase the sexual revolution's failed social experiments. We do ourselves no favors by ignoring the fallout from this false eschatology. Instead, we must have the confidence to pose good questions to those who trust in the sexual revolution's vision of the good life.

Create a Haven of Human Flourishing

The challenge for Christians is that we occupy a cultural moment in time in which the sexual revolution promotes the freedom to express oneself sexually as a major aspect of human flourishing. In contrast, the Christian virtues of chastity or purity are seen not merely as old-fashioned or dated but rather as repressive and harmful to the human psyche. To tell someone not to act on certain sexual desires is to tell them not to be authentic, to deny who they are deep down. In order to respond to this critique, Christians must be equipped to do more than simply stand against the sexual revolution; we must cultivate a different kind of culture, with different assumptions, different expectations, and a deeper vision of "authenticity."

In the meantime, part of the compassionate response required of the church is to cultivate a haven of human flourishing, devoted to God's design for sexuality, marriage, and the family. This creation of a counterculture must not only be a prophetic word against the sexual revolution in society but must also welcome those who have been wounded and betrayed by the failed promises of the revolution.

In a society casting off sexual restraint, we can expect to encounter people who have been wounded by the actions of others. In this worldview

72. Russell Moore, *Onward: Engaging the Culture without Losing the Gospel* (Nashville: B&H, 2015), 171–72.

sexual gratification becomes the good for which everything, including spouse and children and happiness, must be sacrificed. The church's response must be to pick up the pieces left in the wake of authenticity's tidal wave of sadness. When "being true to oneself" tramples everything else, broken hearts litter the path.

A church community that exists as a haven for refugees from the sexual revolution is one of the strongest elements of our response to the sexual revolution. Richard Hays encourages Christians to pursue a prophetic, compassionate response, "We live, then, as a community that embraces sinners as Jesus did, without waiving God's righteousness. . . . In the midst of a culture that worships self-gratification, and in a church that often preaches a false Jesus who panders to our desires, those who seek the narrow way of obedience have a powerful word to speak."[73] Of course, the church as a haven for wounded and sinful people will only be as strong as the church's eschatological vision—recognizing we live now in light of our future. The imagery used in Scripture to refer to the future is one of marriage and new creation, the marriage supper of the Lamb (Revelation 19) and the new world being born (Romans 8).

Summary

In conclusion, the sexual revolution advocates for an eschatological viewpoint that opposes Christian eschatology at various points; it refashions the purpose of life as self-discovery and self-expression; it casts sexual restraint and moral norms as chains from which humans need liberation; it uses technological advances and the influence of entertainment to reshape society's thought on what constitutes progress and what makes a family; and it uses the power of the state to marginalize people who dissent from the cultural orthodoxy. In order for a missionary encounter to occur with a society impacted by the sexual revolution, Christians must embrace eschatological discipleship—the process by which we recognize and reject the sexual revolution's rival conception of time—and then demonstrate in our corporate witness (through words and deeds) how the reality of fulfillment in finding one's identity in Christ vastly supersedes the self-gratification of sexual liberation.

73. Hays, *Moral Vision*, 430.

CHAPTER 8

Christianity and Consumerism

> The third rival eschatology in North American culture concerns the story of consumerism and the journey from poverty to wealth, or from dissatisfaction in "not having" to the satisfaction of having all one can ask. The most difficult task we face with consumerism is seeing it because this outlook, more than the Enlightenment and the sexual revolution, undergirds so many of our actual practices in life. These practices shape us into people who adopt a consumerist eschatology. In this section we attempt to form a definition of *consumerism*, examine consumerism's impact on how people conceive of their identities, seek to discern the consumerist eschatology, and then offer a Christian response.

Defining *Consumerism*

Consumerism as a term serves as an umbrella that encompasses several aspects of contemporary society's worldview. In this section we look at a consumer culture and the differences between consumerism and consumption, as well as the characteristics of consumerism.

A Consumer Culture of Commoditization

Speaking of a culture as consumer is a way of getting to the heart of consumption and what consumption represents. In most cases it refers to a society where cultural objects have become commoditized; that is, they have a perceived value outside the worth of the object itself. Vincent Miller describes "consumer societies" as those in which "consumption plays an important role in establishing social identity and solidarity. These tend to be marked by high levels of Consumerism because the consumption of commodities is linked to such fundamental social functions."[1]

1. Vincent Miller, *Consuming Religion: Christian Faith and Practice in a Consumer Culture* (New York: Bloomsbury Academic, 2005), 30.

Don Slater places this commoditization within a context where "the relation between lived culture and social resources . . . is mediated through markets."[2] A culture in which the markets take on this kind of status leads to "continuous self-creation through the accessibility of things which are themselves presented as new, modish, faddish or fashionable, always improved and improving."[3] Slater believes unending consumption has brought about the most profound secularization of the modern world, stating, "If there is no principle restricting who can consume what, there is also no principled constraint on what can be consumed: all social relations, activities, and objects can in principle be exchanged as commodities."[4] The core of a consumer culture, then, is this tendency to commoditize anything. A consumer culture in which everything can become a commodity reinforces the idea that nothing has intrinsic value. We find value in whatever is *useful* to us, not in what it is itself.

One of the results of a consumer culture is the tendency to commoditize relationships, to consider them in "transactional terms." We have seen how the sexual revolution's emphasis on fulfillment and self-expression leads to a transformed understanding of the role of marriage and how it must help people "find themselves" and be the kind of people they are called to be. The consumer culture compounds this problem, leading us no longer to consider friendship or marriage as relationships with intrinsic value but as opportunities to have our own needs satisfied. When they no longer fulfill their function, we put our energy and efforts into other relationships that are considered to be "a better use of our resources."[5]

In politics and economics the effect of consumerism is that human activity becomes primarily about labor, product creation, satisfying of the needs of other consumers. Newbigin claims the modern concept of "built-in obsolescence" indicates the consumer cycle of production and consumption, which minimizes the need to create something that will endure. Instead the cycle encourages politicians to debate the best way to keep the cycle going and keep the largest number of people satisfied. Within this environment, he says, "Questions of ultimate purpose are excluded from

---

2. Don Slater, *Consumer Culture and Modernity* (Cambridge, MA: Polity, 1997), 8.

3. Ibid., 10. One could also say that consumer culture is a natural result of the Enlightenment view of progress, now applied to fashion and what is new versus what is old.

4. Ibid., 27.

5. Wilkens and Sanford, *Hidden Worldviews*, 51.

the public world."[6] In other words, the more we focus on the satisfaction of perceived human needs, the less we are able to see beyond this world to spiritual needs and questions of human significance.

Consumerism Versus Consumption

In reacting against a consumer culture, some might find it easy to slip into what is essentially a dualist understanding of the world in which the created order and the things we consume are seen as dangerous in and of themselves. Accordingly, some might embrace an ascetic philosophy that rejects the materials of this world as inherently evil rather than accepting the created world as good, though with the potential for misdirection. To avoid this pitfall, we should take care to distinguish between consumerism as a mind-set and consumption as an activity, while nevertheless recognizing how consumption as a habit can lead to consumerism as a philosophy. The consumption of goods is not wrong; it is necessary for human survival. The concern is when consumption reinforces a set of presuppositions about the material world, beliefs we never question or critique.[7]

One of the most potent presuppositions is the valuing of something apart from its context. Miller writes, "Our systems of labor, commodity exchange, the single-family home, marketing, and advertising have profound impacts on the way we live our lives and how we relate to culture. . . . Our countless acts of consumption and evaluation of commodities large and small train us daily to value things out of their contexts."[8] The result of valuing something out of its context, without giving thought to where it came from or where it will go once we have finished receiving benefit from it, is "alienation."[9] We think of things as they "are," rather than what they have been or what they will be. We make our purchases, put them to use, and once the purchases no longer satisfy, they can be discarded.

---

6. Newbigin, *Foolishness to the Greeks*, 30; and Frederica Mathewes-Green, *The Illumined Heart* (Brewster, Mass., Paraclete Press, 2001), 34. It is not only in the public discourse that consumerism pushes questions of ultimate purpose to the side. Orthodox writer Frederica Mathewes-Green comments on how individuals also turn to consumerism to avoid dealing with the difficult questions of life, "When we face eternal questions like 'Why is the world so messed up?' and 'How am I part of the problem?' we have a reduced pack of available answers. The quick answer, 'Buy something and forget about it,' is supremely seductive."

7. Skye Jethani, *The Divine Commodity: Discovering a Faith Beyond Consumer Christianity* (Grand Rapids: Zondervan, 2009), 12.

8. Miller, *Consuming Religion*, 71.

9. Jethani, *Divine Commodity*, 41.

This approach to consumption reinforces the ethos of consumerism, defined by Laura Hartman as "a collection of attitudes, values, and cultural constructs—that places great value on shopping and consumption, such that consumption defines the parameters of the good life and the ultimate goals of the human, and concomitant lack of attention to the moral dimension of consumption."[10] To put it another way, consumerism takes something inherently good and necessary (consumption) and then "absolutizes" it to the point that we believe we can find fulfillment by accumulating wealth—our needs can be satisfied by what we consume.[11]

Characteristics of Consumerism

If consumerism is the ethos and consumption is the practice, how can we tell when we have adopted the ethos of consumer culture? Craig Bartholomew offers three characteristics of a consumer culture, and each of these characteristics help us recognize what our consumption represents. It is not the *act* of consumption that makes for a consumer culture but rather what that act *means* and how it is interpreted.

First, Bartholomew claims that, in a consumer culture "the core values of the culture derive from consumption rather than the other way around."[12] In other words, we no longer consume something according to what our culture values, but we value things according to what our culture consumes. A second characteristic of a consumer culture is the privatization of society, following from the Enlightenment's vision of autonomy and the sexual revolution's vision of family. Further, Bartholomew states, "Freedom is equated with individual choice and private life."[13] The reversal is also true, that limitation of individual choices or questioning our private moral decisions is tantamount to robbing us of freedom.

Bartholomew's third characteristic deserves further attention. It is the idea of supply and demand where "needs are unlimited and insatiable."[14] One could mistakenly interpret this characteristic as referring to shallow people who have a shallow attachment to things earthly, but in a consumer

10. Laura M. Hartman, *The Christian Consumer: Living Faithfully in a Fragile World* (New York: Oxford University Press, 2011), 6.

11. Wilkens and Sanford, *Hidden Worldviews*, 45.

12. Craig Bartholomew, "Christ and Consumerism: An Introduction," in *Christ and Consumerism: A Critical Analysis of the Spirit of the Age* (ed. Craig Bartholomew and Thorsten Moritz; Crownhill, UK: Paternoster, 2000), 6.

13. Ibid., 8.

14. Ibid., 9.

culture the desire itself is not a shallow demand to receive products in order to be fulfilled. The desire itself is the source of joy.[15] The "insatiable" aspect becomes part of the appeal, like someone who is well fed and yet hungrily looking forward to the next meal. Once needs are multiplied (as well as products to fulfill them), we have moved into a consumer society of commodification, and consumers are rewarded for wanting more and more things, whether they originally saw a need for them.[16]

While Craig Bartholomew offers three characteristics of consumer culture, Craig Gay narrows his understanding to two fundamental commitments. Gay's first commitment corresponds largely with Bartholomew's second characteristic (about freedom redefined within the framework of individual choice and private life). He describes this commitment as one of "self-creation" and "autonomous self-definition," stating:

> We are told today that we are, or at least ought to be, entirely free to make whatever we would of ourselves; and so long as our projects of self-construction do not obviously interfere with anyone else's, we must not be hindered by tradition, custom, law or outmoded notions of 'human nature' as we fashion our own identities. This commitment amounts finally to a repudiation of the belief in moral order.[17]

The final part of Gay's analysis in that paragraph is what leads to the second fundamental commitment, the desire to shrink "the range of possible human aspirations to those circumscribed by secular existence." He explains, "We may construct ourselves entirely as we see fit, so we are also told today, as long as we remain within the confines of this world and within the limits of the here and now."[18] According to this characteristic of consumerism, then, we are limited to a view of the world that keeps us from approaching horizons of transcendence.

---

15. Miller, *Consuming Religion*, 144.

16. Paul Louis Metzger, *Consuming Jesus: Beyond Race and Class Divisions in a Consumer Church* (Grand Rapids: Eerdmans, 2007), 40.

17. Craig M. Gay, "Sensualists without Heart: Contemporary Consumerism in Light of the Modern Project," in *The Consuming Passion: Christianity and the Consumer Culture* (ed. Rodney Clapp; Downers Grove, IL: IVP, 1998), 20.

18. Ibid., 20.

Consumerism's Appeal to Identity

Just as the sexual revolution links sexual fulfillment to identity, so also does consumerism, although in the latter worldview humans are perceived as successful when they are self-made, self-sufficient individuals. In short, consumerism provides a system of meaning through which we interpret ourselves as individuals, define ourselves by the brands we purchase, and then assess our value in terms of economic and social status or whatever we are able to accomplish in the workforce.

A System of Meaning

As seen above, consumption is not the same thing as consumerism, for consumption is necessary for human survival. The turn from consumption to consumerism lies in what Jean Baudrillard refers to as the "system of meaning" one attaches to one's consumption.[19] Consumerism's impact on our identity takes place when the system of meaning we have assigned to our consumption begins to define us. The result of this move is a subtle process of dehumanization.[20] Slater points out how this affects the individual, explaining, "Society comes to dominate the individual, not least through the material world of objects and interests, which are now essential not merely for meeting needs but for being or finding a self."[21] Thus, although in contemporary society the freedom to consume appears to be a terrific example of the free, self-sufficient individual making autonomous choices, the reality is often less attractive, as the consumer culture begins to enslave us to our own desires and invented needs, subjecting us to social scrutiny and interpersonal competition.

The system of meaning we assign to our consumption is often associated with the brands we consume. "Brands are the new religion," says Douglas Atkin, writing about customer loyalty.[22] Because of the identity-shaping impact of brands and purchases, shopping takes on an increasingly important role in helping people discover meaning and construct

---

19. Jean Baudrillard, *Jean Baudrillard: Selected Writings* (ed. Mark Poster, trans. Jacques Mourrain et al.; Palo Alto, Calif: Stanford University Press, 2001), 49.

20. Mathewes-Green, *Illumined Heart*, 32–33. Orthodox writer Frederica Mathewes-Green describes this dehumanization as being rooted in search for meaning and significance in what we consume rather than who we are. The result of such dehumanization is a downward spiral where "self-esteem is wrecked by self-indulgence, because a million self-indulgences add up to a person you can't respect very much."

21. Slater, *Consumer Culture and Modernity*, 83.

22. Douglas Atkin, *The Culting of Brands: When Customers Become True Believers* (New York: Portfolio, 2004), xi.

their own identities.[23] Shopping becomes less about consumption itself and more about the meaning and significance we find in that consumption.

A System of Self-Expression

When studying the sexual revolution, we saw that the Age of Authenticity describes the purpose of life as discovering and expressing one's unique essence, over against societal restraints that demand conformity. When applying this pursuit of authenticity to a consumer culture, we see how people are likely to construct and express their own identities through what they buy. Jethani states, "Individuality is the new conformity."[24] Choice is a powerful factor in a consumer society because more choices provide more ways for consumers to demonstrate their uniqueness.

How does this emphasis on self-expression take place? In a consumer culture, desire is a powerful force expressed in seduction and misdirection. In the first case *seduction* does not refer to a customer's gravitating to one particular object; it refers to a customer's feeling the desire for multiple, endless choices of objects. Miller observes, "Seduction spurs consumption by prolonging desire and channeling its inevitable disappointments into further desires."[25] In the second case *misdirection* refers to marketing and advertising strategies that associate a product with needs or desires that are not related to the product. The marketing tactic leads consumers to see the consumption of a product as a way to fulfill more profound needs.[26] With seduction and misdirection a consumer society is an intricate web of methods to make meaning, with life reinterpreted as a means of self-expression and self-fulfillment.[27]

Consumerist Eschatology

Tracing the eschatological outlook of a consumer culture is a difficult task, primarily because no one point in time exists to which consumer society can point. The Enlightenment's eschatology associates the turning point of

---

23. Jethani, *Divine Commodity*, 53.

24. Ibid., 126.

25. Miller, *Consuming Religion*, 109.

26. Ibid.

27. Oliver O'Donovan, *Begotten or Made? Human Procreation and Medical Technique* (New York: Oxford University Press, 1984). A consumer culture radically affects humans' most intimate relationships. Once the family is reenvisioned as a means of self-expression, people are likely to see children as the way to express and fulfill themselves and not according to their own intrinsic value. Oliver O'Donovan believes a danger exists of seeing children as something to be manufactured, not created, something we make, not beget.

history with the dawn of the age of reason and the journey out of the "dark ages." The sexual revolution's eschatology tracks closely beside the Enlightenment, although there seems to be a clear acceleration in the 1960s when the moral consensus of the early and middle years of the twentieth century began to fall apart. With consumerism we might assume the eschatological viewpoint concerns the conditions of poverty in past generations and the promise of abundant wealth in the future. Yet there still seems to be no particular turning point in world history, a climactic moment of before and after or any event after which nothing will ever be the same again.

Christians should not be surprised to discover, considering its high priority on individual autonomy, that consumerism's eschatology is grounded less in the events of world history and more in the story line of an individual's pursuit of wealth accumulation.[28] There are, of course, collective elements of a consumer calendar (as will be explored below), but overall a consumer culture may best be seen as a radical individualizing of personal eschatology. Furthermore, consumerism's individualistic eschatology may be the only idea still sustaining the Enlightenment myth of progress. Christopher Lasch believes "the incorporation of the masses into the culture of abundance" is what has enabled the Enlightenment concept of progress to survive "the rigors of the twentieth century."[29] Consumerism, then, is a radical individualization of eschatology that serves as a pillar holding up the overarching Enlightenment eschatology of progress for a secular society.

The Consumerist Ordering of Society's Calendar

The eschatology of consumerism reveals itself at two levels: ritualistic and individual. The interplay between these two levels is instructive for our present purposes. Medieval times were filled with holy days and feasts commemorating saints and festivals. Today the calendar is structured around consumerism. Thanksgiving is the precursor to Black Friday and Cyber Monday sales, carrying us through the shopping season of Christmas, to all sorts of exercise and dieting offers in January (which is a purge of consumerist excess, but even the purge is sold to us in consumer terms), to Valentine's Day, Mother's Day, Father's Day, Memorial Day, and Labor Day

---

28. Gay, "Sensualists without Heart," 20. Craig M. Gay sums up the shrinking eschatological horizon within consumerism, writing, "Our culture invites us to locate the sum total of human happiness here and now and in the consumption of the fruits of the technological economy."

29. Christopher Lasch, *The True and Only Heaven: Progress and Its Critics* (New York: Norton, 1991), 78.

(which become less about what we are remembering and more about the kickoff and end of the summer season). These are the seasons, the rhythms that give shape to contemporary society. Note how most of these "holidays" are not "holy days" in the old sense but "shopping days" in the new sense. When the purpose of life is consumption, then time is refigured to help people consume more and better.

The consumerist eschatology for society is also seen in the words used in advertising copy. Pointing to the eschatological desire for the new world, advertisers rely on words such as *new*, *radical*, *innovative*, and *revolutionary*. Miller notes, "As we habitually turn to the future, apocalyptic expectation is absorbed into the confused quest of consumer desire."[30] The advertising copy serves the purpose of creating dissatisfaction with the current product owned by the consumer while simultaneously promising an improved experience that will *finally* satisfy the consumer's needs and desires. We should not overlook the eschatological dimension of marketing.

The Consumerist Interpretation of Individual Hope

Rituals help us see how consumerism plays out at the societal level, but we must go one more level down in order to get to the individual narrative, the calendar that influences the decisions people make. The individual narrative is that every person is on a journey from lack to plenty, from inauspicious beginnings to the "successful life" of wealth and recognition. This story shapes how we see the world and how we make decisions. The "before" is a relative state of poverty, and the "after" is financial security, seen in what has been consumed. Susan White sums up the story this way:

> If there is any overarching metanarrative that purports to explain reality in the late 20th century, it is surely the narrative of the free-market economy. In the beginning of this narrative is the self-made, self-sufficient human being. At the end of this narrative is the big house, the big car, and the expensive clothes. In the middle is the struggle for success, the greed, the getting-and-spending in a world in which there is no such thing as a free lunch. Most of us have made this so thoroughly "our story" that we are hardly aware of its influence.[31]

---

30. Miller, *Consuming Religion*, 132.
31. Susan White, "A New Story to Live By?" *Bible in TransMission* (Spring 1998): 3–4.

According to this narrative, an eschatological dimension exists in our purchases when we see ourselves on a ladder of success, moving higher and higher, depending on our abilities to acquire more stuff. Because stuff represents status, we measure our progress toward the eschatological hope of financial security and success by the status of things we have attained or are now able to afford.

Alan Storkey helps us see an eschatological dimension of consumer societies by differentiating between present-oriented consumption and future-oriented consumption. Present-oriented consumption is the hedonistic desire for maximum fulfillment now, no matter where the current purchases may leave us in the future. The result of this kind of consumption is, not surprisingly, debt. Future-oriented consumption is different because in this case the consumer is willing to forgo certain present satisfactions in light of the future hope of reward. Storkey explains:

> On this view, work is the means to the consumption end. It is negative utility that will yield a later positive reward. Economic life is just a calculated effort towards these ultimate consumption ends, a massive process of throughput. And, of course, this is what many people feel. The strain of work, of production, is often negative, even unbearable, were it not for the consumption rewards which eventually emerge. But more than this, we are trained to push the ends, the consumption rewards, even more into the future—a bigger house, a better job which will mean higher rewards, a smoother car, more holidays, a cruise, a good pension, a nice burial. The pressure towards the future is so powerful that there is no room for the present. . . . People are not able to live in the present, because the future with its ends and goals has so big a claim on them.[32]

Future-oriented consumption is the eschatological dimension of an individual consumerist. It is the willing surrender of present comforts because of the confidence that such sacrifice will lead to reward, which in this case is a big payoff. This surrender resembles Christian eschatology in that it inspires a person to self-denial in light of future reward, but it is a distortion of eschatology because the hope it places in front of the consumer

32. Alan Storkey, "Postmodernism Is Consumption," in *Christ and Consumerism: A Critical Analysis of the Spirit of the Age* (Crownhill, UK: Paternoster Press, 2000), 110.

continues to move forward like a carrot on a stick. As the consumer agrees to more and more discomfort in the present, the possibility of long-lasting joy shrinks.

The Consumerist Quest for Fulfillment

Another way the eschatology of consumerism reveals itself is in the individual's search for and acquiring of fulfillment in a commodity. "I once was lost but now am found," words from the old hymn "Amazing Grace," is about God's search for humanity. In a consumer society the words to the hymn would be, "I once was searching but now have found." However, the hymn line would need additional verses because in the consumer ethos the joy is not in *possessing* something but in *seeking* it. Unlike Augustine who speaks of the heart's being restless until it finds itself in God, the consumer enjoys the restless search. Restlessness has become a source of pleasure, which is the reason we are always second-guessing ourselves and our belongings and wondering if what we have is enough.[33]

The therapeutic understanding of sin and salvation, and the recasting of life as a journey—a quest for self-fulfillment, is the unstated element that drives along the narrative for many individuals in a consumer culture. The Enlightenment believes the solution to the problem is found in reason and science, and the sexual revolution believes the problems would be more manageable if only they found sexual self-fulfillment, but consumerism sees the solution as fulfillment found in the consumption of commodities. Because consumption is now the way of fulfilling certain psychological and social needs, it becomes a rival to other sources of significance, such as the community and religious adherence.[34]

Consumerism's Effect on Christianity

In considering a consumer culture, we do well to remind ourselves that we swim in this water. No doubt exists that the church in the West is affected by consumerism, even if Christians do not realize to what extent. When everything is commoditized, the church itself is refashioned into a place for delivering religious products and services rather than being seen as the people through whom God's transcendence challenges our shallow and superficial ways of life. In a consumerist society, worship becomes a means

33. Miller, *Consuming Religion*, 128.
34. Ibid., 88.

to an end (increasing satisfaction, albeit of the religious sense), and individualism hinders the church's ability to be a corporate witness to the gospel.

We inhabit this cultural world, and, unless we are called to a society or culture in which this kind of commoditization is less present or less prominent, we will continue to live in a consumer culture.[35] Still, Christians are not required to embrace a consumer worldview. Yes, we are consumers. We eat, make purchases, enjoy entertainment, dress ourselves, and join the common activity of a consumer culture, but living in a consumer culture and adopting a consumerist outlook on life are two different things, and we must be careful to discern the difference. Just as we live in a world deeply in debt to Enlightenment philosophy but reject the Enlightenment's rival vision of progress and just as we live in a sexualized culture that sees personal fulfillment as the goal of life but reject this rival vision of happiness, we must now distinguish between the current cultural setting and Christianity. Only in this way will we know how to engage in a "missionary encounter" in a consumerist world.

Recasting Christianity as a Means to Self-Fulfillment

Sociologists and psychologists do not shy away from speaking of consumerism as a rival religion that provides a way of life, as well as a vision of salvation through consumption. Stephen Miles claims the "parallel with religion is not an accidental one," primarily because of consumerism's prevalence and power on society. He says, "It is arguably *the* religion of the late twentieth century."[36] Thus, how does the consumer eschatology confront and conform our understanding of Christianity? Vincent Miller uses the metaphor of a railroad, illustrating, "The conflict between Christianity and consumer culture lacks the definitiveness of a head-on collision; rather it has about as much drama as a train switching tracks and going in a slightly different direction. This deflection is of a piece with consumer culture's capacity to exploit any narrative, belief, or value."[37]

---

35. Femi Bitrus Adeleye, *Preachers of a Different Gospel: A Pilgrim's Reflections on Contemporary Trends in Christianity* (Nairobi, Kenya: Hippo Books, 2011), 20. The promise of consumerist eschatology has infected even those cultures that one would expect to resist commoditization. In his trenchant critique of the "prosperity gospel" spreading throughout Africa, African leader Femi Bitrus Adeleye contrasts "the gospel of the cross" with the "gospel of champagne," the latter of which he sees as the call for "a lifestyle committed to gullible celebration and self-indulgence with pleasures opposed to kingdom values."

36. Stephen Miles, *Consumerism as a Way of Life* (London, UK: Sage, 1998), 2.

37. Miller, *Consuming Religion*, 108.

Rather than a head-on collision with Christianity, similar to the way the Enlightenment emphasis on reason collides with Christian views of divine revelation, or the way the sexual revolution's emphasis on self-fulfillment collides with Christian views of moral behavior, consumerism's confrontation with Christianity is subtler. It does not reject Christianity outright but rather recasts it. Perhaps the reason for the subtler confrontation is that many of the desires cultivated by consumerism resemble Christian forms of desire.

The way consumerism recasts Christianity is by turning the gospel into a commodity, something we believe because it is useful, not because it is true. The therapeutic purpose of life leads us, already formed by our search for self-fulfillment through consumption, to require of religion the same kind of freedom of choice and opportunity to have our needs met. Sri Lankan theologian Vinoth Ramachandra comments on how consumerist faith becomes a parody of true Christianity:

> What is promoted as "faith in God" often turns out, on closer inspection, to be a means for obtaining emotional security or material blessing in this life and an insurance policy for the next. This kind of preaching leaves the status quo untouched. It does not raise fundamental and disturbing questions about the assumptions on which people build their lives. It does not threaten the false gods in whose name the creation of God has been taken over; indeed it actually reinforces their hold on their worshippers.[38]

If Ramachandra is correct, then we would expect believers today to require the church's traditions—preaching, Bible study, fellowship, and outreach—to be justified on consumer terms. Unfortunately, when this takes place and value is found in what is immediately useful, churches begin to emphasize doctrines and practices that provide an immediate payoff. Neglected are the parts of Christian faith not viewed as immediately "practical," including the big story of Scripture and the attributes of God.[39]

Meanwhile, in churches that do retain their traditional emphases on preaching, Bible study, prayer, and so forth, the practitioners of these traditions recast their significance. No longer are spiritual disciplines or the

---

38. Ramachandra, *Gods that Fail*, 40.
39. Jethani, *Divine Commodity*, 41.

doctrines of salvation seen as valuable in and of themselves but in what they represent to the consumer who engages in them. Dallas Willard notes, "The consumer Christian is one who utilizes the grace of God for forgiveness or the services of the church for special occasions, but does not give his or her life and innermost thoughts, feelings, and intentions over to the kingdom of the heavens. Such Christians are not inwardly transformed and not committed to it."[40] Our involvement in church traditions and spiritual disciplines becomes a badge, a brand, something that can be applied within the realm of our own preferences but is usually divorced from the context in which they arose.

Segregating Christianity according to Consumer Preferences

Perhaps an even greater danger in the recasting of Christianity is the way consumerism divides the church and keeps it segregated. "[The consumerist spirit] cleverly shapes race and class divisions in the evangelical church and beyond, and it makes conquering these depersonalizing and dehumanizing forces increasingly difficult," writes Paul Louis Metzger, adding, "It divides churches along the lines of race and class."[41] Consumerism proves divisive for the church in multiple ways. It separates churches from their members (by creating a class of clergy who dispense religious goods as commodities), separates one church from another (by casting them as competitors in delivering the best goods and programs), and separates churches by race and class (by catering to the desires of one group over another).[42]

The socioeconomic divisions of the church are compounded by consumerism as well. Even wealthier churches that promote mercy ministry or social work as an antidote to consumerism (a way to give rather than consume) can miss the ways believers' social involvement is often infected by consumerist ideology. People are most likely to choose to be involved in ministries where they work alongside like-minded, upwardly mobile Christians who see their role as ministering *to* the poor rather than *with* or *alongside* the poor as participants of the same group.[43]

---

40. Dallas Willard, *The Divine Conspiracy: Rediscovering Our Hidden Life in God* (New York: Harper, 1998), 342.
41. Metzger, *Consuming Jesus*, 40.
42. Ibid., 135.
43. Ibid., 65.

Not surprisingly, homogeneity is the outcome when the values of consumerism dominate a church. As Jethani notes, "When given the choice, most people will pick a community that conforms to their style, perspective, life-stage, and ethnicity."[44] This does not mean Christians are actively and consciously discriminating against people who belong to other ethnicities, cultural backgrounds, socioeconomic spheres, or generations. Many believers sincerely state they would never turn anyone away from their churches, but digging deeper into the church's open posture, one finds that many believers welcome diverse people to join *their* church, "as long as they embrace the majority culture and do not try to bring another culture (namely, their own) with them."[45] Perhaps the most difficult element of this analysis is that many Christians do not see this as a problem. While rightfully decrying racial and ethnic divisions and stereotypes, we can easily miss the subtle and sinister ways consumerism keeps the church divided, even when racial animosity has declined.

The Shriveled Eschatology of Moralistic Therapeutic Deism

In the mid-2000s, after many years of research into the spiritual lives of American teenagers, sociologist Christian Smith made the claim that the dominant religion among contemporary U.S. teenagers is "Moralistic Therapeutic Deism." He codified the creed of this religion in five major affirmations. First, "a God exists who created and orders the world and watches over human life on earth" (an essentially deist understanding of a generic God as Creator). Second, "God wants people to be good, nice, and fair to each other, as taught in the Bible and by most world religions" (the moralistic understanding that sees the purpose of life in adhering to morals that make the world a better place). The third affirmation concerns the "central goal of life," which is "to be happy and to feel good about oneself." (Here the therapeutic element comes to the forefront, since the purpose of life is reworked around one's ability to be fulfilled.) The fourth affirmation combines the deistic view of God with the therapeutic purpose for existence, that "God does not need to be particularly involved in one's life except when God is needed to resolve a problem." Finally, the last

44. Jethani, *Divine Commodity*, 127.

45. Mark DeYmaz, *Building a Healthy Multi-Ethnic Church: Mandate, Commitments, and Practices of a Diverse Congregation* (Hoboken, NJ: John Wiley and Sons, 2007), 58.

affirmation reaffirms the moralistic understanding of salvation that "good people go to heaven when they die."[46]

Moralistic Therapeutic Deism, at its heart, is opposed to the gospel because it makes grace unnecessary, robs God of his glory, and recasts the purpose of life in terms that are solely self-centered. If this summary of the religious beliefs of contemporary American young people is accurate, then it is not surprising to see the gospel's call to personal sacrifice seem like something that calls into question the benevolent heart of God.[47] One would also expect to see this kind of consumerist-influenced philosophy prevalent in churches. Nigel Scotland writes:

> The starting point of many has become my needs, my self-interest and my satisfaction. Much of contemporary evangelism tells people Jesus will make them happy and fulfilled. People therefore look for a church that meets their needs and they go to worship for what they can get out of it. Indeed the comment "I didn't get much out of that service" is often passed without even a thought that there might have to be a sacrifice of praise and thanksgiving or a concerted effort to worship God with all of one's heart, mind, soul and strength. Thus for many churchgoers Christianity has become primarily a lifestyle, an ethos, a culture or a club, rather than a faith or relationship with a Lord who demands total commitment on the part of his followers and who wants them to live in community relationships with others.[48]

Smith does not claim that all teenagers in North America are firm believers in Moralistic Therapeutic Deism. He does not suggest an official religion exists by this name or that most teenagers have adopted it. Instead, he sees the main tenets of this rival worldview as "colonizing" established religious traditions and congregations. The consumerist ethos at the heart of Moralistic Therapeutic Deism is the "new spirit living in the old body" of traditional religion.[49]

How does the consumerist ethos and Moralistic Therapeutic Deism affect Christianity's eschatology? It shrivels up eschatological hope in

46. Smith and Denton, *Soul Searching*, 162–63.

47. Jethani, *Divine Commodity*, 118.

48. Nigel Scotland, "Shopping for a Church: Consumerism and the Churches," in *Christ and Consumerism: A Critical Analysis of the Spirit of the Age* (Crownhill, UK: Paternoster Press, 2000), 145.

49. Smith and Denton, *Soul Searching*, 165–66.

the coming of God's new world.[50] Marva Dawn describes materialistic consumerism as "the most popular of eschatological replacements" and "the worst substitute for heaven of all."[51] Furthermore, Moralistic Therapeutic Deism affects eschatology by sabotaging the long-term pursuit of justice. Vincent Miller writes, "The synthesis of deferral and anticipation that marks seduction is likely to reduce eschatological hope to an impotent desire for improvement that, because it is by nature not invested in any particular object or program, can envision nothing new, only endless superficial changes in the present order." He adds, "The absorption of concern for the other into commodification likewise threatens to route the disruptive power of the eschatological and apocalyptic desire for justice into shopping."[52] Moralistic Therapeutic Deism leaves people with the shell of Christianity, a message that can no longer be proclaimed, only marketed.

Marketing Christianity in a Pluralist Society

The pluralism of Western culture makes marketing the church an inevitable necessity. Now that the days of imposing one's religious tradition on others in society have faded away, churches are forced into the situation of marketing their congregational benefits to people who may or may not be interested. As Peter Berger observes, "The pluralist situation is, above all, a market situation. In it, the religious institutions become marketing agencies and the religious traditions become consumer commodities."[53] In order to strengthen the marketing potential of a congregation, the institution begins to focus attention on its programs rather than on its people, with the institutional benefits of the church outweighing the flesh-and-blood relationships that form the heart of God's mission for the world.[54]

The idea of marketing the church seems, at first, almost sacrilegious. After all, the gospel is not a commodity to be pushed on consumers but the truth about the world to be believed by sinners. Conceiving of Christianity as a product to be marketed can compromise the gospel and undermine the core values of the faith. Furthermore, in a marketing environment, the

50. Robert Smith Jr., *Doctrine that Dances: Bringing Doctrinal Preaching and Teaching to Life* (Nashville: B&H, 2008), 117, 169–70. Smith recommends preachers ask of every Scripture passage, "Where is the eschaton in this text?" as a way of lifting the hearts of the people from earth to heaven and from time to eternity.

51. Dawn, *Royal "Waste" of Time*, 360.

52. Miller, *Consuming Religion*, 130.

53. Peter Berger, *The Sacred Canopy: Elements of a Sociological Theory of Religion* (New York: Doubleday, 1967), 138.

54. Jethani, *Divine Commodity*, 92.

church tends to sacrifice its individuality in order to become a copy or clone of some other ministry's success, leading to individualism and a stronger entrenchment of the consumerist ethos, especially among the attendees who chose the church after having gone "church shopping." Soong-Chan Rah explains how enticing consumers into the church creates the additional problem of maintaining the growth of a church full of consumers:

> The acquiescence to consumer culture means that churches fall into the vicious cycle of trying to keep the attendees happy. When a church entices consumers by using marketing techniques and materialistic considerations, is it possible to change that approach after the individual begins attending the church? Or has it set up the church in such a way that the church attendee expects the same level of accommodation that was available when they were church shopping? Can a relationship that began on the level of an exchange of goods and services transition to a deeper level of commitment?[55]

The answer to Rah's last question implies a no, but what if the answer to that question is, "Yes, but it will be difficult"? Keeping in mind all of the pitfalls of a marketed Christianity, we should look for ways the consequences of "marketing" the church may have unexpected benefits. For example, consumerism challenges the church to clarify its vision and purpose and forces churches and their leaders to ask, "Why does our church exist, and what is our mission?" Because a congregation can no longer assume its role in society or impose its vision on others, the church must make a case for its existence, and this process—forced on us by consumerist assumptions—can be immensely clarifying for congregants. Those who work their way through the process of justifying and establishing a motivation for their church are more likely to be dedicated to fulfilling its vision.

While not denying the troublesome elements of consumerism, Nigel Scotland points out three potential benefits. It leads congregations to clarify their vision; it calls them to better serve the people in their communities and congregations; and it challenges apathy by causing them consistently to "reassess their environment and strategies."[56] Scotland is right to provide

55. Soong-Chan Rah, *The Next Evangelicalism: Freeing the Church from Western Cultural Captivity* (Downers Grove, IL: InterVarsity Press, 2009), 55.

56. Scotland, "Shopping for a Church," 146–49.

this counterpoint to those who would too quickly dismiss every element of consumerism. Though this rival worldview contains falsehoods and dangers, consumerism also provides an opportunity for a clear and consistent Christian witness. The question before the church now is, How can Christians maximize the opportunity of consumerism while simultaneously confronting its idolatries?

A Missionary Encounter with Consumerist Eschatology

The pervasive influence of consumerism can lead Christians to feel that the way forward is almost impossible, as if we would do better to throw up our hands, admit the problem, and then bemoan the challenges rather than tackle them in a futile attempt to overcome them. Consumerism does, indeed, present considerable obstacles for Christianity, and the reduction of eschatology to an individual accumulation of wealth is one of the most pernicious elements of this rival worldview.

We do ourselves no favors, however, by complaining about the eschatology we must resist. In contemporary North America we face *this* challenge, not another. It is ours to counter, not to bemoan. Besides, as Charles Taylor reminds us, "Doesn't every dispensation have its own favored forms of deviation? If ours tends to multiply somewhat shallow and undemanding spiritual options, we shouldn't forget the spiritual costs of various kinds of forced conformity: hypocrisy, spiritual stultification, inner revolt against the gospel, the confusion of faith and power, and even worse." In light of the challenges the Christian church has faced in the past, Taylor concludes, "Even if we had a choice, I'm not sure we wouldn't be wiser to stick with the present dispensation."[57] Part of asking the worldview question, "What time is it?," implies that once we discover the time of our current cultural setting, we accept this moment as ours and then seek to live accordingly.

Concerning consumerism's pull on the heart of our society, if it is true that discipleship and desire are intertwined,[58] then we must be ever-aware of how our desires are formed. Making disciples will include the formation of desires. Skye Jethani emphasizes the role of the imagination in this process, "If we are to effectively make disciples of Jesus Christ and teach them to obey everything he commanded, we cannot neglect the imagination. Knowledge and skills are important, but neither will be employable

57. Charles Taylor, *Varieties of Religion Today: William James Revisited* (Cambridge: Harvard University Press, 2002), 114.

58. Miller, *Consuming Religion*, 138.

if the mind is still imprisoned by the conventionality of the surrounding culture."[59] To replace one set of desires with another does not take place by force of will but by force of attraction. Christians must find beauty in something other than the products that are peddled to us by marketers and citizens who see consumption as the purpose of life.

In the following section we consider three ways for Christians to counter the rival eschatology of consumerism. First, we see how the individual eschatology of growing in wealth should be replaced with our eschatological hope of growing in Christ. Second, we see how the consumer's eschatological hope of finding wealth and fulfillment in the future should be replaced with the proper enjoyment of God's gifts in the present. Third, we see how churches can reorder time in ways that direct our gaze away from the collective consumerism of our culture and toward the redemptive acts of Jesus Christ.

Reclaim the Goal of Christlikeness in a World of Choices

If consumerist eschatology tells the story of the self-made individual moving from a place of financial poverty to wealth and status and success, then the church must tell the story of an individual moving from spiritual death to new life in Christ, from immaturity in Christ to representing him well before the world. Growth in holiness, from one's conversion until one's death or Christ's return, must become the dominant narrative by which Christians live. The goal of discipleship is Christlikeness; therefore, we cannot judge our growth or success by the world's standards but rather by God's. The question can never be, "Are we keeping up with the Joneses?," but, "Are we looking more like Jesus?"

Individuals alone will not be able to reclaim this goal of discipleship. It will require the alternative story of the community of faith, believers who see both the danger of consumerism and the opportunity. The danger is to recast Christianity in self-focused terms; the opportunity is to reclaim Christianity's truly transformative vision for human flourishing. Instead of dismissing all consumer evaluations of a church (summed up in the question, What does this congregation offer me?) as if they are shallow and self-centered, we should rise to the challenge and offer serious answers. The church does offer something transformative to the seeker, and instead of judging the seeker, the church should welcome the difficult questions that

59. Jethani, *Divine Commodity*, 27.

arise in a consumer culture, "Seekers want to know precisely why a particular community exists. What does it stand for? What is its mission? How is that accomplished? A culture of choice is not necessarily antithetical to commitment."[60] In fact, we may even find that a culture of choice is one in which commitment is stronger in the long run, precisely because the choice has been made consciously.

Reclaiming the goal of discipleship also means we must see our discipleship efforts as taking place in a context in which freedom of choice reigns supreme. We recognize that the people we disciple, including our own children, will be confronted with a large number of religious and nonreligious choices. The danger of experimenting with endless variations of spirituality is that Christianity can become subservient to our pursuit of personal fulfillment and no longer be about leading people to, in the words of the Westminster Catechism, "glorify God and enjoy him forever."[61] The opportunity, however, is that once we are aware that Moralistic Therapeutic Deism is "converting believers in the old faiths to its alternative religious vision of divinely underwritten personal happiness and interpersonal niceness,"[62] we are better equipped to help churches consistently and intentionally cultivate Christian identity as based in Christ's cross and resurrection.

Another way to challenge consumer identity is intentionally to pursue diversity in the makeup of the church congregation and church leadership, whenever possible, whether that diversity is expressed in multiple ethnicities, people from different socioeconomic spheres, different types of professions, or different stages of life.[63] Pursuing diversity within a congregation challenges the homogeneity of consumerist preferences when the leaders embrace and model interdependence. Mark DeYmaz notes how Americans have an independent streak that leads them to value self-sufficiency and the ability to control one's life and future, but the challenges of a diverse congregation are such that Christians are put in situations where they must depend on one another personally.[64] Furthermore, a church that

---

60. Miller, *Consuming Religion*, 90.

61. Ibid., 139. Miller states, "The self that goes unchallenged here is precisely the consumer self. It is on a quest not for self-transformation but for spiritual experience."

62. Smith and Denton, *Soul Searching*, 171.

63. Mark DeYmaz and Harry Li, *Ethnic Blends: Mixing Diversity into Your Local Church* (Grand Rapids: Zondervan, 2010), 39. DeYmaz and Li use the term "multiethnic" instead of "multicultural" in order to avoid the baggage the latter term carries. They do, however, use the term "multiethnic" to encompass more than just ethnicity; they include economic, educational, and generational diversity under that umbrella.

64. DeYmaz, *Building a Healthy Multi-Ethnic Church*, 47–48.

pursues diversity soon learns the difference between assimilation (integrating the newcomer into a larger body) and accommodation (adapting the congregation to receive the newcomer).[65] The practice of accommodating expressions of faith and worship beyond one's own personal experience or preference is one of the best ways to break the idea of church as a place for a consumer to receive goods and services.[66]

Reclaiming discipleship as *eschatological* requires us to avoid speaking of the gospel in ways that focus solely or primarily on therapeutic results to the exclusion or minimalizing of the gospel's public nature. To be clear, the gospel as public truth does not exclude therapeutic benefits to believers, but it is only because the gospel is public truth that those therapeutic benefits are available. Newbigin warns, "There can be no true evangelism except that which announces what is not only good news but true news." He continues, "It is a very serious matter when the gospel is marketed primarily as a panacea for personal or public ills. We believe that it is indeed for the healing of the nations, but it cannot be this if it is not true."[67] In other words, present the gospel as true, and people will find it helpful. Present the gospel as merely helpful, and people will consider it to be neither.

The challenge of endless spiritual choices is not new for Christians. The early Christians in Rome lived in a time of moral decadence and religious pluralism. These Christians knew, however, who was the true King of the world, and they rejected the eschatology of Roman imperialism no matter how many coins bore the image of Caesar or how many priests exalted his glories.[68] They belonged to Christ and his family.

Belonging, which goes beyond brands, status, and economic results, is key to overcoming the divisions fostered by a consumer mind-set. New creation is seen in the death of prejudices and personal demands. The way for Christians to reclaim the goal of discipleship is to provide a foretaste of the eschatological feast, glimpsed in every celebration of the Lord's Supper,

---

65. Ibid., 59–60; and DeYmaz and Li, *Ethnic Blends*, 81.

66. Jarvis Williams, *One New Man: The Cross and Racial Reconciliation in Pauline Theology* (Nashville: B&H, 2010), 136.While pursuing ethnic diversity is laudable, it is not the ultimate goal. African-American scholar Jarvis Williams contrasts "ethnic diversity," which brings people from different races into one environment, with "racial reconciliation," which emphasizes the oneness of the spiritual family of Christ. He says, "Practicing racial reconciliation means that I regard a white Christian as my brother . . . but not an African-American who is a non-Christian. Hence, my love and service to my Christian brothers and sisters should transcend any love, affection, favoritism, devotion, and service that I offer someone from my race, because Christians are part of the family of God."

67. Newbigin, *Truth to Tell*, 52.

68. Robert Webber, *Who Gets to Narrate the World: Contending for the Christian Story in an Age of Rivals* (Downers Grove, IL: InterVarsity Press, 2008), 51.

by putting aside personal tastes purposefully, intentionally, and clearly for the benefit of others.[69]

Lift Up Examples of Proper Stewardship

We cannot expect to absorb our community's values simply by osmosis. Instead we must combine vibrant Christian fellowship with intentional Christian indoctrination, providing examples and counterpoints to the consumerist eschatology that promotes a narrative of "rags to riches," and always puts off fulfillment until the next stage of wealth has arrived. The ethics of the kingdom challenge the ethics of consumerism.

Some may think the best way to counter consumerist eschatology is by promoting asceticism. However, the immediate desire to divest oneself of wealth may be a sign that we have misunderstood the proper relationship between the things of earth and ourselves as human creatures. The Old Testament does not include a rejection of creation's good things. On the contrary, the images of paradise are often related to plentiful goods and abundance of possessions.[70] A biblical perspective that considers the inherent goodness of creation recognizes that all of God's good gifts are here to be enjoyed; the issue is *how* they are to be enjoyed.[71]

Laura Hartman encourages consumption (which she defines as "the physical throughput of materials and goods in human lives")[72] shaped by a Christian perspective. According to Hartman, the way Christians are to consume is driven by four primary characteristics, "to avoid sin," "to embrace creation," "to love the neighbor," and "to envision the future."[73] That final suggestion is the one that most corresponds to a Christian's countering of consumerist eschatology. Hartman believes Christians can envision the future by seeking to make practical economic choices grounded in "a sense of God's desire for the world's fulfillment."[74] The two areas in which Christian theology lean into this sort of eschatological consumption are the

---

69. Dawn, *Royal "Waste" of Time*, 99, says, "It seems to me that if we eat the body and blood of Christ in expensive churches without care for the hungry, the sacrament is no longer a foretaste of the feast to come, but a trivialized picnic to which not everyone is invited."

70. Craig Blomberg, *Neither Poverty nor Riches: A Biblical Theology of Possessions* (Downers Grove, IL: InterVarsity Press, 1999).

71. J. Gordon McConnville, "The Old Testament and the Enjoyment of Wealth," in *Christ and Consumerism: A Critical Analysis of the Spirit of the Age* (ed. Craig Bartholomew and Thorsten Moritz; Crownhill, UK: Paternoster, 2000), 50.

72. Hartman, *Christian Consumer*, 9, uses the word "throughput" to "denote the flow of materials used and waste discarded."

73. Ibid., 21–24.

74. Ibid., 24.

Sabbath and the Eucharist, where believers receive a foretaste of a world finally fulfilled, where Christ is all in all.[75]

In light of Jesus's instruction to lay up treasures in heaven (Matt 6:20), all earthly enjoyment of God's good gifts should be oriented toward a future of abundance. Marva Dawn calls this "eschatological stewardship," a belief that God's kingdom will prevail in the future and is now being spread in the stewardship of their lives and possessions.[76] She writes:

> Eschatology teaches us that there are no other gods in whom we can trust for the fulfillment of the cosmic future. . . . Glorifying only God kicks out all other idolatries. If all thanksgiving goes to God, we can't be greedy. Gratitude and greed won't coexist, for thanksgiving frees us from scrambling, enables us to relax in the provision of God. Obviously that will affect our stewardship, for if we don't deify money, we are set free to give it away for the purposes of God.[77]

Indeed, Dawn is right to show how the consumerist eschatology is constraining rather than liberating. The challenge for contemporary believers is to see ourselves as stewards, not consumers.

Key to lifting up examples of good stewardship is the emphasis on freedom. We are free from our entanglement with commodities when we receive them as provisional and not as ultimate. That freedom is what makes us stand out in a world of excess. Samuel Escobar links evangelistic faithfulness to Christians' treatment of wealth, stating, "No missionary is a true missionary if he does not live and announce the gospel in a way that makes clear that he does not worship Mammon or Caesar."[78] The Christian response to a consumer culture is to seek ways of cultivating a proper relationship with God's good gifts, countering a culture that idolizes possessions.

Reordering Our Time

A third way of countering the consumerist eschatology is by cultivating communities that reorder time around the great redemptive actions of

---

75. Ibid., 130.
76. Dawn, *Royal "Waste" of Time*, 276.
77. Ibid., 273.
78. Samuel Escobar and John Driver, *Christian Mission and Social Justice* (Scottdale, PA: Herald Press, 1978), 82.

God, not the shopping holidays of a consumer culture. James K. A. Smith recommends we change our practices, not just our thinking. He urges us to

> reactivate and renew those liturgies, rituals, and disciplines that intentionally embody the story of the gospel and enact a vision of the coming kingdom of God in such a way that they'll seep into our bones and become the background for our perceptions, the baseline for our dispositions, and the basis for our (often unthought) action in the world.[79]

Although Smith's counsel refers to more than Christian worship and liturgy, believers should not overlook the formative influence our worship and engagement in spiritual disciplines can have when we recognize our need to be free from the cultural imagination of consumerism. "We need to be regularly immersed in the 'true story of the whole world,'" Smith writes, "that is, our imaginations need to be restored, recalibrated, and realigned by an affective immersion in the story of God in Christ reconciling the world to himself."[80] Otherwise, without this emphasis on the story of God, Christians run the risk of immersing our religious experiences with the consumerist eschatology in which we already believe. If our worship does not counter our consumerism, our consumerism will colonize our worship.

One practical way of immersing people into the grand narrative of Scripture is by using the ancient church calendar. Protestants are divided regarding the use of ancient liturgical devices. Some see the requirements of fasting and celebration as legalistic excess while others see these traditions as helpful in the spiritual life.[81] Those who may resist ordering time by a church calendar are right to point out the lack of explicit biblical basis for this practice, but considering the current consumer society in which Christians live, the question should not be, "Will we adopt a church calendar?," but rather, "Which church calendar is better?" Many churches that spurn the high church's liturgical calendars are often the most beholden to

79. Smith, *Imagining the Kingdom*, 40.

80. Ibid., 163.

81. Robert Webber, *Ancient-Future Time: Forming Spirituality through the Christian Year* (Grand Rapids: Baker Books, 2004), 24. Robert Webber distinguishes between the Christian calendar as the source of spiritual formation and Christ himself. He says the Christian year is "an instrument through which we may be shaped by God's saving events in Christ," but Christ himself is the One who transforms. Webber recommends use of the Christian year because "the very heartbeat of time, the source of meaning and power for the cycle of all time, *derives from* and *returns to* the death and resurrection of Christ."

consumerist ways of ordering time, including celebrations for the Fourth of July, Mother's Day, or Veterans Day, and so forth. For all churches to order their spiritual lives together the same way is not mandatory, but every pastor and church leader should consider how the church orders time and what it communicates.[82]

Meanwhile, Protestants who have adopted some elements of the liturgical church year will need to be careful that they are not picking and choosing elements from church history, not for their own sake but as a way of distinguishing themselves as one brand of church over against another. The retrieval of insights and practices from church history is an excellent way to push against the rootlessness of our consumer culture and to arm ourselves with the resources from the past that will help us face the present. It is good for us not to describe ourselves as "radical" and "new" and "innovative" and "fresh" but rather as wise disciples who stand in a long line of saints who have been faithful to the gospel. However, the perennial problem we face in retrieving insights and practices from church history is that a consumer culture is likely to reach back into the past for antiques that become "window dressing for capitulation to the status quo of everyday life."[83] The ability to participate truly in the "democracy of the dead" is lost,[84] as Chesterton described tradition, because we are only interested in the past for how it makes us feel in the present, not for the pointed challenge it might give us.

The idea that the past would be something we would learn from, something to guide us into the future, is uncommon in a consumer culture focused so heavily on what is new. The temptation for Christians seeking to combat consumerism is that our practices of fasting and our adoption of the church calendar can morph into just another accommodation to the consumerism from which we are hoping to be delivered. Divorced from the community life in which these kinds of practices find their fullest meaning, the spiritual disciplines become another "purchase"—something we turn to in order to find fulfillment, which inoculates us to the strong medicine they offer.

---

82. Mark Galli, *Beyond Smells and Bells: The Wonder and Power of Christian Liturgy* (Brewster, MA: Paraclete Press, 2008), 20-27, 65. Mark Galli describes the aim of a Christian church calendar as changing the way Christians "experience time and perceive reality." Christian worship should be like "entering a new time zone," where the "cosmic calendar" of God's redemptive work is re-presented.

83. Miller, *Consuming Religion*, 81.

84. G. K. Chesterton, *Orthodoxy* (Chicago, Ill.: Moody, 2009), 74, says, "Tradition means giving a vote to most obscure of all classes, our ancestors. It is the democracy of the dead."

Tailoring worship *only* to consumer preferences without considering what a consumer truly needs will bring in a congregation, but it will never send out disciples. Marva Dawn casts a vision for what this eschatological focus on worship might do in biblical churches:

> If our worship is oriented by the present and future reign of God, it will form us to be dependent on him—in contrast to our culture, which always wants to be in control. We will be formed to be churches that are humble, instead of competing to be successful. We will be nurtured to be people who are repentant, Joy-full in our forgiveness, and eager for direction—aware of our insignificance and yet of our critical importance for God's purposes, aware of the immensity of God's sovereignty and yet of his intimate care for us. . . . How would it affect the society around us if all the people in our congregations knew that wherever they go they bring with them the presence of God in proleptic envisioning of the fulfillment in glory and power of all his promises? . . . We live distinctly if we live eschatologically.[85]

Dawn is right to ground Christian worship in Christian eschatology and to view that worship as formative for the Christian's life of obedience. Similarly, James K. A. Smith claims that "Christian worship is an intentionally decentering practice, calling us out of ourselves into the very life of God."[86] Christian worship is radically God focused. Our corporate gatherings should bring us out of ourselves. In a world in which we are constantly told we are the center of the universe, from the devices buzzing in our pockets, the notifications from our social media spheres, and the advertising that is now geared to our preferences, we need time in which we are just one of many voices raised to the heavens, bursting through the immanent, consumerist frame that leads us to judge all our time by its usefulness or pleasure

Summary

Consumerism shrinks the eschatological vision of an individual to the personal pursuit of wealth, and it opposes Christian eschatology at various points; it transforms products and relationships into commodities valued

85. Dawn, *Royal "Waste" of Time*, 366.
86. Smith, *Imagining the Kingdom*, 149.

for their usefulness to people; it recasts religious observance in therapeutic terms of self-fulfillment; it reorients the collective calendar of society around shopping; and it leaves believers with a shriveled eschatology that is unable to confront segregation by race, socioeconomic status, or life stage. For a missionary encounter with a society impacted by consumerism to occur, Christians must embrace eschatological discipleship—the process by which we recognize and reject consumerism's rival conception of time—and then demonstrate in our corporate witness (through their unity in Christ and our generous stewardship of resources) how the goal of becoming like Christ vastly supersedes the journey toward wealth.

PART 4

Eschatological Discipleship for Evangelicalism

CHAPTER 9

Evangelical Conceptions of Discipleship

In the previous chapters we have outlined a vision of discipleship that takes into consideration the New Testament's holistic approach to teaching and learning, as well as the need for wisdom as we seek to follow Christ faithfully in our own generation. This discipleship is "eschatological" because it pursues wisdom by asking the worldview question, "What time is it?," and seeks to discern the best way forward in light of the biblical vision of world history. We have examined various New Testament authors' appeals to eschatology when exhorting Christians to live according to biblical ethics, and I have made the case that living on mission requires Christians to understand their contemporary setting, particularly in relation to rival conceptions of time and progress.

In this section we place eschatological discipleship next to current conceptions of spiritual formation within evangelicalism to see how they may interact in ways that strengthen these evangelical views of discipleship. As we apply the vision of eschatological discipleship to common conceptions of disciple making in evangelical churches, we will advocate for churches to see disciple making as spiritual formation that goes beyond the adoption of personal spiritual disciplines or engagement in church-related activities to a missionary encounter and confrontation with the world.[1]

Placing discipleship processes into categories poses a difficult challenge, perhaps because so many Christian authors and pastors use the word without giving it a specific definition. A sparseness exists of books and resources devoted solely to the definition of a disciple or the laying out of a discipleship

1. Due to the constraints of space, I have narrowed my focus to evangelical views of spiritual formation. A good resource that examines the differences in spiritual formation among Roman Catholics, Eastern Orthodox, mainline Protestants, and evangelicals is Bruce Demarest and Stanley Gundry, eds., *Four Views on Christian Spirituality* (Grand Rapids: Zondervan, 2012).

process. In their book *Transformational Discipleship*, Eric Geiger, Michael Kelley, and Philip Nation echo this frustration, "*Discipleship* is a word that is often hijacked and haphazardly tossed around to describe a multitude of things. And because it has become such a nebulous term, people launch complaints about a ministry described as 'discipleship' that may not have the slightest resemblance to what is possible in delivering transformation to people."[2] Of course, some may argue that the lack of resources devoted specifically to discipleship is a sign that evangelicals view all of their resources as connected in some way to evangelizing unbelievers or edifying believers so that discipleship is "baked in," so to speak, among various resources that may not focus on the term. If such is indeed the case, categorizing and summarizing various approaches to discipleship become even more difficult since different aspects of the process will inevitably vary from leader to leader.

Despite these difficulties I believe there is value in seeking to place different conceptions of discipleship within a framework that reveals the distinctions between groups without minimizing their similarities. To that end I will survey common evangelical conceptions of discipleship that fall into three distinct categories: (1) discipleship conceived of as evangelistic reproduction, (2) discipleship in terms of personal piety (expressed through the adoption of spiritual disciplines), and (3) discipleship that is gospel centered in its motivation. For each category we will narrow our analysis to only a few representatives for each group.

This survey is not intended to be exhaustive, nor should we assume no overlap exists between the groups. Those who see discipleship in terms of spiritual disciplines and personal piety would, of course, affirm the need for evangelism; likewise, those who call for gospel-driven obedience do not necessarily eschew certain spiritual disciplines, and so forth. The purpose of this brief survey is not to argue for one approach to discipleship over another or even to make the case that these three conceptions are the most common ones found in evangelicalism, but rather to show how each approach would benefit from training Christians to think eschatologically, to ask and answer the worldview question of "what time it is" in the culture in which we are called to submit to Jesus as Lord. Our goal is to take all of the philosophical and theological work we have engaged in up to this point and begin to apply it to common conceptions of discipleship within

2. Eric Geiger, Michael Kelley, and Philip Nation, *Transformational Discipleship: How People Really Grow* (Nashville: B&H, 2012), 17.

evangelicalism today and thus avoid reductionist views of discipleship that fail to provide a cohesive and coherent vision for the church.

Discipleship as Evangelistic Reproduction

Our first approach to discipleship can be labeled as "evangelistic reproduction." The focus of this discipleship process is on people being evangelized. Once people have repented of sin and trusted Christ, they must learn how to become evangelists themselves. If we were to sum up the idea in one phrase, we might say, "Disciples are followers of Jesus who make disciples" or "converts making converts." The initial element of making a disciple (conversion) becomes a major part of defining discipleship because it is what a disciple seeks on behalf of others. A nonreproducing disciple is an oxymoron. *By definition* disciples reproduce through evangelism.

Evangelistic passion is not unique to this vision of making disciples, but the emphasis on evangelism and the need for disciples to know how to evangelize is strongest in this conception, as compared to the others we will study. In this section we will examine how "evangelistic reproduction" focuses on discipling converts to the point they can make converts. We will also look at the strengths and weaknesses of this emphasis and then offer some thoughts as to how eschatological discipleship might improve the conception.

Converts Who Make Converts

Disciple Making Is . . ., edited by Dave Earley and Rod Dempsey, features contributions from various scholars on the issue of how discipleship should be defined and how the process should take place. This book is one of the finest representations of the "evangelistic reproduction" understanding of discipleship.

In an early chapter Rod Dempsey warns against evangelistic fervor that is not rooted in a clear vision of what discipleship is or how a disciple looks. He points out the flaw in seeking to make disciples without a clear understanding of what a disciple is:

> Many times churches try to make disciples without a clear understanding of what a disciple actually looks like. As a result, many churches are running, and running very hard, but not making progress in the disciple-making process. Therefore, the starting

> point for disciple making is to examine carefully what the Master had to say about disciple making.[3]

Dempsey is correct to bring us back to the Gospels and to Jesus's own words about disciples and discipleship. In the end, looking at Jesus and the disciples' example, the authors see a strong emphasis on reproduction, or multiplication.

Evangelistic reproduction emphasizes the truth that disciples make disciples. The evangelized must begin to evangelize. Earley sums up the "evangelistic reproduction" approach: "Disciplemaking is about comprehensive training in obedience leading to reproduction and multiplication. When many speak of fulfilling the Great Commission, they are talking only about evangelism. Yet, Jesus was quite clear that disciplemaking is not complete until the disciple is practicing everything Jesus commanded, including the command to make more disciples."[4] Notice Earley's emphasis on the goal of discipleship as reproduction and multiplication. Notice how he subsumes the command to make disciples underneath the Great Commission's call to practice "everything Jesus commanded." *Comprehensive* training is necessary. For Earley, then, discipleship is obedience to Christ, and since evangelism is part of that obedience, no true disciple making occurs apart from calling others to faith.[5]

What is evangelism? The first goal in the disciple-making process is to "win the lost." Winning the lost takes place through evangelism, which Earley claims is "to communicate good news . . . that Jesus died on the cross to pay for our sins and open the way for us to get to God."[6] Evangelists spread this good news the way farmers harvest a crop of corn. The ground must be plowed; the seeds must be planted, watered, and weeded, and then given time to grow. Earley encourages believers to see everyone around them as a "spiritual field" and to "cooperate with God and others to plow the soil of their heart, plant the seed of the gospel, water the seed, and wait

---

3. Rod Dempsey, "Beginning on a Sure Foundation," in *Disciple Making Is . . . : How to Live the Great Commission with Passion and Confidence* (ed. Dave Earley and Rod Dempsey; Nashville: B&H, 2013), 22.

4. Dave Earley, "Introduction: Fulfilling the Great Commission," in *Disciple Making Is . . .*, 5.

5. Dave Earley, "Obeying Everything Jesus Commanded," in *Disciple Making Is . . .*, 19. Earley claims that Jesus's commissioning of the disciples assumed they were already living as disciples, claiming, "In commanding them to obey everything He had demanded, He was assuming they were already obeying everything He had commanded. Therefore, before you can make a disciple, you need to *be* a disciple." This distinction between "being a disciple" and "making disciples" contradicts Earley's earlier insistence that discipleship always includes the making of disciples. It appears that his point, then, is that one must *be* something before one can *do* something.

6. Dave Earley, "Helping Others Go to the Next Level," in *Disciple Making Is . . .*, 130.

for God to bring the harvest,"[7] which is the method of evangelization seen in the ministry of Jesus, the apostle Paul, and leaders in church history, such as William Booth and John Wesley.[8]

What does the process of discipleship look like? We should not assume the evangelistic reproduction approach to discipleship narrows its vision of obedience *only* to evangelism, as if seeking converts is all disciple making entails. Dempsey adds a wider-angled view of a disciple by crafting a definition that lines up with what is seen in Jesus's work with the disciples in the Gospels. He lists the aspects of a disciple in the following way. A disciple is someone who: (1) seriously considers the cost before following Christ; (2) is totally committed to Christ; (3) is willing to carry his or her individual burden to sacrifice for Christ and his cause; (4) is willing to give up all earthly possessions; (5) continues in God's Word and experiences freedom in Christ; (6) genuinely loves other believers; (7) abides in Christ, prays, bears fruit, and glorifies God; (8) is full of the Holy Spirit; (9) obediently follows the desires of the Master; and (10) is intimately involved in the mission of Jesus to make disciples.[9]

Still, even with these added descriptions, Dempsey does not want us to lose sight of how discipleship connects to reproduction in terms of Christ's mission of seeking and saving the lost. He says, "A disciple is a person who has trusted Christ for salvation and has *surrendered* completely to Him. He or she is committed to practicing the spiritual disciplines in *community* and *developing to their full potential for Christ and His mission*."[10] Here we see the holistic vision of discipleship (surrendering every part of life to Christ), as well as the need for spiritual disciplines and Christian growth. But notice how both of these elements (holistic obedience and spiritual disciplines) are oriented toward the potential of evangelization—they are to become useful for Christ and his mission. Earley does not deny the other elements of discipleship; he does, however, give them an evangelistic *telos*.

Building on A. B. Bruce's book *The Training of the Twelve*, the contributors to *Disciple Making Is . . .* describe disciple making in terms of progression. Bruce writes, "The twelve arrived at their final intimate relation to Jesus only by degrees, three stages in the history of their fellowship

7. Ibid., 131.
8. Ibid., 131–36.
9. Dempsey, "Beginning on a Sure Foundation," 22–26.
10. Ibid., 28 (emphasis in original).

with Him being distinguishable."[11] Stage 1 refers to declaration—"investigation leading to repentance and faith in Jesus." Stage 2 refers to development—"immersion, abandonment, and apprenticeship into ministry." Stage 3 refers to deployment—"intentional global commissioning." The vision of salvation is one in which believers grow in "intimacy with Jesus" and move up the ladder of "believer" to "disciple" to "disciple maker." The questions asked at each stage are: "Will you *believe* in Jesus?" (believer), "Will you *follow* Jesus?" (disciple), and "Will you *go* for Jesus?" (disciple maker).[12] This idea of the discipleship process being a progression from convert, to disciple, to disciple maker is common in the evangelistic reproduction approach to discipleship, and it is also evident in chapter titles that use words like "first step" and "next level."

In summary, the "evangelistic reproduction" approach to discipleship is seen most clearly in its emphasis on the goal of making disciples who, in turn, make disciples. As Anthony Gittins writes, "The purpose of discipleship is mission. . . . The fruits of authentic discipleship will be manifest in the continuing commitment of those who have first encountered Jesus and then been sent by him on mission"—*mission* here defined primarily in the activity of personal evangelism.[13] This leads to a strong focus on evangelistic reproduction through multiplication.[14]

Strengths and Weaknesses

In what follows we look at some of the strengths and weaknesses of the evangelistic reproduction approach to discipleship. Like each of these conceptions, we should expect to find laudable aspects as well as elements that could be improved. The goal is not to give an exhaustive summary of strengths and weaknesses but rather to explore how eschatological discipleship might address and assist any deficiencies in these perspectives on discipleship.

First, we should commend the admirable passion that exists for proclaiming the gospel in order that others may come to faith in Christ and take their places as fellow proclaimers of the gospel. The church's calling is not merely to "make disciples," but to make disciples who, in turn, make

---

11. A. B. Bruce, *The Training of the Twelve* (Grand Rapids: Kregel, 1988), 11.

12. A chart laying out the detailed stages of "discipleship requirements of Jesus" is included in Earley and Dempsey, *Disciple Making Is . . .*, 61.

13. Anthony Gittins, *Called to Be Sent* (Liguori, MO: Liguori Press, 2008), 1, 15.

14. Dave Earley, "Focusing on a Multiplied Harvest," in *Disciple Making Is . . .*, 175.

disciples. The advocates of this approach are correct in seeing the built-in reproductive elements of discipleship as part of the healthy Christian life.

Second, we should affirm advocates of this model of discipleship in their claim that evangelism is not a requirement reserved only for elite believers but must be characteristic of all who follow Jesus. To apply Jesus's commissioning texts only to the apostles in the first century would blunt their force. The role of the apostles is unique and foundational to the witness of the church, and to speak of our role today in apostolic terms is to cause potential confusion regarding the authoritative nature of their witness and writings. Christians today are *sent* just as the apostles were, but we are sent in the footsteps of those who walked with the Lord and blazed the trail of mission before us. We should recognize the unique identity and authority given to the apostles, but, as the proponents of the evangelistic reproduction approach affirm, we should not limit the application of the Great Commissioning texts to those who were physically present in the scene. Otherwise, we seek to force too strong a distinction between the missional identity of Christ's first followers and the missional identity of those who follow today. Michael Goheen explains why limiting the commissioning to the apostles is a mistake:

> No doubt this is the first reference: the apostolic witness to the resurrection of Jesus Christ is unique, unrepeatable, and foundational for the church. But the apostles also form "the beginning, the nucleus of the eschatological people of God around the Messiah;" they are the missionary church *in partu* (in childbirth)—that is, the missional church as it is born. Or, again, the apostolic band is the missional church pars *pro toto* (the part that represents the whole). Thus this promise is given to them as they represent the whole people of God. Witness begins with this small apostolic group but extends as the calling of the whole church.[15]

This way of understanding and applying Christ's commissioning of the disciples maintains the foundational nature of the apostles and the extension of their identities to all who name the name of Christ. The advocates of the evangelistic reproduction approach to discipleship are right to focus their attention on this aspect of disciple making.

15. Goheen, *Light to the Nations*, 127.

Third, the advocates of this approach are correct to view discipleship as oriented necessarily toward mission. This focus on mission provides an outward, evangelistic orientation for all aspects of our obedience. Furthermore, this approach can keep us from turning inward, from becoming focused only on ourselves and our own spiritual growth. Earley writes, "Disciples live as missionaries. If you are going to be a disciple of Jesus Christ, you will be a missionary. Living on mission is not the career of a select few. It is the calling of *all* disciples, commission to *all* disciples, and command for *all* disciples. We are all called as missionaries. The question is: Will we be obedient or disobedient?"[16] Other scholars might choose to define *missionary* differently than Dave Earley (the term *missionary* might be better reserved for cross-cultural missions and the broader term "live on mission" as a description of all Christians), but many would agree with the mission-focused sentiment he puts forth.

We find two primary weaknesses in the "evangelistic reproduction" approach to discipleship. First, there is an inherent dissonance in affirming, on the one hand, that discipleship is divided into stages (believer, disciple, and disciple maker), while at the same time claiming that disciples, by definition, are missionaries actively seeking to make disciples. If discipleship begins with converts, who eventually become disciples by following Christ's instructions and only later arrive at the stage of disciple maker, then how can we simultaneously say that no one is truly a disciple unless he or she is making more disciples? On the one hand, we are told that evangelism is not the responsibility reserved for an elitist class, and yet on the other hand, disciple maker is clearly the most advanced level of discipleship. The division of discipleship into stages contradicts the mission-focused definition these contributors give to disciple making.

The second weakness to this approach is that "living on mission" is largely reduced to evangelism, without sufficient attention given to how cross-cultural missionaries approach that task of evangelism. An outward missionary posture toward the world is a key characteristic of discipleship.[17] However, the problem surfaces in the general way that evangelism or "life

---

16. Dave Earley, "Accepting the Third Step of Obedience," in *Disciple Making Is . . .*, 78.

17. Bruce Ashford, "The Church in the Mission of God," in *The Community of Jesus: A Theology of the Church* (ed. Kendall Easley and Christopher Morgan; Nashville: B&H, 2014). Ashford recommends viewing the missional church as pointed in five directions: (1) upward (to God as the source of mission); (2) inward (to ourselves as those who manifest God's mission); (3) backward (to God's creational design for the world); (4) forward (to the coming of God's promised kingdom); and (5) outward (to the nations as we proclaim and promote God's salvation).

on mission" is described. Advocates of evangelistic reproduction suggest evangelists ask questions with the intent to "really listen" to lost people, but this listening is exclusively framed within the context of building a relationship. The "listening" here is not Stott's idea of "double listening" with its emphasis on speaking the gospel in a way that is culturally sensitive and effective but rather the idea of getting to know neighbors in order to have credibility to share the gospel. Of course, both purposes (relational credibility and missional contextualization) are important, but advocates of this vision of discipleship give insufficient attention to the element of contextualizing our presentation of the gospel.

A missionary who seeks to proclaim the gospel effectively in another culture must learn the language and understand the culture in which the gospel will confront idolatries and offer hope and purpose. This is the reason missionaries undergo training in the worldview and philosophy of the culture they are seeking to reach. The evangelistic reproduction approach, for all its emphasis on every Christian as a missionary, could be stronger in showing how "living on mission" includes understanding a cultural setting, a culture's idols, and how to bring the truth of the gospel to bear on society, both personally in evangelistic proclamation and corporately in the church's wider witness to the world in embodying the reality of God's kingdom in all spheres of life.

The Strengthening Addition of Eschatological Discipleship

The evangelistic reproduction approach is commendable in its focus on personal evangelism and the idea of "living on mission." However, this conception of discipleship would be improved if it were to rely less on "stages" of discipleship and more on the need for contextualization, particularly in asking and answering the question of "what time it is" in the culture in which the evangelist seeks to share and exhibit the gospel. Here are two ways in which eschatological discipleship can strengthen and support the evangelistic reproduction approach.

Strengthened Evangelistic Effectiveness from Contextualization. First, for those who see discipleship primarily as "converts making converts," asking "what time it is" will aid in the evangelistic process as well as take into account rival eschatologies, which might diminish a disciple's impact. Tim Keller's *Center Church* includes a helpful definition of *contextualization*, which includes "giving people the Bible's answers, which they may not at all want to hear, to questions about life that people in their particular time and place are asking, in language and forms they can comprehend, and through appeals and arguments with force they can feel, even if they reject them."[18] The strength of Keller's definition is its focus on the necessity of making the gospel comprehensible to people who inhabit a culture. It recognizes the impossibility of a cultureless gospel presentation or church. Asking, "What time is it?" will help those who adopt the evangelistic reproduction approach to discipleship find a proper place for contextualization in twenty-first-century North America.

The proponents of evangelistic reproduction are right to emphasize the need to listen carefully to lost people as they share their stories. Eschatological discipleship would ensure that this listening goes beyond the building of relationship to the development of a personalized presentation of gospel truth to an individual, a presentation that is personalized in light of the dominant narratives of society that have shaped the potential convert. Jonathan Dodson points out the diversity of biblical metaphors for handling the gospel and recommends that evangelistic strategies be adapted to the cultural backgrounds of unbelievers. He writes, "Good evangelism removes the stones and shares the truth in such a way that the light of God's grace can travel down a shaft, into the grave of a darkened heart."[19] The type of listening he advocates goes beyond the strengthening of a relationship; it includes the apologetic necessity of listening to "new questions people are asking" and learning "how to translate the language of the gospel into words and concepts that speak to the heart."[20] Active listening aims at understanding "what people hear and how they speak" so that, as evangelists, we can "communicate the gospel in intelligible ways."[21]

Asking "what time it is" helps us adapt to a postmodern culture in which institutions and authorities are viewed with suspicion. When doctrine and dogma are downplayed or resisted as power plays from people with vested interests in religious outcomes, or when people are more likely to adopt an amalgam of differing, sometimes contradictory, beliefs and not feel pressed by logic to consider their core values and how they line up with their beliefs and actions, evangelists must be aware of the challenges and adapt our methodologies appropriately. Tim Keller describes this "contextual

18. Keller, *Center Church*, 89.

19. Jonathan Dodson, *The Unbelievable Gospel: Say Something Worth Believing* (Grand Rapids: Zondervan, 2014), 127.

20. Ibid., 136.

21. Ibid., 138.

communication" as the intention of resonating with yet defying the culture, stating, "It means to antagonize a society's idols while showing respect for its people and many of its hopes and aspirations. It means expressing the gospel in a way that is not only comprehensible but also convincing."[22]

Keller lists six practices one should do in evangelistic preaching: (1) use accessible or well-explained vocabulary; (2) employ respected authorities to strengthen the theses; (3) demonstrate an understanding of doubts and objections; (4) affirm in order to challenge baseline cultural narratives; (5) make gospel offers that push on the culture's pressure points; and (6) call for gospel motivation.[23] None of these practices are possible apart from eschatological discipleship and asking the question, "What time is it?" from a worldview perspective. Not surprisingly, Keller then explains how to accomplish these practices in preaching to the "(late) modern mind," which is his contextualized application of evangelistic ministry for the twenty-first century.[24]

Holistic View of Witness. A second way eschatological discipleship could strengthen the evangelistic reproduction approach to discipleship is by promoting a vision of "witness" that goes beyond verbal proclamation. Among some advocates of an evangelistic reproduction approach to discipleship, the fervor for evangelism can lead to a reduced vision of what the church's overall mission is. Once this reduction takes place, Christians who focus on the need for good works as part of the church's mission may be viewed with suspicion for "watering down" the priority placed on verbal proclamation. (On the flip side, those who focus on the need for evangelistic words may be viewed with disdain for "neglecting compassion" and failing to see the role of good works in their promotion of the gospel.)

Eschatological discipleship helps avoid the wedge between word and deed, a wedge that is unfortunate primarily because it is truly impossible to fully distinguish the two. Anyone who shares the gospel verbally is doing so as an embodied individual. Facial expressions, vocal inflection, and the tone of the conversation all contribute (as deeds) to the words being spoken. To focus only on words or only on deeds is impossible. Taking into consideration the meaning of "witnesses" in Acts and the priority given to

22. Keller, *Preaching*, 99.

23. Ibid., 99–120.

24. Ibid., 121–56; and Clark, *To Know and Love God*, 99–132, especially chapter 3, "Theology in Cultural Context." Contextualization is not something a preacher or missionary can accomplish alone, especially when the person communicating the gospel is seeking to reach people in a different culture or, in the case of Western societies, multiple cultures and subcultures. A dialogical approach is necessary for contextualization to take place.

identity over the task means that believers are simultaneously "witnesses who witness." David Peterson explains the need for the church's corporate witness to be extended through verbal proclamation, insisting:

> It is not simply the corporate or ecclesial testimony of vibrant Christian faith issuing in good works, important though this may be in convincing unbelievers about the truth of Christianity. Fundamentally, it involves proclaiming the kingdom of God and teaching about the Lord Jesus Christ as the apostles did. It means using the apostolic witness to persuade people of the need to turn to Jesus, relying upon God to provide his own confirming witness to the proclamation of this message through the work of his Spirit in believers.[25]

Because the task of witnessing flows from Christians' identities as witnesses, a relationship exists between living as Christ's followers and speaking as Christ's followers, a relationship that cannot and must not be broken.

Eschatological discipleship would strengthen the evangelistic reproduction approach to discipleship, helping its advocates avoid false dichotomies and instead see how actions and words mutually relate. Christians must take care to ensure that our words are backed up by our actions and that our actions give way to words. Only in this way is ministry truly holistic. A deeds-based conception of "witness" fails to do justice to the prominence given to gospel "speech" in the New Testament. A words-based conception of "witness" fails to do justice to the prominence given to witnessing "identity" in the commissioning texts of Jesus. Eschatological discipleship leads us away from choosing between one or the other and toward a view of evangelism that envisions the local church as the backdrop and evidence for the verbal proclamation of its members.

Discipleship as Personal Piety

Another common approach to discipleship conceives of the church's task primarily in terms of personal piety and obedience to Christ, developed over time through the cultivation of spiritual disciplines. For some the term *pietistic* may have negative connotations, with *piousness* implying a self-righteous aloofness or a diligent, rigorous life of super-spirituality. However, I use the term *piety* in its positive connotation, recognizing that

25. Peterson, *Acts*, 82–83.

at its best piety includes acts of service toward others and a posture of love toward one's neighbors. In this section we examine the work of Dallas Willard, who calls us to the use of spiritual disciplines in shaping our spirituality so that we begin to appear more like Christ.

Disciples and the Disciplines

The personal-piety approach to discipleship is represented well by authors such as Richard Foster, Dallas Willard, and Donald Whitney. We will focus primarily on Willard's work, while occasionally drawing from other sources. The personal-piety approach emphasizes a person's spiritual progression in holiness and Christlikeness, and this progression takes place through the exercise of spiritual disciplines.

Discipleship in Stages. One of the ways to distinguish between the "evangelistic reproduction" and "personal piety" views of discipleship is that the latter resists the impulse to separate obedience into stages, a common feature in books such as Bruce's *The Training of the Twelve*[26] or Leroy Eims's *The Lost Art of Disciple Making*, the latter of which presents the Christian life in levels of "convert," "disciple," and "worker.[27]

Dallas Willard responds to Eims's work by pointing out that, according to Eims's framework, one could potentially be a convert and yet never become a "disciple" or "worker," thus implying that these latter stages are "optional" for a Christian. This leads Willard to diagnose what he believes is a tragic problem, a "great omission" in contemporary church teaching, that Christians do not consider themselves disciples. He writes:

> The greatest issue facing the world today, with all its heartbreaking needs is, whether those who, by profession or culture, are identified as "Christians" will become *disciples*—students, apprentices, practitioners *of Jesus Christ*, steadily learning from him how to live the life of the Kingdom of the Heavens into every corner of human existence. Will they break out of the churches to be his Church—to be, without human force or violence, his mighty force for good on earth, drawing the churches after them toward the eternal purposes of God?[28]

---

26. Bruce, *Training of the Twelve*.
27. Leroy Eims, *The Lost Art of Disciple Making* (Grand Rapids: Zondervan, 1978).
28. Dallas Willard, *The Great Omission: Reclaiming Jesus's Essential Teachings on Discipleship* (New York: HarperOne, 2006), xv (emphasis in original).

Willard is deeply concerned about nominalism—the idea that one can be called by the name of Christ (Christian) without truly following him as Lord. The motivation behind all of his work is to bring the spiritual disciplines back to the center of spiritual development, and thus rectify this problem.[29]

Interestingly enough, although Willard contrasts his own vision of discipleship against the "stages" mentioned in books like Bruce and Eims, Willard does not negate all talk of "stages." He speaks openly about stages "on the spiritual way" and also differentiates between conversion and transformation, stating, "It is necessary to say that conversion, as understood in Christian circles, is *not* the same thing as *the required transformation of the self*. The fact that a long course of experience is needed for the transformation is not set aside when we are touched by the new life from above."[30] Willard uses the apostle Peter as an example of someone who was converted and yet who stumbled and fell and grew until he later became a mighty force for the kingdom of God. Willard describes Peter as an apostle who progressed in holiness.[31]

If there are stages to discipleship, and they are not the stages Eims mentioned (convert, disciple, worker), what kind of progression is in view here? Willard sees three stages to personal redemption. In the first case, "We were baptized *into* Christ and brought to 'experiential union' with him."[32] This framework seems to correspond rather closely with Eims's understanding of "conversion." It refers to the stage whereby someone comes out of the kingdom of darkness and into the kingdom of light, now with an established relationship with God.

At the second stage of personal redemption, Willard points to "a specific act on our part that develops into an enduring attitude."[33] Here Willard is referring to spiritual disciplines. Christians must act; we seek to follow Jesus as our Lord, to imitate him; and these actions form us until we exhibit the attitudes that accompany them.

The third stage is when "we consciously direct our bodies in a manner that will ensure that it eventually will come 'automatically' to serve

---

29. Dallas Willard, *The Spirit of the Disciplines: Understanding How God Changes Lives* (San Francisco, CA: Harper & Row, 1988), xi. "This book is a plea for the Christian community to place the disciplines for the spiritual life at the heart of the gospel."

30. Ibid., 70.

31. Ibid., 70–74.

32. Ibid., 114.

33. Ibid., 115.

righteousness as it previously served sin automatically."[34] This stage is when the disciplines and intentional attitudes of the believer have become second nature. Willard believes a real and enduring psychological process takes place as a person seeks to follow Christ. The stages of personal redemption lead from initial conversion to full transformation of the person, with the spiritual disciplines as a bridge from one to the other.

We might wonder how Willard can, on the one hand, criticize an author for separating "convert" from "disciple," while, on the other hand, describe discipleship as a process that includes three stages. The key difference is that Willard includes all of this under the label of "redemption." In other words, he sees redemption as the umbrella under which the initial conversion and the subsequent actions and disciplines find their place. Though he sees discipleship as a process with various stages, he would reject the idea that one can be a convert but not a disciple. He wants us to see a holistic connection between initial salvation and long-term sanctification, and thus he pushes against views of discipleship that make "disciple" seem like an option for those who are spiritually minded, who have already been "converted."

Discipleship and Christlikeness. The personal-piety approach to discipleship is perceptive in articulating how every human being is a disciple of some sort. Willard points out that all human beings are "the kind of creatures that have to learn and keep learning from others how to live."[35] This approach wisely takes into consideration the formative influences of culture in shaping who we are and how we behave. We are all being formed by someone or something.

According to Willard, the disciple of Jesus is "one who, intent upon becoming Christ-like and so dwelling in *his* 'faith and practice,' systematically and progressively rearranges his affairs to that end."[36] Notice the emphasis on becoming like Jesus. This understanding of discipleship does not exclude the evangelistic reproduction approach examined earlier, but its emphasis clearly falls on growing personally in Christlikeness so that the life of Christ is the most formative influence on our hearts and behavior.

Willard describes spiritual formation in three meanings or moments, different from the "stages" of redemption considered previously. According to Willard, spiritual formation should be seen as a diamond and viewed from various angles. He says:

---

34. Ibid., 117.
35. Willard, *Great Omission*, 7.
36. Ibid.

> First, identifying certain activities as spiritual work or exercise, one can think of *spiritual formation as training in these special spiritual activities*. . . . Second, spiritual formation may be thought of as the *shaping of the inner life, the spirit, or the spiritual side of the human being*. . . . Third, spiritual formation may be thought of as a *shaping by the spirit or by the spiritual realm, and by the Holy Spirit and other spiritual agencies* in the kingdom of God, especially the Word of God.[37]

One can see from Willard's approach that spiritual formation is following Jesus through the implementation of concrete actions, or disciplines, until the actions shape us, by the power of the Spirit, into the Christlike people God has called us to be. Before moving on, we must take a closer look at the disciplines Willard mentions.

Disciples and the Spiritual Disciplines. How do we go about accomplishing this goal of discipleship? The evangelistic reproduction approach focused on training people to "live on mission" by evangelizing unbelievers, just as Jesus did, but this type of activity may not necessarily result in people who are much like Christ. It is possible to share the message of Christ without the manner of Christ. Willard warns about this danger. Summing up the landscape of evangelical spirituality, Willard writes, "Most Christians had been told by me as by others to attend the services of the church, give of time and money, pray, read the Bible, do good to others, and witness to their faith. And certainly they should do these things. But just as certainly something more was needed."[38] That "something more" is found in the spiritual disciplines—seeking to follow Christ and imitate his behavior through the intentional cultivation of the inner life through various disciplines. He writes:

> We can, through faith and grace, become like Christ by practicing the types of activities he engaged in, by arranging our whole lives around the activities he himself practiced in order to remain constantly at home in the fellowship of his Father. What activities did Jesus practice? Such things as solitude and silence, prayer,

37. Ibid., 70, 71.
38. Willard, *Spirit of the Disciplines*, 19.

> simple and sacrificial living, intense study and meditation upon God's Word and God's ways, and service others.[39]

Willard claims that only through the appropriate exercise of the disciplines can "full participation in the life of God's kingdom and in the vivid companionship of Christ" come.[40]

How do these disciplines help shape the disciple into Christlikeness? The personal-piety approach focuses on helping people become like Jesus through the use of what Willard calls "the Golden Triangle," a threefold way of growing in Christlikeness. The first side of the triangle is the "faithful acceptance of everyday problems." Willard explains, "By enduring trials with patience, we can reach an assurance of the fullness of heaven's rule in our lives."[41] The second side of the triangle is "interaction with God's Spirit in and around us," benefiting from and cultivating the Spirit's gifts and the Spirit's fruit.[42] The third side of the triangle is the implementation of spiritual disciplines, the means by which the Holy Spirit forms our hearts and minds so that our behavior begins to mirror that of Christ. The list of spiritual disciplines differs among the advocates of the personal-piety approach,[43] but some of the activities most commonly recommended are prayer, Bible reading, fasting, solitude, and generosity.[44]

---

39. Ibid., ix; and Donald Whitney, *Spiritual Disciplines for the Christian Life* (rev. [SBLH 7.2.15] and updated ed.; Colorado Springs, Colo.: NavPress, 2014), 9. Donald Whitney sees a similar purpose, "The Spiritual Disciplines are *means, not ends*. The end—that is, the purpose of practicing the Disciplines—is godliness. I define *godliness* as both closeness to Christ and conformity to Christ, a conformity that's both inward and outward, a growing conformity to both the heart of Christ and the life of Christ. This Christlikeness is the goal, the reason we should practice the Disciplines."

40. Willard, *Spirit of the Disciplines*, 26.

41. Willard, *Great Omission*, 26.

42. Ibid., 27–28.

43. Willard, *Spirit of the Disciplines*, 158-59; Richard Foster, *Celebration of Discipline: The Path to Spiritual Growth* (rev. ed., San Francisco, CA: HarperSanFrancisco, 1988); and Whitney, *Spiritual Disciplines for the Christian Life*, 5. Willard divides the disciplines by "abstinence" and "engagement." The disciplines of abstinence are solitude, silence, fasting, frugality, chastity, secrecy, and sacrifice. The disciplines of engagement are study, worship, celebration, service, prayer, fellowship, confession, and submission. Richard Foster divides the disciplines into three categories, inward (meditation, prayer, fasting, study), outward (simplicity, solitude, submission, service), and corporate (confession, worship, guidance, celebration). Donald Whitney believes the Bible prescribes both personal and interpersonal spiritual disciplines, the former being practiced alone and the latter being practiced with others. His treatment of the disciplines includes Bible intake, prayer, worship, evangelism, serving, stewardship, fasting, silence and solitude, journaling, and learning.

44. Willard, *Spirit of the Disciplines*, 159. The disciplines of abstaining (from noise, from company, from food) should not be interpreted as an asceticism that sees these activities as bad, inferior, or morally problematic. Willard says the disciplines of abstention are a way of countering "today's distorted condition of humanity" in which "these basic desires that have been allowed to run a rebellious and harmful course, ultimately serving as the primary hosts of sin in our personalities" (ibid).

In sum, the personal-piety approach to discipleship sees the heart of evangelical faith as "Christ-centered piety" consisting of three substantive elements: "conviction of sin, conversion to a godly life of faith, and testimony to the saving work of God in the soul."[45] But what about evangelism? Willard believes a missionary outlook is essential, but the means of attaining such evangelistic fervor is not by stressing what believers must do but who they are as evangelists. He says, "There is a special evangelistic work to be done, of course, and there are special callings to it. But if those in the churches really are enjoying fullness of life, evangelism will be unstoppable and largely automatic."[46] Evangelistic fruitfulness, then, is the result of an interior life that is richly ordered and seeks Christlikeness.

Strengths and Weaknesses

The personal-piety approach to discipleship has two primary strengths. First, these writers are perceptive in their analysis of the role of culture in personal formation. We are constantly being formed by something. The only question is, what is forming our desires and actions? Any Christian who seeks to be formed into the image of Christ should be aware of the countervailing influences that prevent growth in Christlikeness. Much of evangelicalism assumes that discipleship is a matter of knowledge rather than practice, the idea that if we know what we should do, we will do it. However, the emphasis on spiritual disciplines recognizes the formative impact of habits.

Second, the personal-piety advocates see mission as flowing out of Christlikeness. By focusing on spiritual disciplines that help us become more like Christ, this approach begins with "who we are" before turning to "testimony to the saving work of God" (what we do). At first this almost seems like a contradiction. After all, the previous strength focused on how our habits shape our inward life. How then can we say that the inward life comes first? In other words, how is it possible to say that what we do shapes who we are and also say that who we are must shape what we do? The difference is in what comes naturally. The habits are ways of expressing the intention to be like Christ, and the habits form us into the kind of people who—by nature—follow Christ with joy. This interplay between habits

45. Willard, *Great Omission*, 162.
46. Willard, *Spirit of the Disciplines*, 247.

and heart, virtue and action, is one of the strengths of the personal-piety approach to discipleship.

A downside exists, however, to this emphasis on spiritual discipline. Whereas the evangelistic reproduction conception of discipleship points outward to neighbors in need of Christ, the personal-piety approach points inward to the cultivation of spiritual disciplines that give shape to God's work in individual souls. Notice how Willard uses the term "testimony to the saving work of God *in the soul*" as the outcome of discipleship.[47] No one should deny that part of the disciple-making process focuses on God's work in an individual's life, but this emphasis seems lopsided when compared with the apostolic proclamation seen in Acts, for example,[48] or even the letters of Paul and his continuous proclamation of giving testimony to the saving work of God *in history*.[49]

In his defense Willard makes clear that spirituality is not a "superior" mode of existence and is not only about inward acts. Rather, he says, it is "a relationship of our embodied selves to God that has the natural and irrepressible effect of making us alive to the kingdom of God—here and now in the material world."[50] The disciple must turn inward in order to turn upward and outward. Thus, the personal-piety approach to discipleship does not deny Christian eschatology or worldview,[51] but it places less emphasis on our current cultural setting, leaving us vulnerable to the possibility of practicing "spiritual disciplines" while living according to another calendar altogether, another vision of eschatological destiny.

Especially considering the Enlightenment's split between facts and values, public truth and private faith, we must be on guard for ways spiritual disciplines can be hijacked by rival eschatologies. Perhaps this is the reason many Christians who are pious in their personal devotion still advocate for implementing aspects of the sexual revolution begun in the 1960s or make peace with an increasing secularism, due to their reliance on the Enlightenment worldview. Perhaps it is also the reason for Christian silence among many of the Germans during the rise of Hitler's holocaust or the silence of Southern Christians in the United States during the Jim Crow

47. Willard, *Great Omission*, 162.

48. Acts 2:14–39; 3:12–26; 4:8–12; 5:29–32; 7:2–53; 10:34–43; 13:16-42; and 17:22–31.

49. Rom 1:1–6 and 1 Corinthians 15.

50. Willard, *Spirit of the Disciplines*, 31.

51. Ibid., 37–38. Willard believes the resurrection is the central fact of the gospel, a cosmic event that validates Jesus's preaching of the kingdom of God and imparts to believers' new life.

era. It is possible to so shrink our focus to the practice of personal piety that the claim of Jesus as Lord over all—not just our soul—is muted.

Willard himself would not countenance such an individualized view. He sees the cultivation of interior righteousness as the element that makes Christian people salt and light in a world of evil. Willard says,

> The righteous can stop the wave before it starts, *if* they are stable in their righteousness, empowered by God, and distributed through society appropriately. The impersonal power structures in the world are, though independent of any one person's will and experience, nevertheless dependent for their force upon *the general readiness of normal people to do evil.*[52]

Still, the books Willard recommends on spiritual living (*Letters by a Modern Mystic* by Frank Laubach, *The Interior Castle* by Teresa of Ávila, and *Invitation to Solitude and Silence* by Ruth Haley Barton) are all inwardly focused. It is difficult to imagine any of these books equipping people with wisdom to answer the "What time is it?" question or to know how to live as Christians in light of current cultural realities. Retreating to the "interior castle" poses no threat to the world's towers of Babel.

The Strengthening Addition of Eschatological Discipleship

As we have seen, the personal-piety approach to discipleship possesses strengths and weaknesses. Eschatological discipleship would aid advocates of this approach by grounding a person's experience of God's transformative work in the soul within the bigger framework of God's future restoration of all of creation.

Keeping Spiritual Disciplines from Becoming Self-Help Consumerism. Because it is grounded in God's redemptive events in the past and the future, eschatological discipleship widens the focus of personal piety from the inward focus on God's transformation of the soul to the outward focus on God's transformation of the cosmos. This widening from the soul to the universe gives personal piety advocates a healthier understanding of how spiritual disciplines work and also their limits—how, in and of themselves, they do not necessarily keep one from being assimilated to the culture. In his critique of pietism, Keller writes,

52. Ibid., 231.

> The reality is that if the church does not think much about culture—about what parts are good, bad, or indifferent according to the Bible—its members will begin to uncritically imbibe the values of the culture. They will become assimilated to culture, despite intentions to the contrary. Culture is complex, subtle, and inescapable, as we have seen in our treatment of contextualization. And if we are not *deliberately* thinking about our culture, we will simply be conformed to it without ever knowing it is happening.[53]

Spiritual disciplines are one way to keep from being formed by the world, of course, but eschatological discipleship would alert personal-piety advocates to the danger of allowing our spiritual practices to be colonized by another worldview or eschatology.

For example, one of the ways consumerism affects Christians is by transforming our adoption of spiritual disciplines into just another way of branding ourselves. Just as people work out at the gym so as to look and feel a certain way, a consumerist can begin to see spiritual disciplines as a means to a personal benefit. Eschatological discipleship would aid the personal-piety approach by giving it additional tools to ensure that spiritual disciplines are not subsumed under wider cultural currents to the point they neutralize their spiritual effect.

The spiritual disciplines approach to formation needs an end point—something to look forward to—and this end point should go beyond the individual's personal holiness to the grand finale of the biblical narrative of God's redemptive acts. Without this grounding in cosmic history, Christians are likely to exert themselves through spiritual discipline without ever capturing a vision for what the goal is. It is difficult to keep up the motivation required for spiritual exertion if we do not keep before us a *telos*, one that includes both personal Christlikeness and the sovereign reign of Christ over the universe. Antoine de Saint-Exupery, the author of *The Little Prince* is quoted as saying, "If you want to build a ship, don't drum up people to collect wood and don't assign them tasks and work, but rather teach them to long for the endless immensity of the sea."[54] Something similar should be said for the personal-piety approach. One can focus on spiritual disciplines as a "rule," but perhaps the better way forward would be for eschatological

53. Keller, *Center Church*, 184–85.
54. Smith, *Imagining the Kingdom*, 7.

discipleship to bring back into the picture the eschatological future—the *telos* that gives motivation to these exercises and keeps them from being co-opted by rival worldviews.

Flexibility of Spiritual Disciplines Based on the Need within Culture. A second way eschatological discipleship would strengthen the personal-piety approach to discipleship is by showing how the exercise of disciplines may need to vary from culture to culture. In a society where ascetic philosophy is viewed as a way to appease God, it may be wise to emphasize disciplines of celebration over abstention. In a society filled with noise (as is ours), a discipline like solitude can be a helpful addition to the spiritual life, but even that discipline would need to be explained as something more than a "purge" from "real life." It is, instead, the kind of discipline that should impact how we address "real life," just as fasting should impact our relationship with food.

John Stott is especially helpful in maintaining the essential contribution of the personal-piety approach to discipleship while including aspects that inevitably point toward a culturally situated understanding of how we live as disciples in the time in which God has placed us. He defines discipleship as "a many-faceted lifestyle, an amalgam of several ingredients," which includes "worship, faith, obedience and hope."[55] In unpacking what discipleship must look like today, Stott calls us to a "radical nonconformity to the surrounding culture," in which we resist contemporary trends of pluralism, materialism, ethical relativism, and narcissism.[56] Stott writes:

> The church has a double responsibility in relation to the world around us. On the one hand we are to live, serve, and witness in the world. On the other hand we are to avoid becoming contaminated by the world. So we are neither to seek to preserve our holiness by escaping from the world nor to sacrifice our holiness by conforming to the world. Escapism and conformism are thus both forbidden to us.[57]

Why must we ask, "What time is it?" Because the church is called not to withdraw into the inner recesses of the personal transformations of its

55. Stott, *Contemporary Christian*, 174.

56. John R. W. Stott, *The Radical Disciple: Some Neglected Aspects of Our Calling* (Downers Grove, IL: InterVarsity Press, 2010), 19.

57. Stott, *Contemporary Christian*, 17.

members' hearts but rather to live publicly according to the gospel so that other worldviews are seen as false.

Eschatological discipleship helps ensure that the flexibility of using the spiritual disciplines keeps us from choosing an escapist or conformist path. The worldview question "What time is it?" grounds our practices of discipline in our current cultural settings and keeps them from drifting into timeless, ethereal practices divorced from contemporary society.

Discipleship as Gospel-Centered Motivation

A recent trend in discipleship is a return to the gospel as the motivating force for individual change.[58] This understanding of discipleship includes aspects of evangelistic reproduction and personal piety, but its focus is on the gospel as the difference maker, the motivating message that makes true transformation possible.

The Gospel Fuels Obedience

Transformational Discipleship is an example of the gospel-centered approach. Positioning themselves between two common yet flawed views of discipleship, the authors point out the weaknesses in "equating information with discipleship" or "viewing discipleship merely as behavioral modification." When churches conceive of discipleship in terms of transferring knowledge, the end result is a Christian who knows all Jesus commanded but does not necessarily obey the commands. When churches conceive of discipleship in terms of tweaking behavior, then the end result is a Christian who changes his or her actions but does not have a changed heart.[59]

The solution is a comprehensive approach to living according to the implications of the gospel.[60] In a similar manner to the personal-piety approach, Pastor Thabiti Anyabwile views growth in Christlikeness as the evidence of discipleship. He says:

> The growth we wish to see, the growth that is not finally external and superficial, is growth in godliness or holiness, growth in "the stature of the fullness of Christ." A growing church member is

58. Collin Hansen, *Young, Restless, and Reformed: A Journalist's Journey with the New Calvinists* (Wheaton, IL: Crossway, 2008). This movement has been described as the "young, restless, and Reformed," and is closely associated with the Gospel Coalition and leaders such as Tim Keller, D. A. Carson, and John Piper.

59. Geiger, Kelley, and Nation, *Transformational Discipleship*, 18, 28.

60. Ibid., 84.

> someone who looks more and more like Jesus in attitude of heart, thought, speech, and action. That's what we long to be and long for our churches to be.[61]

What distinguishes the gospel-driven-obedience approach to discipleship is its emphasis on the gospel as the motivating factor in developing Christlikeness. There is less talk about specific spiritual disciplines that develop personal piety and more conversation about deepening our understanding of what God has done for humanity in Christ.

A good example is Timothy S. Lane and Paul David Tripp's *How People Change*,[62] which uses the gospel story as the spiritually motivating and spiritually forming message that transforms the heart. Lane and Tripp believe the process of change in the life of a disciple happens as the gospel of grace touches the different spheres of life. Three redemptive truths ground the experience of believers. The "redemptive fact" is that we have been crucified with Christ, who broke the spiritual power sin had over us. We no longer have to give in to sin because Christ has conquered it on our behalf. The second redemptive truth is the "present reality" that Christ now lives in us. Our hearts are new because Christ lives in us, and this reality is what gives us the potential for growing in holiness. The third redemptive truth is "the results for daily living" in obedience, by the new principle of the power and grace of Jesus. The cross and resurrection of Christ ground our obedience in God, not in ourselves, and the gospel becomes the motivation for a life of grateful submission.[63]

This grounding of the believer's obedience in the work of Christ is what is frequently referred to as the distinction between imperatives and indicatives. The imperatives of Scripture (the commands) are grounded in the indicatives of Scripture (the truth of what God has done). One can see the journey from indicative to imperative running throughout Paul's letters, most often turning on the word "therefore." "You are not under the law but under grace," and you are "those who are alive from the dead" (indicatives, Rom 6:14, 13), *therefore* "do not let sin reign in your mortal body. . . . Do not offer any parts of it to sin as weapons for unrighteousness. But . . . offer

61. Thabiti Anyabwile, *What Is a Healthy Church Member?* (Wheaton, IL: Crossway, 2008), 89.

62. Timothy S. Lane and Paul David Tripp, *How People Change* (Greensboro, NC: New Growth Press, 2008).

63. Ibid., 150–52.

yourselves to God, and all the parts of yourselves to God as weapons for righteousness." (imperatives, Rom 6:12–13).

The first three chapters of Ephesians explain the gospel in terms of God's redemptive plan, our powerlessness to save ourselves, and God's bringing together Jew and Gentile alike. Then in chapter 4, Paul begins to list ways to apply the gospel message. "Therefore," he says and proceeds to give commands that are grounded in the gospel. The same is true of Galatians 5:24 and 5:16: "Those who belong to Christ Jesus have crucified the flesh with its passions and desires" (indicative), *therefore*, "walk by the Spirit and you will certainly not carry out the desire of the flesh" (imperative).[64]

According to the gospel-centered approach to discipleship, much of evangelicalism's current malaise is due to an overemphasis on the imperatives of Scripture, divorced from their rootedness in the indicatives of the gospel.[65] Simply telling people what to do is insufficient; what is necessary is for Christians to hear again and again what Christ has done.[66] This transformative understanding of discipleship, grounded in God's work through the cross and resurrection of Christ, is what truly changes a life. Any other attempt to force life change, either by motivating someone through guilt or through fear, will be short-lived and inferior. Lane and Tripp claim that "fruit grows out of a heart that drinks in the gospel."[67] True life change takes place through the gospel as a motivating force, and the gospel is what makes Christians more like Jesus.[68]

Christlikeness is a key component of gospel-centered theology. Pastors Mike Cosper and Daniel Montgomery, both considered part of the gospel-centered movement, focus on becoming like Christ, with their conception of discipleship heavily indebted to Willard. They state, "To be a disciple of Jesus, then, means that we not only learn about Jesus (studying

64. Jared C. Wilson, *Gospel Wakefulness* (Wheaton, IL: Crossway, 2011), 122, 130. According to Jared Wilson, "The difference between gospel-shaped obedience and law-driven obedience is the difference between a Christian life rooted in God's love and a self-salvation project. . . . Sanctification is wrought in us by the Spirit working through our obedience, but this catalyzed in the Spirit's approving of us as we return again and again to the gospel."

65. This is the main claim of the first part of J. D. Greear's book, *Gospel: Recovering the Power that Made Christianity Revolutionary* (Nashville: B&H, 2011).

66. Wilson, *Gospel Wakefulness*, 140. "Grace-driven effort springs from parking ourselves at the gospel and beholding. People who truly behold the beatific vision of Christ's finished work on their behalf move into mission."

67. Lane and Tripp, *How People Change*, 181.

68. J. A. Medders, *Gospel Formed: Living a Grace-Addicted, Truth-Filled, Jesus-Exalting Life* (Grand Rapids: Kregel, 2014), 23. Pastor J. A. Medders believes the gospel message focuses on right thinking, while motivation "hones in on right doing for the right reasons. Jesus shapes what we do and why we do it."

the Bible, learning doctrine, etc.) but that we look to the pattern of his life to learn how we ourselves should live. It means that we will not only be able to answer questions about him, but through the work of his Spirit, we will actually begin to look like him."[69]

Again the major difference in Cosper and Montgomery's work is that they see this obedience as lasting and transformative only when the gospel is the motivation, as they state, "The path to growth and transformation as disciples of Jesus is to put ourselves in a place where the floodlights of God's spirit can shine. Change happens in the human heart when we see Jesus as 'more beautiful and more believable' than all our addictions to sin and self."[70] In summary, the gospel-centered approach to discipleship focuses on the gospel as the motivating factor and fuel for obedience to the commands of Christ and the development of Christlikeness.

Strengths and Weaknesses

The strengths of the gospel-centered approach are as follows. First, advocates of this approach are apt to connect personal transformation to engagement in God's mission (offering a balance of inward and outward activity). Mission is to be the natural outworking of a heart transformed by grace. A strong missional component exists for many of the advocates for gospel-centered Christianity. No gospel-centeredness exists apart from mission because the gospel is the story of a missionary God.[71] The focus on gospel motivation for obedience is intended to inspire Christians to obey out of a delight-filled relationship with God rather than from a dutiful, drudgery of obligation.

Second, this approach provides a helpful corrective to a mechanical understanding of personal growth that could be implied by the personal-piety approach. Transformation is not a mechanical process of steps and stages and levels; rather, it is driven by a relationship with Christ who transforms us from the inside out. Furthermore, the emphasis on delighting in God is important if the sustaining of spiritual exertion is to be made possible. As Timothy Lane and Paul David Tripp remind, "A new lifestyle—the outward Fruit of a believer's life—does not grow out of a stoic obedience to

69. Daniel Montgomery and Mike Cosper, *Faithmapping: A Gospel Atlas for Your Spiritual Journey* (Wheaton, IL: Crossway, 2013), 160.

70. Ibid., 167.

71. I make this point in my book, *Gospel Centered Teaching: Showing Christ in All the Scripture* (Nashville: B&H, 2013), 95–109. See also the outward posture of a Gospel-centered Christian described in Geiger, Kelley, and Nation, *Transformational Discipleship*, 175–200.

God's commands, but from a heart that has been captured and captivated by the Giver of those commands."[72]

Along with these strengths are two weaknesses to the gospel-driven obedience approach. First, applying the gospel to all of life sometimes gets reduced to all of one's personal life, not necessarily to all spheres of culture, which is the reason the authors of *Transformational Discipleship* can, on the one hand, affirm that the gospel is for all of life, and yet, on the other hand, leave traces of a deeschatologized, otherworldly understanding of salvation, where "this world and its pursuits are fleeting."[73] This type of statement is helpful insofar as the authors' goal is to remind us that our ultimate allegiance is to the kingdom of God. However, too often Christians tend to move from the question of allegiance to the question of importance and, thereby, undercut these worldly aspects of bringing Christ's rule to bear in all spheres of life.

Likewise, when advocates of gospel-driven obedience refer to eschatology, they often do so in an individualistic way. Even when authors correctly observe how often the New Testament connects a Christian's spiritual growth to the truth of Christ's second coming, they may interpret these eschatological references in a personal and individualistic way, encouraging disciples to grow in holiness by simply meditating on these truths. The application stays personal rather than cosmic in scope. It is not explicitly connected to the in-breaking of God's kingdom into human history and the calling of Christians to live under Christ's lordship in all spheres of life.

A second weakness is the reliance on the gospel when the personalized Spirit should be at the forefront. Many of the statements commonly associated with the gospel-centered approach ("Our obedience is *fueled* by the gospel." "The gospel is what *motivates* our obedience." "We need to be captured again by the gospel." Or, "We need be refreshed in the gospel every day.") could just as easily refer to the Spirit's working. The statement, "The gospel fuels our obedience," is shorthand for the truth that the Spirit captures our affections with the gospel in order to fuel our obedience.

Certainly a biblical precedent exists for thinking of the gospel as having a power of its own, an innate power inherent to its message. Paul spoke of it as "the power of God for salvation" (Rom 1:16), and Luke refers

72. Lane and Tripp, *How People Change*, 173.

73. Geiger, Kelley, and Nation, *Transformational Discipleship*, 107, state, for example, "Leaders who view discipleship through the lens of identity help the people they serve realize this world is not their ultimate home."

to the Word "increasing and multiplying" (Acts 12:24 NET). There is nothing unbiblical about using the gospel in a way that gives the good news a personification, but gospel-centered proponents who think of power as flowing from the gospel (which is a message) can unintentionally communicate that believers are changed by knowledge of a message and not by personal acquaintance with the Messenger. We run into problems when we use "gospel reflection" language as buzz words that reduce the Christian life to continual reflection on a set of propositional truths instead of the dynamic Word that brings people into relationship with Persons—the Father, the Son, and the Spirit.

The Strengthening Addition of Eschatological Discipleship

For those who take a gospel-driven-obedience approach to discipleship, asking what time it is ensures that our understanding of the gospel is not reduced to an individual's personal forgiveness of sins but also includes the significance of Christ's resurrection and exaltation as Lord of the world. Asking what time it is also increases our need for the Spirit's wisdom and guidance as we seek to obey.

The Gospel as Public Truth. Mike Cosper and Daniel Montgomery do well in synthesizing the best aspects of the converts-making-converts approach to discipleship, the personal-piety reliance on spiritual disciplines, and the need for all one's obedience to be motivated by the gospel. In *Faithmapping*, they ask worldview questions at the end of each chapter, exploring the role of the church as worshipers, family, servants, disciples, and witnesses. Their questions are: "Who am I?," "Where am I?," and "What am I to do?" They write, "When someone wakes up one day and realizes that his whole world matters to God, and sees the whole gospel unfold in his life, it truly changes everything. His sins are forgiven. The pressure is off. He has a message to share. He's now part of something bigger."[74] The dimensions of discipleship (location, vocation, recreation, restoration, and multiplication) stem from the cosmic implications of the gospel message.

Because of their emphasis on the grand narrative of Scripture, Timothy Lane and Paul David Tripp recognize the need for eschatology. They write about how the biblical story helps believers live with the destination in view. Knowing how the biblical story ends is important for three reasons: (1) going in the right direction presupposes knowledge of the destination,

74. Montgomery and Cosper, *Faithmapping*, 202.

(2) the perspective of eternity is necessary to make sense of the details of one's life, and (3) eternity teaches what is most important in life.[75] Lane and Tripp continue, "Christian joy is not about avoiding life while dreaming about heaven. It is about taking an utterly honest look at all earthly life through heaven's lens."[76] This concept is close to the eschatological discipleship we have been pursuing. The only thing it needs is a stronger dose of *cosmic* eschatology that does more than focus on the destination of the individual. Part of what aids us in understanding how we are to live in the present is knowing what God's plan for the entire world is, not just our individual sanctification.

The question "What time is it?" has deeply personal implications, as Tripp and Lane's commenting on living in light of eternity reveals, but it is not first and foremost a personal question. Rather, it is a world question, a cosmic question; it demands we consider ourselves in light of biblical history and view our culture from within a biblical eschatology. By speaking of how eschatology affects us only personally, we are left with this view alone—that because we will be glorified, we should live toward that future.

Eschatological discipleship widens the horizon so we see the world will be renewed. If the vision of our personal glorification and ultimate Christlikeness gives hope and direction for our personal obedience, so also the vision of the world's renewal should give hope and direction for our actions in the world. Our good works in the world take on an eschatological dimension when we see ourselves as anticipating the coming renewal of all things. Furthermore, widening this eschatological horizon causes us to lean more heavily on the Spirit who gives wisdom in determining the best way to live toward that future. Eschatological discipleship commends both the personal and cosmic visions of the future—consideration of the believer's own glorification and the world's ultimate future in Jesus Christ.

Obedience in Light of What God Will Do. Along these lines the gospel-driven-obedience approach would be helped not just by personal meditation on the reality of Christ's second coming but also on the significance of Christ's future reign for our actions in the present. As seen in this study of eschatological discipleship in the New Testament, the exhortations of

75. Lane and Tripp, *How People Change*, 37.
76. Ibid., 44.

Scripture are often based on "what time it is"—the indicatives of what God has promised to do in the future, not just what God has done in the past.

The gospel-centered approach to discipleship consistently pushes Christians to consider God's redemptive work in the past. For example, Jared Wilson writes, "We will not experience freedom in religion's three words. 'Get to work' doesn't work. We must first be set free by the gospel's three words. 'It is finished.'"[77] Eschatological discipleship would add another phrase that liberates Christians to live in light of God's future work, "I am making all things new" (Rev 21:5 ESV). Grounding present imperatives in past indicatives is only half of the New Testament's witness. Present imperatives are also grounded in future promises. As Marianne Meye Thompson writes:

> The Bible anticipates and leans into the future; it is replete with yearnings for the coming of the future realm of blessedness, when swords are beaten into plowshares, when the earth yields its crops abundantly, when God wipes away every tear from our eyes, when human beings dwell together in harmony with each other and with their God, when God's work to call together this holy, worshiping, loving people will be brought to fruition. For that new beginning we trust in the God who made the world and who will redeem it through Jesus Christ. Then the story will not only have its ending, but its new beginning too.[78]

Once the scope of indicatives is widened to the future of the cosmos, one is left with more reasons for involvement in the world.

Conclusion

Evangelicalism has a myriad of helpful resources that define and delineate the process of discipleship. The three categories of discipleship examined—evangelistic reproduction, personal piety, and gospel-driven obedience—each has strengths and weaknesses, but all of them would benefit from a healthy dose of worldview thinking regarding eschatological implications for the church. This dimension would ground each of these approaches to

77. Wilson, *Gospel Wakefulness*, 133.

78. Marianne Meye Thompson, "What Holds the Bible Together?," in *Conversations at the Edges of Things: Reflections for the Church in Honor of John Goldingay* (Eugene, Ore.: Wipf and Stock, 2012), 48.

discipleship in history in such a way that Christians would increasingly be salt and light, obeying all that Christ has commanded by resisting the unbiblical worldviews thrust forth in contemporary society.

Conclusion

Christian eschatology forms a basic and necessary component of discipleship, and contemporary conceptions of discipleship among evangelicals would be strengthened by a stronger emphasis on the cosmic eschatological perspective found in the Bible's grand narrative. In order to make this case, I have sought to build strong biblical foundations from both the Old and New Testaments in order to demonstrate the eschatological motivation behind many of the biblical authors' ethical considerations. I have also sought to apply these insights into eschatological discipleship within the context of North America by examining Christian eschatology in light of the rival eschatologies of the Enlightenment, sexual revolution, and consumerism.

In conclusion, I would like to point readers toward further avenues of research that will strengthen the understanding of eschatological discipleship and how it can apply in a North American context. First, there is need for a fuller treatment of the wisdom literature of the Old Testament in light of Israel's eschatological situation. The relationship of timeless maxims and timely application deserves further consideration, especially considering the importance of Spirit-guided wisdom and discernment, which is a necessary and integral component of eschatological discipleship. It would be helpful to see the various similarities and contrasts between wisdom's role in Israel's obedience in the Old Testament and wisdom's role in the Church's obedience in the New Testament and how contemporary Christians can apply these insights in a contemporary setting where Spirit-guided wisdom is sorely needed.

Another avenue of fruitful research would be to flesh out the biblical foundations for eschatological discipleship in order to provide a deeper and richer exploration of how the New Testament's ethical exhortations contain eschatological underpinnings. Our study focused primarily on

Matthew's and Luke's commissioning and Matthew's parables. Further studies could demonstrate the eschatological motivation behind the exhortations in Jesus's didactic teachings, including those of the Gospel of John. Much more could be said about how Paul's vision for church life and his counsel to the churches are both grounded in his hope for the realization of new creation now, in anticipation of the consummation of the new creation in the future. Other non-Pauline New Testament letters should also be considered, including Peter's instructions to the early Christians, in which we see the same vision of obedience through suffering (and identity as exiles).

The danger of asking the question "What time is it?" is that it could potentially lead to syncretism or a relativism based on one's time period. Just as it is possible for someone to relativize Christian teaching based on cultural location ("what is right in one culture may be wrong in another"), it is also possible for someone to use the "What time is it?" question to relativize Christian teaching based on historical epoch ("what was considered wrong in one period of time should be considered right in another"). More exploration should be done to ensure that eschatological discipleship leads to a stronger and more effective contextualization of the Christian faith *while simultaneously* avoiding syncretism, a creeping relativism that would undercut the church's historic witness across cultures and generations to a common foundation of Christian ethics.

Regarding the Enlightenment eschatology of progress, there is need for a more comprehensive historical study of how post-Enlightenment revolutions have used the eschatology of progress in order to implement social change. From the American Revolution, to the Napoleonic wars and the French Revolution, to the rise of the Soviet Union, we see a common thread of historical inevitability, which accompanies an explicit and implicit view of progress and the future of world history. We need more research into how this vision of progress works rhetorically, culturally, and sociologically.

Finally, we need a more comprehensive study of the role of cosmic eschatology in evangelical conceptions of discipleship. As seen in the previous chapter, the three common conceptions of discipleship we considered showed only slight interaction with the role that cosmic eschatology plays in our everyday obedience. More attention should be devoted to how distinctive visions of holiness and Christian faithfulness depend on and are influenced by our view of world history according to Christian eschatology, not merely our view of a believer's personal destiny.

Christ, Sovereign Over Time

My prayer at the close of this book is that Christians will incorporate the question "What time is it?" into their conception of discipleship in order to reduce the likelihood of our being seduced by the world. As we fulfill the call to be transformed, not conformed to this world that is passing away, we must learn to discern our times properly in order to have a missionary encounter that shines light on the true eschatology of the gospel that proclaims Jesus Christ as the hope of the world. This missionary encounter is the proclamation of hope—true hope in a world of myths. As Dietrich Bonhoeffer wrote, "The difference between the Christian hope and a mythological hope is that the Christian hope sends a man back to his life on earth in a wholly new way. . . . Myths of salvation arise from human experience of the boundary condition. Christ takes hold of a man in the center of his life."[1]

Abraham Kuyper famously said, "There is not a square inch in the whole domain of our human existence over which Christ, who is sovereign over all, does not cry, Mine!"[2] Eschatological discipleship adds to that famous phrase, "There is not a split second in the whole history of our cosmos over which Christ, who is sovereign over time, does not cry, Mine!" Christ—sovereign over every acre, sovereign over every hour—redeems the time and confronts any calendar that would displace his cross and resurrection from the center of history.

1. Bonhoeffer, *Letters and Papers*, 112–13.
2. Abraham Kuyper, *Lectures on Calvinism* (Grand Rapids: Eerdmans, 1987), 11.

Selected Bibliography

Adeleye, Femi Bitrus. *Preachers of a Different Gospel: A Pilgrim's Reflections on Contemporary Trends in Christianity*. Nairobi, Kenya: Hippo Books, 2011.

Akin, Daniel L., ed. *A Theology for the Church*. Rev. ed. Nashville: B&H Academic, 2014.

Allen, Roland. *Missionary Methods: St. Paul's or Ours?* Grand Rapids: Eerdmans, 1962.

Allison, Dale C. *The Sermon on the Mount: Inspiring the Moral Imagination*. New York: Crossroad Publishing, 1999.

______. *Studies in Matthew: Interpretation Past and Present*. Grand Rapids: Baker Academic, 2005.

Allison, Gregg. *Historical Theology: An Introduction to Christian Doctrine*. Grand Rapids: Zondervan, 2011.

______. *Sojourners and Strangers: The Doctrine of the Church*. Wheaton, IL: Crossway, 2012.

Andria, Solomon. *Romans*. Africa Bible Commentary Series. Edited by Samuel Ngewa. Grand Rapids: Zondervan, 2012.

Anyabwile, Thabiti. *What Is a Healthy Church Member?* Wheaton, IL: Crossway, 2008.

Armstrong, Jennifer Keishin. *Mary and Lou and Rhoda and Ted: And All the Brilliant Minds Who Made the Mary Tyler Moore Show a Classic*. New York: Simon and Schuster, 2013.

Ashford, Bruce Riley. "The Church in the Mission of God." Pages 237–60 in *The Community of Jesus*. Edited by Kendell H. Easley and Christopher W. Morgan. Nashville: B&H, 2013.

______, ed. *Theology and Practice of Mission: God, the Church, and the Nations*. Nashville: B&H, 2011.

Atkin, Douglas. *The Culting of Brands: When Customers Become True Believers*. New York: Portfolio, 2004.

Augustine of Hippo. *City of God*. New York: Doubleday, 1958.

______. *Confessions*. Nashville: Thomas Nelson, 1999.

______. *In Epistulam Iohannis*. 4.6. Accessed September 28, 2015. http://www.ewtn.com/library/PATRISTC/PNI7-8.TXT.

______. *Sermon on the Mount*. 2.24.87. Accessed September 28, 2015. http://www. ewtn.com/library/PATRISTC/PNI6-1.TXT.

Bailey, Kenneth E. *Jacob and the Prodigal: How Jesus Retold Israel's Story*. Downers Grove, IL: InterVarsity Press, 2003.

______. *Jesus through Middle Eastern Eyes: Cultural Studies in the Gospels*. Downers Grove, IL: IVP Academic, 2008.

______. *Poet and Peasant* and *Through Peasant Eyes: A Literary-Cultural Approach to the Parables in Luke*. Combined ed. Grand Rapids: Eerdmans, 1983.

Barnes, Julian. *Nothing to Be Frightened Of*. New York: Alfred A. Knopf, 2008.

Barth, Karl. *The Epistle to the Romans*. London: Oxford University Press, 1933.

Bartholomew, Craig. "Christ and Consumerism: An Introduction." Pages 1–12 in *Christ and Consumerism: A Critical Analysis of the Spirit of the Age*. Edited by Craig Bartholomew and Thorsten Moritz. Crownhill, UK: Paternoster Press, 2000.

______, and Michael Goheen. *Christian Philosophy: A Systematic and Narrative Introduction*. Grand Rapids: Baker Academic, 2013.

Bartholomew, Craig G. *Ecclesiastes*. Baker Commentary on the Old Testament: Wisdom and Psalms. Edited by Tremper Longman III. Grand Rapids: Baker Academic, 2009.

______. *Where Mortals Dwell: A Christian View of Place for Today*. Grand Rapids: Baker Academic, 2011.

______. *The Drama of Scripture: Finding Our Place in the Biblical Story*. Grand Rapids: Baker Academic, 2004.

______. *Living at the Crossroads: An Introduction to Christian Worldview*. Grand Rapids: Baker Academic, 2008.

______, and Ryan O'Dowd. *Old Testament Wisdom Literature: A Theological Introduction*. Downers Grove, IL: IVP Academic, 2011.

Bauckham, Richard. *Jesus and the Eyewitnesses: The Gospel as Eyewitness Testimony*. Grand Rapids: Eerdmans, 2006.

Baudrillard, Jean. *Jean Baudrillard: Selected Writings*. Edited by Mark Poster. Translated by Jacques Mourrain. Palo Alto, CA: Stanford University Press, 2011.

Beale, G. K. *We Become What We Worship: A Biblical Theology of Idolatry*. Downers Grove, IL: InterVarsity Press, 2008.

______, and Benjamin L. Gladd. *Hidden but Now Revealed: A Biblical Theology of Mystery*. Downers Grove, IL: IVP Academic, 2014.

Beck, Brian E. *Christian Character in the Gospel of Luke*. London: Epworth Press, 1989.

Beilby, James K., and Paul Rhodes Eddy, eds. *The Historical Jesus: Five Views*. Downers Grove, IL: IVP Academic, 2009.

Bellah, Robert N., Richard Madsen, William M. Sullivan, Ann Swidler, and Steven M. Tipton. *Habits of the Heart: Individualism and Commitment in American Life*. 2008. Oakland, CA: Regents of the University of California, 2008.

Benedict XVI (pope). *Jesus of Nazareth: From the Baptism in the Jordan to the Transfiguration*. Translated from the German by Adrian J. Walker. New York: Doubleday, 2007.

Berger, Peter. *The Sacred Canopy: Elements of a Sociological Theory of Religion*. New York: Doubleday, 1967.

Berlin, Isaiah. *The Crooked Timber of Humanity: Chapters in the History of Ideas*. 2nd ed. Princeton, NJ: Princeton University Press, 2013.

Bevans, Stephen B. *Models of Contextual Theology*. Rev. and exp. ed. Maryknoll, NY: Orbis Books, 2002.

Bird, Michael. *Evangelical Theology*. Grand Rapids: Zondervan, 2013.

Blickenstaff, Marianne. "Matthew's Parable of the Wedding Feast (Matt 22:1–14)." *Review and Expositor* 109, no. 2 (Spring 2012): 265.

Blomberg, Craig L. *The Historical Reliability of John's Gospel*. Downers Grove, IL: IVP Academic, 2001.

______. *Interpreting the Parables*. Downers Grove, IL: IVP Academic, 1990.

______. *Matthew*. New American Commentary. Vol. 22. Nashville: Broadman 1992.

______. *Neither Poverty Nor Riches: A Biblical Theology of Possessions*. Downers Grove, IL: InterVarsity Press, 1999.

Bloom, Allan. *The Closing of the American Mind*. New York: Simon & Schuster, 1987.

Bock, Darrell L. *Luke*. Grand Rapids: Baker Books, 1996.

______. *A Theology of Luke and Acts: God's Promised Program, Realized for All Nations*. Biblical Theology of the New Testament. Edited by Andreas J. Köstenberger. Grand Rapids: Zondervan, 2012.

Bonhoeffer, Dietrich. *The Cost of Discipleship*. New York: SCM Press, 1959.

______. *Letters and Papers from Prison*. London: Fontana, 1953.

______. *Life Together: The Classic Exploration of Christian Community*. New York: Harper & Row, 1954.

Bornkamm, Gunther. *Paul*. Translated by M. G. Stalker. New York: Harper & Row, 1966.

Bosch, David J. *Transforming Mission: Paradigm Shifts in Theology of Mission*. 20th anniversary ed. Maryknoll, NY: Orbis Books, 2011.

Bowie, Walter Russell. *The Compassionate Christ: Reflections from the Gospel of Luke*. New York: Abingdon Press, 1965.

Brake, Elizabeth. *Minimizing Marriage: Marriage, Morality and the Law*. London: Oxford University Press, 2012.

Bruce, A. B. *The Training of the Twelve*. Grand Rapids: Kregel, 1988.

Bruce, F. F. *1 & 2 Thessalonians*. Word Biblical Commentary. Vol. 45. Nashville: Word, 1982.

Butterfield, Herbert. *The Whig Interpretation of History*. Repr. ed. New York: W. W. Norton, 1965.

Carson, D. A. *Christ and Culture Revisited*. Grand Rapids: Eerdmans, 2008.

______. *Gagging of God: Christianity Confronts Pluralism*. Grand Rapids: Zondervan, 2009.

______. *The God Who Is There: Finding Your Place in God's Story*. Grand Rapids: Baker, 2010.

______. *Matthew*. Expositor's Bible Commentary. Vol. 8. Edited by Frank E. Gaebelein. Grand Rapids: Zondervan, 1984.

______, Walter W. Wessel, and Walter L. Liefeld. *Matthew-Mark-Luke*. Expositor's Bible Commentary. Vol. 8. Edited by Frank E. Gaebelein. Grand Rapids: Zondervan, 1984.

______, and John Woodbridge, eds. *Scripture and Truth*. Grand Rapids: Baker, 1992.

Chan, Simon. *Grassroots Asian Theology: Thinking the Faith from the Ground Up*. Downers Grove, IL: IVP Academic, 2014.

______. *Liturgical Theology: The Church as Worshiping Community*. Downers Grove, IL: IVP Academic, 2006.

______. *Pentecostal Theology and the Christian Spiritual Tradition*. Sheffield, UK: Sheffield Academic Press, 2000.

______. *Spiritual Theology: A Systematic Study of the Christian Life*. Downers Grove, IL: InterVarsity Press, 1998.

Chandler, Diane J. *Christian Spiritual Formation: An Integrated Approach for Personal and Relational Wholeness*. Downers Grove, IL: IVP Academic, 2014.

Chapell, Bryan. *Christ-Centered Preaching: Redeeming the Expository Sermon*. 2nd ed. Grand Rapids: Baker Academic, 2005.

Chapman, Alister. *Godly Ambition: John Stott and the Evangelical Movement*. Oxford: New York: Oxford University Press, 2012.

Chesser, Eustace. *Salvation Through Sex: The Life and Work of Wilhelm Reich*. New York: William Morrow and Co., 1973.

Chester, Tim. *From Creation to New Creation: Making Sense of the Whole Bible Story*. London: Good Book Co., 2010.

______. *You Can Change: God's Transforming Power for Our Sinful Behavior and Negative Emotions*. Wheaton, IL: Crossway, 2011.

______, and Steve Timmis. *Total Church: A Radical Reshaping Around Gospel and Community*. Wheaton, IL: Crossway, 2008.

Chesterton, G. K. *Brave New Family: G. K. Chesterton on Men and Women, Children, Sex, Divorce, Marriage, and the Family*. San Francisco, CA: Ignatius, 1990.

______. *Orthodoxy*. Chicago, IL: Moody, 2009.

______. *The Superstition of Divorce*. New York: John Lane Co., 1920.

Chrysostom, John. *Homily* 24.3. Accessed September 28, 2015. http://www.newadvent.org/fathers/200124.htm.

Clapp, Rodney, ed. *The Consuming Passion: Christianity and the Consumer Culture*. Downers Grove, IL: IVP, 2007.

Clark, David. *To Know and Love God: Method for Theology*. Wheaton, IL: Crossway, 2003.

Clowney, Edmund. *The Church*. Downers Grove, IL: InterVarsity Press, 1995.

______. *The Message of 1 Peter*. Downers Grove, IL: InterVarsity Press, 1988.

______. *The Unfolding Mystery: Discovering Christ in the Old Testament* 2nd ed. Phillipsburg, NJ: P&R, 2013.

Coleman, Robert E. *The Master Plan of Evangelism*. 2nd ed. Grand Rapids: Revell, 1993.

Colson, Charles, and Nancy Pearcey. *How Now Shall We Live?*. Wheaton, IL: Tyndale House, 1998.

Conn, Harvie M. *The Urban Face of Mission: Ministering the Gospel in a Diverse and Changing World*. Phillipsburg, NJ: P&R, 2002.

Conzelmann, Hans. *The Theology of St. Luke*. Translated by Geoffrey Buswell. London: Faber and Faber, 1960.

Copan, Victor A. *Saint Paul as Spiritual Director: An Analysis of the Concept of the Imitation of Paul with Implications and Applications to the Practice of Spiritual Direction*. Eugene, OR: Wipf and Stock Publishers, 2007.

Cowan, Steven, ed. *Five Views on Apologetics*. Zondervan Counterpoints Series. Grand Rapids: Zondervan, 2000.

Crossan, John Dominic. *In Parables: The Challenge of the Historical Jesus*. Sonoma, CA: Polebridge Press, 1992.

Crouch, Andy. *Culture Making: Recovering Our Creative Calling*. Downers Grove, IL: InterVarsity Press, 2008.

______. *Playing God: Redeeming the Gift of Power*. Downers Grove, IL: InterVarsity Press, 2013.

Cyril of Alexandria (saint). *Commentary on the Gospel of Saint Luke*. Translated by R. Payne Smith. Seattle, WA: Studion Publishers, 1983.

Dawkins, Richard. *Unweaving the Rainbow: Science, Delusion, and the Appetite for Wonder*. Geneva, IL: Mariner Books, 2000.

Dawn, Marva. *A Royal "Waste" of Time: The Splendor of Worshiping God and Being Church for the World*. Grand Rapids: Eerdmans, 1999.

Demarest, Bruce, and Stanley Gundry, eds. *Four Views on Christian Spirituality*. Grand Rapids: Zondervan, 2012.

Dever, Mark. *The Church: The Gospel Made Visible*. Nashville: B&H Academic, 2012.

DeYmaz, Mark. *Building a Healthy Multi-Ethnic Church: Mandate, Commitments, and Practices of a Diverse Congregation*. Hoboken, NJ: John Wiley and Sons, 2007.

______, and Harry Li. *Ethnic Blends: Mixing Diversity into Your Local Church*. Grand Rapids: Zondervan, 2010.

Diderot. *Supplement au Voyage de Bougainville*. In *Oeuvres Philosophiques*. Paris, France: Garnier, 1964.

Dodd, C. H. *The Parables of the Kingdom*. London, Nisbett and Co.: Charles Scribner's Sons, 1956.

Dodson, Jonathan. *The Unbelievable Gospel: Say Something Worth Believing*. Grand Rapids: Zondervan, 2014.

Dollar, Harold. *St. Luke's Missiology: A Cross-Cultural Challenge*. Pasadena, CA: William Carey Library, 1996.

Donahue, John R. *The Gospel in Parable*. Minneapolis: Fortress Press, 1988.

Doriani, Daniel M. *The Sermon on the Mount: The Character of a Disciple*. Phillipsburg, NJ: P&R, 2006.

Douthat, Ross. *Bad Religion: How We Became a Nation of Heretics*. New York: Free Press, 2012.

Earley, Dave, and Rod Dempsey, eds. *Disciple Making Is . . . : How to Live the Great Commission with Passion and Confidence*. Nashville: B&H, 2013.

Easley, Kendell H., and Christopher W. Morgan, eds. *The Community of Jesus: A Theology of the Church*. Nashville: B&H Academic, 2013.

Eims, Leroy. *The Lost Art of Disciple Making*. Grand Rapids: Zondervan, 1978.

Ellis, Carl, Jr. *Free at Last? The Gospel in African-American Experience*. Downers Grove, IL: IVP, 2006.

Elmer, Duane. *Cross-Cultural Conflict: Building Relationships for Effective Ministry*. Downers Grove, IL: IVP Academic, 1993.

Erickson, Millard J. *Christian Theology*. 3rd ed. Grand Rapids: Baker Academic, 2013.

Escobar, Samuel. "Mission Studies—Past, Present, and Future." Pages 219–43 in *Landmark Essays in Mission and World Christianity*. Edited by Robert L. Gallagher and Paul Hertig. Maryknoll, NY: Orbis Books, 2009.

______. *The New Global Mission: The Gospel from Everywhere to Everyone*. Downers Grove, IL: IVP Academic, 2003.

______, and John Driver. *Christian Mission and Social Justice*. Scottdale, PA: Herald Press, 1978.

Fabian, Johannes. *Time and the Other: How Anthropology Makes Its Object*. New York: Columbia University Press, 1983.

Fea, John. *Why Study History? Reflecting on the Importance of the Past*. Grand Rapids: Baker Academic, 2013.

Fee, Gordon D. *The First Epistle to the Corinthians*. New International Commentary on the New Testament. Grand Rapids: Eerdmans, 1987.

______. *Paul's Letter to the Philippians*. New International Commentary on the New Testament. Grand Rapids: Eerdmans, 1995.

Fitch, David E., and Geoff Holsclaw. *Prodigal Christianity: 10 Signposts into the Missional Frontier*. San Francisco, CA: Jossey-Bass, 2013.

Ford, David F. *Christian Wisdom: Desiring God and Learning in Love*. Cambridge, MA: Cambridge University Press, 2007.

Forster, Greg. *The Contested Public Square: The Crisis of Christianity and Politics*. Downers Grove, IL: IVP Academic, 2008.

______. *Joy for the World: How Christianity Lost Its Cultural Influence and Can Begin Rebuilding It*. Wheaton, IL: Crossway, 2014.

Forsythe, Clarke D. *Politics for the Greatest Good: The Case for Prudence in the Public Square*. Downers Grove, IL: InterVarsity Press, 2009.

Foster, Richard. *Celebration of Discipline: The Path to Spiritual Growth*. Rev. ed. Downers Grove, IL: InterVarsity Press, 1988.

______. *Money, Sex, and Power: The Challenge of the Disciplined Life*. New York: Harper & Row, 1985.

Foucault, Michel. "Foucault Text: From *The History of Sexuality*." Pages 123-34 in *The Postmodern God: A Theological Reader*. Blackwell Readings in Modern Theology. Edited by Graham Ward. Malden, MA: Blackwell, 1997.

______. *The Use of Pleasure*. The History of Sexuality. Vol. 2. New York: Vintage Books, 1990.

Fourez, Gerard. "The Sexual Revolution in Perspective." Pages 3-10 in *The Sexual Revolution*. Edited by Gregory Baum and John Coleman. Edinburgh, Scotland: T&T Clark, 1984.

Frend, W. H. C. *The Rise of Christianity*. Philadelphia, Pa.: Fortress, 1984.

Gaffin, Richard B., Jr. *By Faith, Not by Sight: Paul and the Order of Salvation*. Phillipsburg, NJ: P&R, 2013.

______. *Resurrection and Redemption: A Study in Paul's Soteriology*. Phillipsburg, NJ: P&R, 1987.

Gay, Craig M. "Sensualists without Heart: Contemporary Consumerism in Light of the Modern Project." Pages 19-38 in *The Consuming Passion: Christianity and the Consumer Culture*. Edited by Rodney Clapp. Downers Grove, IL: IVP, 1998.

Gay, Peter. *The Enlightenment: An Interpretation*. The Rise of Modern Paganism. New York: Alfred A. Knopf, 1966.

Geiger, Eric, Michael Kelley, and Philip Nation. *Transformational Discipleship: How People Really Grow*. Nashville: B&H, 2012.

George, Timothy. "St. Augustine and the Mystery of Time." Pages 27-46 in *What God Knows: Time and the Question of Divine Knowledge*. Edited by Harry Lee Poe and J. Stanley Mattson. Waco, TX: Baylor, 2005.

______. *Theology of the Reformers: 25th Anniversary*. Nashville: B&H Academic, 2013.

Girgis, Sherif, Ryan T. Anderson, and Robert P. George. *What Is Marriage? Man and Woman: A Defense*. New York: Encounter Books, 2012.

Gittins, Anthony. *Called to Be Sent*. Liguori, MO: Liguori Press, 2008.

Goheen, Michael. *Introducing Christian Mission Today: Scripture, History, and Issues*. Downers Grove, IL: IVP Academic, 2014.

______. *A Light to the Nations: The Missional Church and the Biblical Story*. Grand Rapids: Baker Academic, 2011.

Goldingay, John. *Israel's Life*. Old Testament Theology. Vol. 3. Downers Grove, IL: IVP Academic, 2009.

______. *Psalms 90–150*. Psalms. Baker Commentary on the Old Testament: Wisdom and Psalms. Vol. 3. Edited by Tremper Longman III. Grand Rapids: Baker Academic, 2008.

Goldsworthy, Graeme. *Christ-Centered Biblical Theology: Hermeneutical Foundations and Principles*. Downers Grove, IL: InterVarsity Press, 2012.

______. *Gospel and Kingdom*. Crownhill, UK: Paternoster, 2012.

______. *Gospel-Centered Hermeneutics: Foundations and Principles of Evangelical Biblical Interpretation*. Downers Grove, IL: InterVarsity Press, 2006.

Gombis, Timothy G. *The Drama of Ephesians: Participating in the Triumph of God*. Downers Grove, IL: IVP Academic, 2010.

González, Justo L. *Mañana: Christian Theology from a Hispanic Perspective*. Nashville: Abingdon Press, 1990.

Gorospe, Athena E. "Old Testament Narratives and Ethics: A Journey in Understanding." Pages 27–38 in *Conversations at the Edges of Things: Reflections for the Church in Honor of John Goldingay*. Edited by Francis Bridger and James T. Butler. Eugene, OR: Wipf and Stock, 2012.

Gray, John. *Enlightenment's Wake: Politics and Culture at the Close of the Modern Age*. Abingdon, UK: Routledge Classics, 2007.

Greear, J. D. *Gospel: Recovering the Power that Made Christianity Revolutionary*. Nashville: B&H, 2011.

Greidanus, Sidney. *The Modern Preacher and the Ancient Text: Interpreting and Preaching Biblical Literature*. Grand Rapids: Eerdmans, 1988.

Guder, Darrell. *Missional Church: A Vision for the Sending of the Church in North America*. Grand Rapids: Eerdmans, 1998.

Guinness, Os. *The Case for Civility*. New York: HarperOne, 2008.

______. *The Dust of Death: The Sixties Counterculture and How It Changed America Forever*. Wheaton, IL: Crossway Books, 1994.

______. *The Last Christian on Earth: Uncover the Enemy's Plot to Undermine the Church*. Grand Rapids: Baker Books, 2010.

Habermas, Jürgen, and Joseph Ratzinger. *The Dialectics of Secularization: On Reason and Religion*. San Francisco, CA: Ignatius Press, 2006.

Haidt, Jonathan. *The Righteous Mind: Why Good People Are Divided by Politics and Religion*. New York: Vintage Books, 2012.

Hamilton, James M. *God's Glory in Salvation through Judgment*. Wheaton, IL: Crossway Books, 2010.

Hansen, Collin. *Young, Restless, and Reformed: A Journalist's Journey with the New Calvinists*. Wheaton, IL: Crossway, 2008.

Harding, Mark, and Alanna Nobbs, eds. *All Things to All Cultures: Paul among Jews, Greeks, and Romans*. Grand Rapids: Eerdmans, 2013.

Hart, Trevor. "Eschatology." Pages 262–75 in *The Oxford Handbook of Evangelical Theology*. Edited by Gerald R. McDermott. New York: Oxford University Press, 2010.

Hartman, Laura M. *The Christian Consumer: Living Faithfully in a Fragile World*. New York: Oxford University Press, 2011.

Hauerwas, Stanley. *Approaching the End: Eschatological Reflections on Church, Politics, and Life*. Grand Rapids: Eerdmans, 2013.

______, and William H. Willimon. *Resident Aliens: Life in the Christian Colony*. Nashville: Abingdon Press, 1989.

Hawthorne, Gerald F. *Philippians*. Word Biblical Commentary. Vol. 43. Nashville: Thomas Nelson, 1983.

Hays, Richard B. *The Moral Vision of the New Testament: A Contemporary Introduction to New Testament Ethics*. New York: HarperOne, 1996.

Hellerman, Joseph H. *When the Church Was a Family: Recapturing Jesus' Vision for Authentic Christian Community*. Nashville: B&H Academic, 2009.

Helyer, Larry R. *The Life and Witness of Peter*. Downers Grove, IL: IVP Academic, 2012.

Henderscott, Anne. *The Politics of Abortion*. New York: Encounter Books, 2006.

Henry, Carl F. H. *The Uneasy Conscience of Modern Fundamentalism*. Grand Rapids: Eerdmans, 2003.

Hesselgrave, David J. *Planting Churches Cross-Culturally: North America and Beyond*. 2nd ed. Grand Rapids: Baker Academic, 2000.

______, and Edward Rommen. *Contextualization: Meanings, Methods, and Models*. Pasadena, CA: William Carey Library, 2000.

______, and Ed Stetzer, eds. *Mission Shift: Global Mission Issues in the Third Millennium*. Nashville: B&H Academic, 2010.

Hiebert Paul G. *Anthropological Insights for Missionaries*. Grand Rapids: Baker Books, 1985.

______. *The Gospel in Human Contexts: Anthropological Explorations for Contemporary Missions*. Grand Rapids: Baker Academic, 2009.

______. *Transforming Worldviews: An Anthropological Understanding of How People Change*. Grand Rapids: Baker Academic, 2008.

______, R. Daniel Shaw, and Tite Tienou. *Understanding Folk Religion: A Christian Response to Popular Beliefs and Practices*. Grand Rapids: Baker Academic, 2000.

Hiers, Richard H. *Jesus and the Future: Unresolved Questions for Understanding and Faith*. Atlanta, GA: John Knox Press, 1981.

Hirsch, Alan. *The Forgotten Ways: Reactivating the Missional Church*. Grand Rapids: Brazos Press, 2006.

______, and Dave Ferguson. *On the Verge: A Journey into the Apostolic Future of the Church*. Grand Rapids: Zondervan, 2011.

Hoekema, Anthony A. *Created in God's Image*. Grand Rapids: Eerdmans, 1986.

Hood, Jason B. *Imitating God in Christ: Recapturing a Biblical Pattern*. Downers Grove, IL: IVP Academic, 2013.

Horsley, Richard A. *Jesus and Empire: The Kingdom of God and the New World Disorder*. Minneapolis: Fortress Press, 2003.

Hortelano, Antonio. "The Sexual Revolution and the Family." Pages 50–54 in *The Sexual Revolution*. Edited by Gregory Baum and John Coleman. Edinburgh, Scotland: T&T Clark, Edinburgh, 1984.

Horton, Michael. *The Christian Faith: A Systematic Theology for Pilgrims on the Way*. Grand Rapids: Zondervan, 2011.

______. *Christless Christianity: The Alternative Gospel of the American Church*. Grand Rapids: Baker Books, 2012.

Hultgren, Arland. *The Parables of Jesus: A Commentary*. Grand Rapids: Eerdmans, 2000.

______. *Paul's Letter to the Romans*. Grand Rapids: Eerdmans, 2011.

Hunter, James Davison. *To Change the World*. New York: Oxford University Press, 2010.

Jacob, Emmanuel. "Discipleship and Mission: A Perspective on the Gospel of Matthew." *International Review of Mission* 91, no. 360 (2002): 106–10.

Jacobs, Alan. *Original Sin: A Cultural History*. New York: HarperOne, 2008.

Janz, Denis R., ed. *A Reformation Reader: Primary Texts with Introductions*. Minneapolis: Fortress Press, 1999.

Jenkins, Philip. *The Next Christendom: The Coming of Global Christianity*. 3rd ed. Oxford: Oxford University Press, 2011.

Jensen, Peter. *The Revelation of God*. Downers Grove, IL: InterVarsity Press, 2002.

Jeremias, Joachim. *The Parables of Jesus*. 2nd rev. ed. New York: Charles Scribner's Sons, 1972.

Jethani, Skye. *The Divine Commodity: Discovering a Faith Beyond Consumer Christianity*. Grand Rapids: Zondervan, 2009.

Johnson, Dennis. *Him We Proclaim: Proclaiming Christ from All the Scriptures*. Phillipsburg, NJ: P&R, 2007.

Johnson, Luke Timothy. *The Gospel of Luke*. Sacra Pagina Series. Vol. 3. Collegeville, MN.: Liturgical Press, 1991.

Jones, David W. *An Introduction to Biblical Ethics*. Nashville: B&H Academic, 2013.

Jones, Peter Rhea. *Studying the Parables of Jesus*. Macon, GA: Smyth and Helwys, 1999.

Juel, Donald. *Luke-Acts: The Promise of History*. Atlanta: John Knox Press, 1983.

Just, Arthur A., Jr. *Luke 9:51–24:53*. Concordia Commentary: A Theological Exposition of Sacred Scripture. Saint Louis, MO: Concordia Publishing House, 1997.

Kaiser, Walter C., Jr. *Toward Old Testament Ethics*. Grand Rapids: Zondervan, 1983.

Kalb, James. "Technocracy Now." *First Things* (August/September 2015): 25–31.

Kant, Immanuel. *Critique of Judgment*. N.p.: N.p., 1790.

_______. "What Is Enlightenment?" Pages 383–90 in Peter Gay, *The Enlightenment: A Comprehensive Anthology*. New York: Simon & Schuster, 1973.

Kaplan, Fred. *1959: The Year Everything Changed*. Hoboken, NJ: John Wiley and Sons, 2009.

Kaufmann, Eric. *Shall the Religious Inherit the Earth: Demography and Politics in the 21st Century*. London: Profile Books, 2010.

Keener, Craig. *A Commentary on the Gospel of Matthew*. Grand Rapids: Eerdmans, 1999.

______. "Matthew's Missiology: Making Disciples of the Nations." *Asian Journal of Pentecostal Studies* 12, no. 1 (January 2009): 15.

Keller, Timothy. *Center Church: Doing Balanced, Gospel-Centered Ministry in Your City*. Grand Rapids: Zondervan, 2012.

______. *Counterfeit Gods: The Empty Promises of Money, Sex, and Power, and the Only Hope that Matters*. New York: Dutton, 2009.

______. *Generous Justice: How God's Grace Makes Us Just*. New York: Dutton, 2010.

______. *Preaching: Communicating Faith in an Age of Skepticism*. New York: 2015.

Kelly, J. N. D. *Early Christian Doctrines*. Rev. ed. New York: HarperOne, 1978.

Kidner, Derek. *The Message of Jeremiah*. Downers Grove, IL: InterVarsity Press, 1987.

Kilner, John F. *Dignity and Destiny: Humanity in the Image of God*. Grand Rapids: Eerdmans, 2015.

Kim, Seyoon. *Christ and Caesar: The Gospel and the Roman Empire in the Writings of Paul and Luke*. Grand Rapids: Eerdmans, 2008.

Kirk, J. R. Daniel. *Unlocking Romans: Resurrection and the Justification of God*. Grand Rapids: Eerdmans, 2008.

Kistemaker, Simon J. *The Parables: Understanding the Stories Jesus Told*. Grand Rapids: Baker Books, 2002.

Klink, Edward W., III, and Darian R. Lockett. *Understanding Biblical Theology: A Comparison of Theory and Practice*. Grand Rapids: Zondervan, 2012.

Knowles, Michael P. "Everyone Who Hears These Words of Mine." Pages 286–305 in *The Challenge of Jesus' Parables*. McMaster New Testament Series. Edited by Richard N. Longenecker. Grand Rapids: Eerdmans, 2000.

Köstenberger, Andreas J., and Peter T. O'Brien. *Salvation to the Ends of the Earth: A Biblical Theology of Mission*. Downers Grove, IL: InterVarsity Press, 2001.

______, and Robert W. Yarbrough. *Understanding the Times: New Testament Studies in the 21st Century*. Wheaton, IL: Crossway, 2011.

Kreitzer, L. J. "Eschatology." Pages 253-69 in *Dictionary of Paul and His Letters*. Edited by Gerald F. Hawthorne, Ralph P. Martin, and Daniel G. Reid. Downers Grove, IL: IVP, 1993.

Kunyihop, Samuel Waje. *African Christian Theology*. Grand Rapids: Zondervan, 2012.

Kuyper, Abraham. *Lectures on Calvinism*. Grand Rapids: Eerdmans, 1987.

Ladd, George Eldon. *Theology of the New Testament*. Grand Rapids: Eerdmans, 1993.

Lane, Dermot A. "Eschatology." Pages 329-42 in *New Dictionary of Theology*. Edited by Joseph A. Komonchak, Mary Collins, and Dermot A. Lane. Wilmington, DE: Michael Glazier, 1987.

Lane, Timothy S., and Paul David Tripp. *How People Change*. Greensboro, NC: New Growth Press, 2008.

Lane, Tony. *A Concise History of Christian Thought*. Rev. ed. Grand Rapids: Baker Academic, 2006.

Lasch, Christopher. *The True and Only Heaven: Progress and its Critics*. New York: Norton, 1991.

Leeman, Jonathan. *The Church and the Surprising Offense of God's Love: Reintroducing the Doctrines of Church Membership and Discipline*. Wheaton, IL: Crossway, 2010.

Leithart, Peter J. *Between Babel and Beast: America and Empires in Biblical Perspective*. Eugene, OR: Cascade Books, 2012.

Lerman, Robert I., and W. Bradford Wilcox. *For Richer, for Poorer: How Family Structures Economic Success in America*. Charlottesville, VA: Institute for Family Studies, 2015. Accessed September 12, 2015. http://www.aei.org/wp-content/uploads/2014/10/IFS-ForRicherForPoorer-Final_Web.pdf.

Lewis, C. S. *The Abolition of Man*. New York: Touchstone, 1996.

______. *God in the Dock*. Grand Rapids: Eerdmans, 1970.

______. *Mere Christianity*. C. S. Lewis Signature Classics. San Francisco, CA: HarperSanFrancisco, 2009.

Liederbach, Mark, and Alvin R. Reid. *The Convergent Church: Missional Worshipers in an Emerging Culture*. Grand Rapids: Kregel, 2009.

Lincoln, Andrew T. *Paradise Now and Not Yet: Studies in the Role of the Heavenly Dimension in Paul's Thought with Special Reference to His Eschatology*. Grand Rapids: Baker, 1981.

Lindberg, Carter. *The European Reformations*. 2nd ed. Hoboken, NJ: Wiley-Blackwell, 2009.

Loconte, Joseph. *The Searchers: A Quest for Faith in the Valley of Doubt.* Nashville: Thomas Nelson, 2012.

Longenecker, Richard N. *Acts.* Expositor's Bible Commentary. Vol. 9. Edited by Frank E. Gaebelein. Grand Rapids: Zondervan, 1981.

______., ed. *The Challenge of Jesus' Parables.* McMaster New Testament Series. Grand Rapids: Eerdmans, 2000.

Lovelace, Richard F. *Renewal as a Way of Life: A Guidebook for Spiritual Growth.* Eugene, OR: Wipf and Stock Publishers, 1985.

Lull, Timothy F., ed. *Martin Luther's Basic Theological Writings.* 2nd ed. Minneapolis: Fortress Press, 2005.

Luther, Martin. *The Sermon on the Mount (Sermons) and the Magnificat.* Luther's Works. Vol. 21. St. Louis, MO: Concordia, 1956.

Lutz, Christopher. *Reading Alasdair MacIntyre's After Virtue.* New York: Bloomsbury Academic, 2012.

Machen, J. Gresham. *Christianity and Liberalism.* Grand Rapids: Eerdmans, 1923.

MacIntyre, Alasdair. *After Virtue: A Study in Moral Theory.* 3rd ed. Notre Dame, IN: University of Notre Dame Press, 2007.

Marquardt, Elizabeth. *Between Two Worlds: The Inner Lives of Children and Divorce.* New York: Crown Publishers, 2005.

Marsden, George. *The Twilight of the American Enlightenment: The 1950s and the Crisis of Liberal Belief.* New York: Basic Books, 2014.

Marsh, Charles. *Strange Glory: A Life of Dietrich Bonhoeffer.* New York: Knopf, 2014.

Marshall, I. Howard. *Acts.* Tyndale New Testament Commentaries. Grand Rapids: Eerdmans, 1980.

______. *The Gospel of Luke.* New International Greek Testament Commentary. Grand Rapids: Eerdmans, 1978.

______. *Luke: Historian and Theologian.* 3rd ed. Downers Grove, IL: InterVarsity Press, 1988.

Marty, Martin E. *The Modern Schism: Three Paths to the Secular.* New York: Harper & Row, 1969.

Mathewes-Green, Frederica. *The Illumined Heart: Capture the Vibrant Faith of the Ancient Christians.* Brewster, MA.: Paraclete Press, 2001.

Mayer, Milton. *They Thought They Were Free: The Germans 1933–45.* 2nd rev. ed. Chicago, IL: University of Chicago Press, 1966.

McConnville, J. Gordon. "The Old Testament and the Enjoyment of Wealth." Pages 34–53 in *Christ and Consumerism: A Critical Analysis of the Spirit of the Age*. Edited by Craig Bartholomew and Thorsten Moritz. Crownhill, UK: Paternoster, 2000.

McDermott, Gerald R. *The Great Theologians: A Brief Guide*. Downers Grove, IL: IVP Academic, 2010.

______., ed. *The Oxford Handbook of Evangelical Theology*. New York: Oxford University Press, 2010.

______, and Harold A. Netland. *A Trinitarian Theology of Religions: An Evangelical Perspective*. New York: Oxford University Press, 2014.

McDowell, Sean, and John Stonestreet. *Same-Sex Marriage: A Thoughtful Approach to God's Design for Marriage*. Grand Rapids: Baker Books, 2014.

McGavran, Donald A. *Understanding Church Growth*. 3rd ed. Revised and edited by C. Peter Wagner. Grand Rapids: Eerdmans, 1990.

McGrath, Alister E. *Christian Theology: An Introduction*. 4th ed. Malden, MA: Blackwell Publishing, 2007.

______. *Mere Apologetics: How to Help Seekers and Skeptics Find Faith*. Grand Rapids: Baker Books, 2012.

McKnight, Scot. *A Community Called Atonement*. Nashville: Abingdon Press, 2007.

______. *Kingdom Conspiracy: Returning to the Radical Mission of the Local Church*. Grand Rapids: Brazos Press, 2014.

______. *Sermon on the Mount*. Grand Rapids: Zondervan, 2013.

______, and Joseph B. Modica. *Jesus Is Lord, Caesar Is Not: Evaluating Empire in New Testament Studies*. Downers Grove, IL: IVP Academic, 2013.

McQuilkin, Robertson. *An Introduction to Biblical Ethics*. 2nd ed. Wheaton, IL: Tyndale, 1995.

Medders, J. A. *Gospel-Formed: Living a Grace-Addicted, Truth-Filled, Jesus-Exalting Life*. Grand Rapids: Kregel, 2014.

Meeks, Wayne A. *The First Urban Christians: The Social World of the Apostle Paul*. 2nd ed. New Haven, CT: Yale University Press, 2003.

Menand, Louis. *The Metaphysical Club: A Story of Ideas in America*. New York: Farrar, Straus and Giroux, 2001.

Metaxas, Eric. *Bonhoeffer: Pastor, Prophet, Martyr, Spy*. Nashville: Thomas Nelson, 2010.

Metzger, Paul Louis. *Consuming Jesus: Beyond Race and Class Divisions in a Consumer Church*. Grand Rapids: Eerdmans, 2007.

Miles, Stephen. *Consumerism as a Way of Life*. London: Sage, 1998.

Miller, Paul E. *A Praying Life: Connecting with God in a Distracting World*. Colorado Springs, CO: NavPress, 2009.

Miller, Vincent. *Consuming Religion: Christian Faith and Practice in a Consumer Culture*. New York: Bloomsbury Academic, 2005.

Minear, Paul S. *Images of the Church in the New Testament*. Louisville, KY: Westminster/John Knox Press, 1960. Reprint, 2004.

Mitchell, C. Ben, and D. Joy Riley. *Christian Bioethics: A Guide for Pastors, Health Care Professionals, and Families*. Nashville: B&H Academic, 2014.

Moltmann, Jürgen. *Theology of Hope*. Minneapolis: Fortress Press, 1993.

______. *The Way of Jesus Christ*. Minneapolis: Fortress Press, 1993.

Monsma, Steve. *Healing for a Broken World: Christian Perspectives on Public Policy*. Wheaton, IL: Crossway, 2008.

Montgomery, Daniel, and Mike Cosper. *Faithmapping: A Gospel Atlas for Your Spiritual Journey*. Wheaton, IL: Crossway, 2013.

Moo, Douglas J. *The Epistle to the Romans*. New International Commentary on the New Testament. Grand Rapids: Eerdmans, 1996.

Moore, Russell D. *The Kingdom of Christ: The New Evangelical Perspective*. Wheaton, IL: Crossway, 2004.

______. *Onward: Engaging the Culture without Losing the Gospel*. Nashville: B&H, 2015.

Moore, T. M. *Culture Matters: A Call for Consensus on Christian Cultural Engagement*. Grand Rapids: Brazos Press, 2007.

Moorehead, Caroline. *Village of Secrets: Defying the Nazis in Vichy France*. New York: HarperCollins, 2014.

Moreau, A. Scott. *Contextualization in World Missions: Mapping and Assessing Evangelical Models*. Grand Rapids: Kregel, 2012.

______, Gary R. Corwin, and Gary B. McGee. *Introducing World Missions: A Biblical, Historical, and Practical Survey*. Grand Rapids: Baker Academic, 2004.

Moreland, J. P., and William Lane Craig. *Philosophical Foundations for a Christian Worldview*. Downers Grove, IL: IVP Academic, 2003.

Morgan, Christopher W., and Robert A. Peterson, eds. *The Kingdom of God*. Wheaton, IL: Crossway, 2012.

Morris, Leon. *1 Corinthians*. Tyndale New Testament Commentaries. Edited by Leon Morris. Grand Rapids: Eerdmans, 1990.

______. *Luke*. Tyndale New Testament Commentaries. Grand Rapids: Eerdmans, 1988.

Motyer, J. A. *The Message of Philippians*. Bible Speaks Today. Downers Grove, IL: InterVarsity Press, 1984.

Mouw, Richard J. *Abraham Kuyper: A Short and Personal Introduction*. Grand Rapids: Eerdmans, 2011.

______. *The Challenges of Cultural Discipleship: Essays in the Line of Abraham Kuyper*. Grand Rapids: Eerdmans, 2011.

Moxnes, Halvor. *The Economy of the Kingdom: Social Conflict and Economic Relations in Luke's Gospel*. Minneapolis: Fortress Press, 1988.

Naugle, David K., Jr. *Worldview: The History of a Concept*. Grand Rapids: Eerdmans, 2002.

Newbigin, Lesslie. *Foolishness to the Greeks: The Gospel and Western Culture*. Grand Rapids: Eerdmans, 1986.

______. *The Good Shepherd: Meditations on Christian Ministry in Today's World*. Oxford, UK: Mowbray, 1977.

______. *The Gospel in a Pluralist Society*. Grand Rapids: Eerdmans, 1989.

______. *The Household of God: Lectures on the Nature of the Church*. Eugene, OR: Wipf and Stock Publishing, 2008.

______. *The Open Secret: An Introduction to the Theology of Mission*. Grand Rapids: Eerdmans, 1995.

______. "Rapid Social Change and Evangelism." Unpublished paper, 1962. Quoted in *Living at the Crossroads: An Introduction to Christian Worldview*. Grand Rapids: Baker Academic, 2008.

______. *Signs amid the Rubble: The Purposes of God in Human History*. Edited by Geoffrey Wainwright. Grand Rapids: Eerdmans, 2003.

______. *A Walk through the Bible*. Kansas City, MO: Bare Foot Ministries, 1999.

Niebuhr, H. Richard. *Christ and Culture*. New York: Harper & Row, 1951.

Noll, Mark A. *The New Shape of World Christianity: How American Experience Reflects Global Faith*. Downers Grove, IL: IVP Academic, 2009.

______, and Carolyn Nystrom. *Clouds of Witnesses: Christian Voices from Africa and Asia*. Downers Grove, IL: InterVarsity Press, 2011.

Nussbaum, Stan. *A Reader's Guide to Transforming Mission: A Concise, Accessible Companion to David Bosch's Classic Book*. Maryknoll, NY: Orbis Books, 2005.

O'Donovan, Oliver. *Begotten or Made? Human Procreation and Medical Technique*. New York: Oxford University Press, 1984.

______. *The Desire of the Nations: Rediscovering the Roots of Political Theology*. Cambridge, MA: Cambridge University Press, 1999.

______. *Finding and Seeking: Ethics as Theology*. Vol. 2. Grand Rapids: Eerdmans, 2014.

______. *Resurrection and Moral Order: An Outline for Evangelical Ethics*. Grand Rapids: Eerdmans, 1994.

______. *Self, World and Time: Ethics as Theology*. Vol. 1. Grand Rapids: Eerdmans, 2013.

O'Donovan, Wilbur. *Biblical Christianity in African Perspective*. Carlisle, PA: Paternoster Press, 1996.

Osborne, Grant R. *The Hermeneutical Spiral: A Comprehensive Introduction to Biblical Interpretation*. Downers Grove, IL: InterVarsity Press, 2006.

Paris, Jenell Williams. *The End of Sexual Identity: Why Sex Is Too Important to Define Who We Are*. Downers Grove, IL: IVP, 2011.

Parsons, Mikeal C. *Luke: Storyteller, Interpreter, Evangelist*. Peabody, MA: Hendrickson Publishers, 2007.

______, and Richard I. Pervo. *Rethinking the Unity of Luke and Acts*. Minneapolis: Fortress Press, 1993.

Patterson, R. D., Hermann J. Austel, J. Barton Payne, Edwin Yamauchi, F. B. Huey Jr., and Elmer B. Smick. *1 & 2 Kings—1 & 2 Chronicles—Ezra, Nehemiah—Esther—Job*. Expositor's Bible Commentary. Vol. 4. Edited by Frank E. Gaebelein. Grand Rapids: Zondervan, 1988.

Pearcey, Nancy. *Finding Truth: 5 Principles for Unmasking Atheism, Secularism, and Other God Substitutes*. Colorado Springs, CO: David C. Cook, 2015.

______. *Total Truth: Liberating Christianity from Its Cultural Captivity*. Wheaton, IL: Crossway, 2004.

Pennington, Jonathan. *Heaven and Earth in the Gospel of Matthew*. Grand Rapids: Baker Academic, 2009.

______. *Reading the Gospels Wisely: A Narrative and Theological Introduction*. Grand Rapids: Baker Academic, 2012.

Perrin, Nicholas, and Richard B. Hays, eds. *Jesus, Paul, and the People of God: A Theological Dialogue with N. T. Wright*. Downers Grove, IL: IVP Academic, 2011.

Peterson, David G. *The Acts of the Apostles*. Pillar New Testament Commentary. Edited by D. A. Carson. Grand Rapids: Eerdmans, 2009.

______. *Engaging with God: A Biblical Theology of Worship*. Downers Grove, IL: InterVarsity Press, 1992.

Phelan, John E. *Essential Eschatology: Our Present and Future Hope*. Downers Grove, IL: InterVarsity Press, 2013.

Pietsch, B. M. *Dispensational Modernism.* Oxford: Oxford University Press, 2015.

Piper, John. *Desiring God: Meditations of a Christian Hedonist.* 25th Anniversary Reference ed. Colorado Springs, CO: Multnomah, 2011.

______. *Future Grace: The Purifying Power of the Promises of God.* Rev. ed. Colorado Springs, CO: Multnomah, 2012.

______. *Let the Nations Be Glad: The Supremacy of God in Missions.* Grand Rapids: Baker, 2003.

Placher, William C. *From Its Beginnings to the Eve of the Reformation.* Readings in the History of Christian Theology. Vol. 1. Louisville, KY: Westminster/John Knox, 1988.

Plantinga, Cornelius. *Not the Way It's Supposed to Be: A Breviary of Sin.* Grand Rapids: Eerdmans, 1995.

Plummer, Robert L., and John Mark Terry, eds. *Paul's Missionary Methods: In His Time and Ours.* Downers Grove, IL: IVP Academic, 2012.

Polhill, John B. *Acts: An Exegetical and Theological Exposition of Holy Scripture.* New American Commentary. Nashville: Broadman, 1992.

______. *Paul and His Letters.* Nashville: B&H Academic, 1999.

Prothero, Stephen. *God Is Not One: The Eight Rival Religions that Run the World—and Why Their Differences Matter.* New York: HarperOne, 2010.

______. *Religious Literacy: What Every American Needs to Know and Doesn't.* New York: HarperCollins, 2007.

Rah, Soong-Chan. *The Next Evangelicalism: Freeing the Church from Western Cultural Captivity.* Downers Grove, IL: InterVarsity Press, 2009.

Ramachandra, Vinoth. *Gods that Fail: Modern Idolatry and Christian Mission.* Downers Grove, IL: IVP, 1996.

______. *Subverting Global Myths: Theology and the Public Issues Shaping Our World.* Downers Grove, IL: IVP Academic, 2008.

Raschke, Carl. *The Next Reformation: Why Evangelicals Must Embrace Postmodernity.* Grand Rapids: Baker Academic, 2004.

Rea, Robert F. *Why Church History Matters: An Invitation to Love and Learn from Our Past.* Downers Grove, IL: IVP Academic, 2014.

Reich, Wilhelm. *The Sexual Revolution: Toward a Self-Regulating Character Structure.* Translated by Therese Pol. New York: Farrar, Straus and Giroux, 1974.

Rieff, Philip. *Triumph of the Therapeutic: Uses of Faith after Freud*. Intercollegiate Studies Institute. Chicago, IL: University of Chicago Press, 2006.

Rommen, Edward, and Gary Corwin, eds. *Missiology and the Social Sciences: Contributions, Cautions, and Conclusions*. Pasadena, CA: William Carey Library, 1996.

Ruden, Sarah. *Paul among the People: The Apostle Reinterpreted and Reimagined in His Own Time*. New York: Pantheon Books, 2010.

Schaeffer, Francis A. *The Complete Works of Francis Schaeffer*. Wheaton, IL: Crossway Books, 1982.

______. *Letters of Francis A. Schaeffer: Spiritual Reality in the Personal Christian Life*. Edited by Lane T. Dennis. Wheaton, IL: Crossway Books, 1985.

Schnabel, Eckhard J. *Paul the Missionary: Realities, Strategies and Methods*. Downers Grove, IL: IVP Academic, 2008.

Schreiner, Thomas R. *New Testament Theology: Magnifying God in Christ*. Grand Rapids: Baker Academic, 2008.

______. *Romans*. Baker Exegetical Commentary on the New Testament. Grand Rapids: Baker Academic, 1998.

Schwarz, Hans. *Eschatology*. Grand Rapids: Eerdmans, 2000.

Schweitzer, Albert. *The Quest of the Historical Jesus*. Mineola, NY: Dover Publications, 2005.

Scotland, Nigel. "Shopping for a Church: Consumerism and the Churches." Pages 135-51 in *Christ and Consumerism: A Critical Analysis of the Spirit of the Age*. Crownhill, UK: Paternoster Press, 2000.

Scruton, Roger. "Is Sex Necessary? On the Poverty of Progressivism's Fixation on Sexual Liberation." *First Things* (December 2014): 33-37.

Sheldon, Charles. *In His Steps*. Greensboro, NC: Empire Books, 2012.

Shiflett, Dave. *Exodus: Why Americans are Fleeing Liberal Churches for Conservative Christianity*. New York: Penguin, 2005.

Siebert, Rudolf. "The Frankfurt School: Enlightenment and Sexuality." Pages 27-37 in *The Sexual Revolution*. Edited by Gregory Baum and John Coleman. Edinburgh, Scotland: T&T Clark, 1984.

Sills, David. "Mission and Discipleship." Pages 186-99 in *Theology and Practice of Mission: God, the Church, and the Nations*. Edited by Bruce Riley Ashford. Nashville: B&H, 2011.

Silva, Moisés. *Philippians*. Baker Exegetical Commentary on the New Testament. Grand Rapids: Baker Academic, 2005.

Sire, James W. *Naming the Elephant: Worldview as a Concept*. 2nd ed. Downers Grove, IL: IVP Academic, 2015.

______. *The Universe Next Door: A Basic Worldview Catalog*. 5th ed. Downers Grove, IL: IVP Academic, 2009.

Slater, Don. *Consumer Culture and Modernity*. Cambridge, MA: Polity, 1997.

Smith, C. Fred. *Developing a Biblical Worldview: Seeing Things God's Way*. Nashville: B&H Academic, 2015.

Smith, Christian, and Melinda Lundquist Denton. *Soul Searching: The Religious and Spiritual Lives of American Teenagers*. Oxford, UK: Oxford University Press, 2005.

Smith, Gordon T. *Called to Be Saints: An Invitation to Christian Maturity*. Downers Grove, IL: IVP Academic, 2014.

Smith, Ian K. "The Later Pauline Letters." Pages 302–27 in *All Things to All Cultures: Paul among Jews, Greeks, and Romans*, ed. Mark Harding and Alanna Nobbs. Grand Rapids: Eerdmans, 2013.

Smith, James K. A. *Desiring the Kingdom: Worship, Worldview and Cultural Formation (Cultural Liturgies)*. Grand Rapids: Baker Academic, 2009.

______. *Discipleship in the Present Tense: Reflections on Faith and Culture*. Grand Rapids: Calvin College Press, 2013.

______. *How (Not) to Be Secular: Reading Charles Taylor*. Grand Rapids: Eerdmans, 2014.

______. *Imagining the Kingdom: How Worship Works (Cultural Liturgies)*. Grand Rapids: Baker Academic, 2013.

Smith, Murray J. "The Thessalonian Correspondence." Pages 269–301 in *All Things to All Cultures: Paul among Jews, Greeks, and Romans*. Edited by Mark Harding and Alanna Nobbs. Grand Rapids: Eerdmans, 2013.

Smith, Robert, Jr. *Doctrine that Dances: Bringing Doctrinal Preaching and Teaching to Life*. Nashville: B&H, 2008.

Snodgrass, Klyne. "Key Questions on the Parables of Jesus." *Review and Expositor* 109, no. 2 (Spring 2012): 173–85.

______. *Stories with Intent: A Comprehensive Guide to the Parables of Jesus*. Grand Rapids: Eerdmans, 2008.

Stark, Rodney. *The Rise of Christianity: How the Obscure, Marginal Jesus Movement Became the Dominant Religious Force in the Western World in a Few Centuries*. New York: HarperOne, 1996.

Stauffer, Ethelbert. *Christ and the Caesars*. Eugene, OR: Wipf and Stock, 1952.

Stein, Robert H. *An Introduction to the Parables of Jesus*. Philadelphia, PA: Westminster, 1981.

______. *Jesus the Messiah*. Downers Grove, IL: IVP Academic, 1996.

______. *Luke: An Exegetical and Theological Exposition of Holy Scripture*. New American Commentary. Nashville: Broadman, 1992.

Stetzer, Ed. *Planting Missional Churches: Planting a Church That's Biblically Sound and Reaching People in Culture*. Nashville: B&H Academic, 2006.

Storkey, Alan. "Postmodernism is Consumption." Pages 100-17 in *Christ and Consumerism: A Critical Analysis of the Spirit of the Age*. Crownhill, UK: Paternoster Press, 2000.

Storms, Sam. *Kingdom Come: The Amillennial Alternative*. Fearn, Rosshire, Scotland: Mentor, 2013.

Stott, John R. W. *Between Two Worlds: The Challenge of Preaching Today*. Grand Rapids: Eerdmans, 1982.

______. *Christian Mission in the Modern World*. Downers Grove, IL: InterVarsity Press, 2008.

______. *The Contemporary Christian: Applying God's Word to Today's World*. Downers Grove, IL: InterVarsity Press, 1995.

______. *The Message of Acts: The Spirit, the Church, and the World*. Bible Speaks Today. Downers Grove, IL: InterVarsity Press, 1990.

______. *The Message of the Sermon on the Mount*. Downers Grove, IL: InterVarsity Press, 1978.

______. *The Radical Disciple: Some Neglected Aspects of Our Calling*. Downers Grove, IL: InterVarsity Press, 2010.

Stroud, Dean G., ed. *Preaching in Hitler's Shadow: Sermons of Resistance in the Third Reich*. Grand Rapids: Eerdmans, 2013.

Tarnas, Richard. *The Passion of the Western Mind: Understanding the Ideas that Have Shaped Our World View*. New York: Ballantine Books, 1991.

Taylor, Charles. *Dilemmas and Connections: Selected Essays*. Boston, MA: Harvard University Press, 2011.

______. *A Secular Age*. Boston, MA: Harvard University Press, 2007.

______. *Sources of the Self: The Making of Modern Identity*. Boston, MA: Harvard University Press, 1992.

______. *Varieties of Religion Today: William James Revisited*. Cambridge, MA: Harvard University Press, 2002.

Taylor, Mark. *1 Corinthians*. New American Commentary. Nashville: B&H, 2014.

Teetsel, Eric, and Andrew Walker. *Marriage Is*. Nashville: B&H, 2015. Kindle edition.

Tennent, Timothy. *Theology in the Context of World Christianity: How the Global Church Is Influencing the Way We Think about and Discuss Theology*. Grand Rapids: Zondervan, 2009.

Thiselton, Anthony C. *Hermeneutics of Doctrine*. Grand Rapids: Eerdmans, 2007.

Thompson, Marianne Meye. "What Holds the Bible Together?" Pages 39–48 in *Conversations at the Edges of Things: Reflections for the Church in Honor of John Goldingay*. Eugene, OR.: Wipf and Stock, 2012.

Tolbert, Mary Ann. *Perspectives on the Parables: An Approach to Multiple Interpretations*. Philadelphia, PA: Fortress Press, 1979.

Tripp, Paul David. *Instruments in the Redeemer's Hands: People in Need of Change Helping People in Need of Change*. Phillipsburg, NJ: P&R, 2002.

Tucker, Jeffrey T. *Example Stories: Perspectives on Four Parables in the Gospel of Luke*. Sheffield, UK: Sheffield Academic Press, 1998.

Tyra, Gary. *A Missional Orthodoxy: Theology and Ministry in a Post-Christian Context*. Downers Grove, IL: IVP, 2013.

Van Gelder, Craig, and Dwight J. Zscheile. *The Missional Church in Perspective: Mapping Trends and Shaping Conversation*. Grand Rapids: Baker Academic, 2011.

Vanhoozer, Kevin J. *Faith Speaking Understanding: Performing the Drama of Doctrine*. Louisville, KY: Westminster/John Knox, 2014.

______, Charles A. Anderson, and Michael J. Sleasman, eds. *Everyday Theology: How to Read Cultural Texts and Interpret Trends*. Grand Rapids: Baker Academic, 2007.

Veith, Gene Edward. *God at Work: Your Christian Vocation in All of Life*. Wheaton, IL: Crossway, 2012.

Veng, Preben, and Terry Carter. *Telling God's Story: The Biblical Narrative from Beginning to End*. 2nd ed. Nashville: B&H Academic, 2013.

Wakabayashi, Allen Mitsuo. *Kingdom Come: How Jesus Wants to Change the World*. Downers Grove, IL: InterVarsity Press, 2003.

Walsh, Brian J. "From Housing to Homemaking: Worldviews and the Shaping of Home." *Christian Scholar's Review* 35, no. 1 (2006): 237–57.

______, and Sylvia C. Keesmaat. *Colossians Remixed: Subverting the Empire*. Downers Grove, IL: IVP Academic, 2004.

______, and J. Richard Middleton. *Transforming Vision*. Downers Grove, IL: InterVarsity, 1984.

Ward, Graham, ed. *The Postmodern God: A Theological Reader.* Malden, MA: Blackwell Publishers, 1998.

Wax, Trevin. *Gospel Centered Teaching: Showing Christ in All the Scripture.* Nashville: B&H, 2013.

Webber, Robert E. *Ancient-Future Time: Forming Spirituality through the Christian Year.* Grand Rapids: Baker Books, 2014.

______. *Who Gets to Narrate the World: Contending for the Christian Story in an Age of Rivals.* Downers Grove, IL: InterVarsity Press, 2008.

______. *The Younger Evangelicals: Facing the Challenges of the New World.* Grand Rapids: Baker Academic, 2002.

Weigel, George. *Evangelical Catholicism: Deep Reform in the 21st Century Church.* New York: Basic Books, 2014.

Wells, David. *Above All Earthly Pow'rs: Christ in a Postmodern World.* Grand Rapids: Eerdmans, 2005.

White, James Emery. *Christ among the Dragons: Finding Our Way through Cultural Challenges.* Downers Grove, IL: InterVarsity Press, 2010.

White, Susan. "A New Story to Live By?" *Bible in TransMission* (Spring 1998): 3–4.

Whitney, Donald S. *Spiritual Disciplines for the Christian Life.* Rev. and updated. Colorado Springs, CO: NavPress, 2014.

Widder, Wendy L. *"To Teach" in Ancient Israel: A Cognitive Linguistic Study of a Biblical Hebrew Lexical Set.* Boston, MA: Walter de Gruyter, 2014.

Wilkens, Steve, and Mark L. Sanford. *Hidden Worldviews: Eight Cultural Stories that Shape Our Lives.* Downers Grove, IL: IVP Academic, 2009.

Willard, Dallas. *The Divine Conspiracy: Rediscovering Our Hidden Life in God.* New York: Harper, 1998.

______. *The Great Omission: Reclaiming Jesus's Essential Teachings on Discipleship.* New York: HarperOne, 2006.

______. *Knowing Christ Today: Why We Can Trust Spiritual Knowledge.* New York, NY, 2009.

______. *The Spirit of the Disciplines: Understanding How God Changes Lives.* San Francisco, CA: Harper & Row, 1988.

Williams, Jarvis. *One New Man: The Cross and Racial Reconciliation in Pauline Theology.* Nashville: B&H, 2010.

Wilson, Andrew. *If God, Then What? Wondering Aloud about Truth, Origins, and Redemption.* Downers Grove, IL: IVP, 2012.

Wilson, Arthur M. *Diderot.* New York: Oxford University Press, 1972.

Wilson, Jared C. *Gospel Wakefulness.* Wheaton, IL: Crossway, 2011.

Winner, Lauren. *Real Sex: The Naked Truth about Chastity*. Grand Rapids: Brazos Press, 2005.

Witherington, Ben, III. *The Individual Witnesses*. The Indelible Image: The Theological and Ethical Thought World of the New Testament. Vol. 1. Downers Grove, IL: IVP Academic, 2009.

______. *The Rest of Life: Rest, Play, Eating, Studying, Sex from a Kingdom Perspective*. Grand Rapids: Eerdmans, 2012.

______. *Work: A Kingdom Perspective on Labor*. Grand Rapids: Eerdmans, 2011.

Witt, Jonathan. "The Icon of Materialism: Why Scientism's Cherished Progress Narrative Fails." *Touchstone* (March/April 2015): 40-43.

Wolters, Albert M. *Creation Regained: Biblical Basics for a Reformational Worldview*. 2nd ed. Grand Rapids: Eerdmans, 2005.

______. "Gustavo Gutierrez." Pages 229-40 in *Bringing into Captivity Every Thought: Capita Selecta in the History of Christian Evaluations of Non-Christian Philosophy*. Edited by J. Kapwijk, S. Griffioen, and G. Groenewoud. Lanham, MD: University Press of America, 1991.

______. "No Longer Queen: The Theological Disciplines and Their Sisters." Pages 59-79 in *The Bible and the University*. Scripture and Hermeneutics Series. Vol. 8. Edited by David Jeffrey Lyle and C. Stephan Evans. Nashville: Zondervan, 2007.

______. "On the Idea of Worldview and Its Relation to Philosophy." Pages 14-25 in *Stained Glass: Worldviews and Social Science*. Christian Studies Today. Edited by Paul Marshall. Lanham, MD: University Press of America, 1983.

Worthen, Molly. *Apostles of Reason: The Crisis of Authority in American Evangelicalism*. Oxford, UK: Oxford University Press, 2013.

Wright, Christopher J. H. *The Mission of God: Unlocking the Bible's Grand Narrative*. Downers Grove, IL: InterVarsity Press, 2006.

______. *The Mission of God's People: A Biblical Theology of the Church's Mission*. Grand Rapids: Zondervan, 2010.

Wright, N. T. *After You Believe: Why Christian Character Matters*. New York: HarperOne, 2010.

______. *Jesus and the Victory of God*. Christian Origins and the Question of God. Vol. 2. Minneapolis: Fortress, 1996.

______. *New Testament and the People of God*. Christian Origins and the Question of God. Vol. 1. Minneapolis: Fortress Press, 1992.

______. *Paul and the Faithfulness of God*. Christian Origins and the Question of God. Vol. 4. Minneapolis: Fortress Press, 2013.

______. *The Resurrection of the Son of God*. Christian Origins and the Question of God. Vol. 3. Minneapolis: Fortress Press, 2003.

______. *Romans*. New Interpreter's Bible Commentary. Vol. 10. Nashville: Abingdon Press, 2002.

______. *Simply Christian: Why Christianity Makes Sense*. New York: HarperOne, 2006.

______. *Simply Good News: Why the Gospel Is News and What Makes It Good*. New York: HarperOne, 2015.

______. *Surprised by Hope: Rethinking Heaven, the Resurrection, and the Mission of the Church*. New York: HarperOne, 2008.

Wright, Ronald. *A Short History of Progress*. Toronto, Canada: House of Anansi Press, 1994.

Wuthnow, Robert. *After the Baby Boomers: How Twenty- and Thirty-Somethings Are Shaping the Future of American Religion*. Princeton, NJ: Princeton University Press, 2007.

Young, Brad. *The Parables: Jewish Tradition and Christian Interpretation*. Peabody, MA: Hendrickson, 1998.

Scripture Index

Name Index

C

D

E

F

G

S

T–U

V

W–X

Subject Index